The Art of Chivalry

Armor. French, ca. 1600 (cat. no. 28)

THE ART OF CHIVALRY

European Arms and Armor

from The Metropolitan Museum of Art

Helmut Nickel · Stuart W. Pyhrr · Leonid Tarassuk

An Exhibition

Organized by The Metropolitan Museum of Art

and The American Federation of Arts

FUNDING FOR THIS PROJECT WAS PROVIDED BY
SCM CORPORATION, THE NATIONAL ENDOWMENT FOR THE ARTS,
THE NATIONAL PATRONS OF THE AMERICAN FEDERATION OF ARTS,
AND THE MABEL PEW MYRIN TRUST BY A GENEROUS GRANT FOR THE PUBLICATION.

*The American Federation of Arts is a national non-profit, educational organization,
founded in 1909, to broaden the knowledge and appreciation of the arts of the past and present.
Its primary activities are the organization of exhibitions
which travel throughout the United States and abroad,
and the fostering of a better understanding among nations
by the international exchange of art.*

MUSEUMS PARTICIPATING IN THE TOUR

Seattle Art Museum · Seattle, Washington

The Denver Art Museum · Denver, Colorado

San Antonio Museum Association, Witte Museum · San Antonio, Texas

The Minneapolis Institute of Arts · Minneapolis, Minnesota

The Detroit Institute of Arts · Detroit, Michigan

Copyright © 1982 The Metropolitan Museum of Art

*Published by The American Federation of Arts
41 East 65th Street · New York, New York 10021*

LCC: 81-68937   ISBN: 0-917418-67-0

AFA Exhibition 81-3   Circulated March, 1982 – May, 1984

*Design and Typography by Howard I. Gralla
Type set in Galliard by Finn Typographic Service
Printed by William J. Mack Company
Bound by Mueller Trade Bindery
Map and drawings by Joseph P. Ascherl*

COVER: *Sallet. Italian, ca. 1470 (cat. no. 3)*

Contents

Foreword

Numbering almost fourteen thousand objects and spanning the thirteenth through the early nineteenth centuries, the Arms and Armor collection of The Metropolitan Museum of Art is the largest in the Western Hemisphere and one of the most encyclopedic of its kind in the world.

Finely designed and decorated arms and armor were always rare, and the majority of existing pieces are preserved in the great ancestral collections of Europe. Since there are very few public collections of armor in this country, this exhibition will provide a unique opportunity for the national museum visitor to see a selection of exceptional quality and diversity illustrating the broad history of the subject. The objects have been selected not only for their artistic merit but also to present their important function in almost every aspect of chivalric and courtly life during the medieval and later periods. Such objects were used in wars, tournaments, parades, and the hunt. Designed to protect the wearer, they also combined comfort and balance with graceful appearance. From the thirteenth century on, armor and weapons became the objects of elaborate and colorful decoration, and artists of talent and reputation devoted themselves to their design and execution.

This exhibition, organized by The Metropolitan Museum of Art and The American Federation of Arts, continues a recently initiated joint program of traveling exhibitions intended to share the vast artistic resources of this great museum with other institutions across the country.

There are many whom we wish to thank for making this project possible: first, the Trustees of The Metropolitan Museum of Art for their generosity in sharing this collection with other museums across the country; second, Dr. Helmut Nickel, Curator, and Stuart W. Pyhrr, Associate Curator, Department of Arms and Armor, for selecting the objects included in the exhibition and writing the catalogue in collaboration with Leonid Tarassuk, Research Associate in the department.

Thanks are due to Carol Moon Cardon, Special Assistant to the Director, for her patient and thorough coordination of the project. We also acknowledge the important contributions of the following: Robert Carroll, Armorer, and Theodore Cuseo, Senior Restorer, Department of Arms and Armor; Mark D. Cooper and Gene C. Herbert, Manager and Photographer, respectively, of the Metropolitan Museum's Photograph Studio; and Linda Yachnes, free-lance display assistant.

At The American Federation of Arts we wish to express our appreciation to Jane Tai for overseeing all aspects of the project; to Jeffery J. Pavelka who served as the exhibition's coordinator and arranged the tour; and to Amy McEwen who served as the registrar for the project.

We thank Howard Gralla for the design of the catalogue, the poster, and the exhibition graphics. Our appreciation also extends to Margaret Aspinwall for editing the catalogue.

Financial support for this project, for which we are deeply grateful, was received from SCM Corporation, the National Endowment for the Arts, and the National Patrons of The American Federation of Arts. An additional grant from the Mabel Pew Myrin Trust has provided a generous subsidy for the publication.

Philippe de Montebello
Director
The Metropolitan Museum of Art

Wilder Green
Director
The American Federation of Arts

Introduction

THE USE OF TOOLS is one of the characteristics that distinguishes man from animals. The earliest known tools, however, were weapons, which man needed for his survival; with their help he was able to hunt and kill his prey and could also defend his hunting grounds against human competitors. It is sad, but true, that the sword is literally older than the plowshare.

The maker of weapons, for the hunt and for war, is the oldest specialized craftsman. It seems that even during the Stone Age there were specialized professionals such as the chippers of flint blades in prehistoric Britain and Denmark. Certainly the metalsmiths of the Bronze Age were highly qualified specialists, and so are the tribal smiths in societies as yet unchanged by the influence of Western civilization.

Weapons, created by the smith's skill with the help of the divine element, Fire, were regarded with superstitious awe throughout history because they represented the power to kill. This awe also extended to the weapon's creator. In many cultures the smith was considered somewhat like a magician, a notion strengthened by his working methods—he forged the steel at night so he could see the changing colors of the glowing metal and thus control its temperature. The chants he spoke as timing devices in tempering the steel seemed like spells. Significantly, the only god of classical antiquity who plied a human craft was the smith Hephaestus/Vulcan. In Celtic and Germanic Dark Age mythology Culain and Wayland the Smith take their honored place among the heroes, and the craft of the smith is the only one which to learn would not disgrace but rather enhance the status and renown of a hero, such as Siegfried the Dragonslayer or CuChulain, the Hound of Ulster.

In most cultures owning and bearing arms was considered the right and privilege of the free man. Naturally the greatest care and skill had to be given to their technical manufacture because this was literally a matter upon which life and death depended. In addition, beauty of functional form and often precious decoration of weapons combined to make them the jewelry of the free man. Sixteenth-century parade armor was indeed the most extensive—and expensive—body jewelry ever designed. Because of this interaction of emotional, historical, and aesthetical values, arms have long been coveted objects of collecting, as shown for instance in the Tale of the Fight for the Arms of Achilles.

In the aftermath of the war in Vietnam and under repercussions from recent political assassinations, contemporary opinion is understandably in strong disfavor of anything connected with weapons and violence. It must be pointed out, however, that a substantial part of all arms—armor—was protective, that is designed to save lives.

The weapon as such is neither good nor evil but a document and indispensable part of the history of mankind. Aside from their importance in cultural history, arms have a considerable role in art history too. Many outstanding artists such as Hans Holbein, Albrecht Dürer, and Leonardo da Vinci made designs for arms that were functional as well as decorative. As a work of art, a complete armor of the fifteenth or sixteenth century is a moving sculpture, and at the same time it often represents the corporeal image of a historically important person.

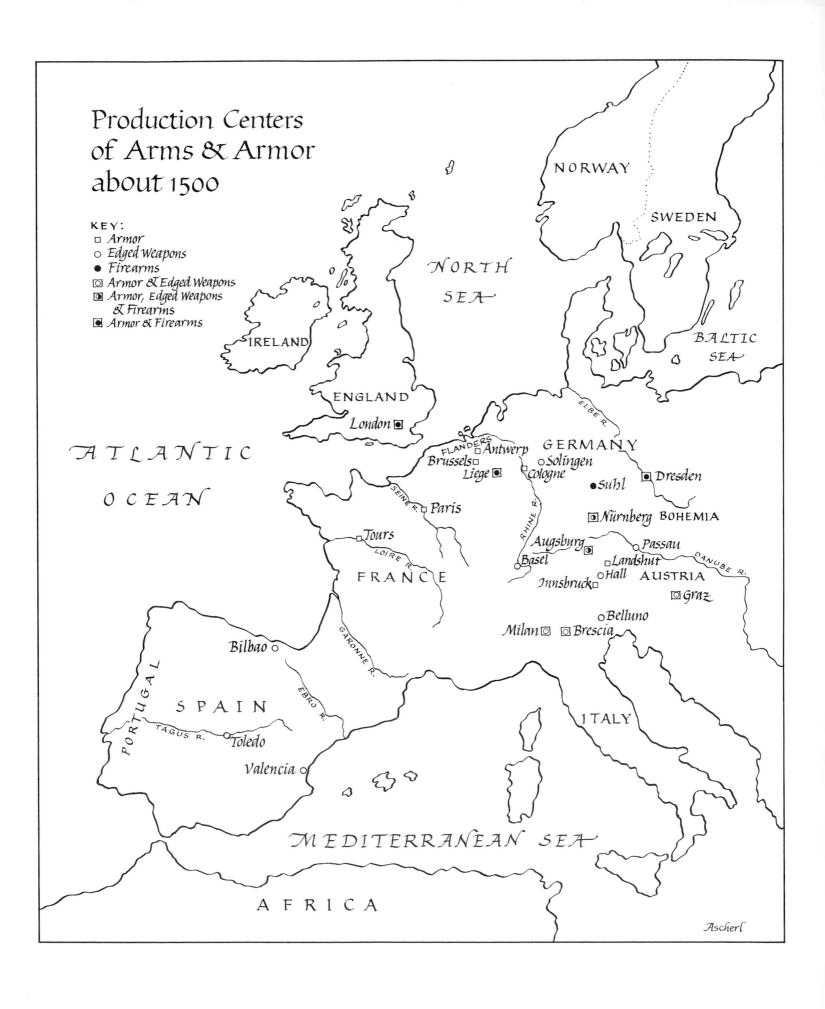

The Art of Chivalry

THE MOST WIDELY accepted embodiment of the spirit of the Middle Ages is the knight, the warrior in shining armor on horseback who lived by the code of chivalry. In most European languages, the word for "knight"–*chevalier, caballero, cavaliere,* and even *Ritter* – refers to horses or horsemanship. In English, chivalry encompasses the entire life-style of these mounted warriors far beyond the purely martial aspect. Chivalry meant more than fairness in battle and generous treatment of noncombatants and innocent bystanders; chivalry was a distinct class culture, which at times even came dangerously close to developing into a counterculture – at least it seemed that way from the point of view of the Church.

In the rigidly structured society of the Middle Ages, the knightly class was the only one, aside from the clergy, that permitted newcomers to join with relative ease. To be a knight was a privilege not automatically bestowed on members of the nobility; it had to be specifically earned and individually given, rather like a commissioned officer's rank today. Every knight had the right to confer the rank on any man he considered worthy, but he also had responsibilities to the novice similar to the ones a godfather would have toward his godson. Since the way of chivalry was based on horsemanship, ownership of a horse – and armor – was the absolute minimum of worldly possessions a knight was expected to have. If he did not possess a castle and lands of his own, he would have to earn his horse's keep in the service of a great lord, most likely the one who had dubbed him a knight in the first place, or else go out as a "free-lance" and do mercenary service wherever there was fighting to be done. Most knights, however, were members of the landed gentry, the established landowners.

To be a knight carried such status, almost mystique, that even wealthy feudal lords and princes considered it a supreme honor to be made a knight and to be included in this international brotherhood. When the novice knight was given the accolade, the three taps on his shoulders with the flat of a sword, he was invested with the sword belt and the golden spurs of his new rank. He in his turn pledged to obey the rules of chivalrous conduct, to be unflinchingly steadfast in his Christian faith and in his loyalty to his feudal lord, to be ready to fight and lay down his life, but to temper his fighting spirit with mercy, to protect the poor and oppressed, to help women and children. This mercy was to be extended even to a vanquished foe; blind revenge was regarded with contempt. These rules of behavior helped make life tolerable in an age when fighting could flare up almost any time and, as in the Hundred Years' War, could go

Fig. 1.
Tournament and the storming of the Castle of Love. Detail of ivory casket, French, early 14th century. Gift of J. Pierpont Morgan (17.190.173). Tournaments were often enhanced by lavish spectacles such as this storming of the Castle of Love, where fair ladies defended the ramparts and both sides used flowers instead of arrows and slingstones.

bards, and Vandals—but they were intermingled with Iranian steppe nomads—Alani and Sarmatians—who had been roaming the plains of Hungary and south Russia. These barbarians established their own kingdoms, with names that survive today such as France, Burgundy, Lombardy, Andalusia (Vandalusia), and Catalonia (Goth-Alania). The nomads were horsemen par excellence. They shared the same cultural complex as the Huns (who are much better known though they played only a very brief role in European history) and were the first heavy armored cavalry the West had seen. The tribal warriors of the Alani and Sarmatians considered themselves all of equally noble birth, infinitely superior to the peasants toiling in the dirt. This disdain for farmers and manual labor by the horse-riding, cattle-breeding nomad is a basic universal attitude, found even in the range wars between cowboys and sodbusters in the Old West. When the tribes got on the move, the Germanic groups, who were basically fighters on foot (as were the Romans), eagerly took up the

Fig. 2.
SAINT GEORGE AND THE DRAGON. *Engraving by the Master of Zwolle, Netherlandish, late 15th century. Harris Brisbane Dick Fund (33.54.6). Saint George was the patron saint of knights and therefore immensely popular; usually he was shown in the finest armor of the period. The patron saint of foot soldiers was Saint Mauritius, of archers, Saint Sebastian, and of artillerymen, Saint Barbara.*

on almost endlessly. Therefore the greatest virtue of a knight was moderation, doing "nothing in excess," and this attitude determined the entire complex of knightly culture.

The origins of this class culture which centered on the warrior on horseback go back to the fall of the Roman Empire in the late fifth century A.D. Barbarian tribes from eastern and central Europe poured into the western provinces of Roman Gaul, Hispania, and Italy. These tribes were mostly Germanic—Goths, Burgundians, Franks, Longo-

Fig. 3.
Two knights about to joust. Stained glass window, German, ca. 1500. Samuel P. Avery Fund (11.120.1). One of the knights bears Lady Love as his crest. In the upper panel are trumpeters on horseback; in the lower are two jesters. These were used as crowd control officers, to keep restless bystanders amused.

mobile cavalry tactics of their nomadic allies. From this blending of the Iranian horseman culture and the Germanic system of mutual loyalty between leaders and followers, plus whatever veneer of culture could be salvaged from the decaying Roman civilization, there eventually resulted the social phenomenon we call chivalry.

Ideally a knight had to own enough property (which in those days meant land worked by his serfs, the despised peasants) to keep himself and his retainers in his castle at a standard of living which made their loyalty to him worthwhile, and in addition to offering protection against enemies. First, he had to supply food and drink, which were judged according to fine points of cuisine. It was part of the formal education of a knight to be sent at an early age – about seven – as a page boy to another noble household, preferably that of his father's feudal lord, where he also served as a convenient hostage for his father's unswerving loyalty. It was part of a page's duties to wait at his master's table – the underlying educational principle was that in order to know how to command, one ought to know first how to serve well – and in the course of this service he would learn how to carve a joint and select the right wine. These household duties were supervised by the lady of the castle and perhaps her older daughters. Thus it was hoped that the young aspiring knight would receive, besides more polished manners, an appreciation of the important part ladies played in the knightly culture. When he was older, about fourteen years, the page boy might be promoted to squire and receive training in the martial arts, starting with caring for the horses and armor of his master. He would also learn fencing, tilting, and the proper ways of the hunt.

Hunting in the Middle Ages was necessary for food, but it was subject to strict rules, some of them clearly ecological: no hunting was allowed during the breeding season, stags and bucks were fair game, but no does. However, no such restrictions extended to wild boars, which bred at an alarming rate and were a serious danger to crops. Severe restrictions against poaching were basically intended to protect game against wholesale slaughter. Among the various methods of hunting, falconry was highly regarded because of its value in teaching patience, while other methods, such as riding to hounds and stalking, made it absolutely essential to have good training in horsemanship, animal care, and archery.

Knightly culture encompassed other important amenities, as for instance art, which – and here the old nomad tradition of the horse warrior makes itself felt – meant poetry and such portable forms of art as tapestries and heraldry. The Age of Chivalry was the age of the great European epics and romances. These were based on historical events which took place around the year 500 A.D. and centered upon persons who actually lived (the most famous group of these epics are the legends about King Arthur and his Knights of the Round Table), but were embroidered with much older motifs which can be traced to the long-vanished epic tradition of the steppe riders. Many of the motifs set epic poetry apart as the art form of a separate class

Fig. 4.
A knight taking leave from his lady. Engraving by Master E S, German, late 15th century. Harris Brisbane Dick Fund (37.3.4). As a final favor and farewell token, the lady fixes a fine ostrich plume in her knight's helmet. The ostrich plume was a symbol of steadfastness because it cannot be ruffled, no matter how hard the wind blows.

within society as a whole; after all, its themes often ran counter to the ethics of Christian morale—battles for war-like glory and/or revenge, blood feuds, search of adventure for personal fame, and also the code of courtly love—and have more in common with the Seven Deadly Sins than with the Ten Commandments. Even the supposedly Christian themes in these epics, such as the Quest for the Holy Grail, have strange features that strongly smack of heresy.

Another knightly art form that aroused the displeasure of the Church was the tournament. Originally, the joust was battle training, but soon it developed into a sport—*the* spectator sport of the Middle Ages, before the days of ball games—with a complicated set of rules designed to make this very rough sport acceptable. In spite of these rules, excesses inevitably occurred, which in turn incurred the wrath of the Establishment, spiritual and even secular; tournaments were banned for one time or another in practically every Christian realm. In spite of these prohibitions, the sport grew evermore popular, with its surrounding spectacle and pageantry expanding to enormous proportions, thereby creating an art form in its own right.

Finally, the knightly theme of courtly love found its finest expression in the lyric poetry of French *trouvères*, Provençal *troubadours*, and German *Minnesingers*, whose songs, composed between the eleventh and fourteenth centuries, were in praise of love (spiritual and earthly) and undying loyalty in the service of ladies. Though some of these poets were landless "free-lances" and others could be princes with vast holdings, they were all members of the same international class culture which bridged even language barriers.

Of course, the lofty standards set in the romances of chivalry and at the courts of love were more often than not difficult to uphold in everyday life, and sad to say many a knight fell woefully short of them. Nevertheless, it was the highest praise for a man, even for a crowned king, to be called—in the tradition of King Arthur and his Knights of the Round Table—the perfect knight.

The ideal persevered even after there were no longer any knights in shining armor riding forth on their white steeds to right wrongs. Though *Don Quixote de la Mancha* (1605) was meant as a satire on the supposedly outmoded romances of chivalry, the immortal fame of the tragicomic Knight of the Sad Countenance has succeeded more than anything else to keep the ideal of knight-errantry alive. In the seventeenth century the spirit of chivalry was upheld by French courtiers and the Musketeers of the King, as well as by the doomed Cavaliers of the English Civil War, and the zeal of the Crusaders was rekindled when the Austrian cuirassiers and Polish hussars turned the Turks back from the gates of Vienna (1683). In the eighteenth century, rococo cavaliers carried elegant small-swords as badges of rank and accessories of their daily dress. They still held "tournaments," now superrefined as a game of skill—tilting at the ring—and they were certainly second to none in the fine art of charming their ladies with polished manners and literate conversation. In the nineteenth century the sword was superseded by the pistol as the dueling weapon, but the romantic knightly spirit showed itself in nostalgic literature such as *Ivanhoe*. In real life it was reawakened by the horseman culture of the American Plains, which in turn brought forth a new form of chivalric romance and a new disguise for the knight-errant who vanquished the Black Knight at the tournament to win the damsel in distress—the cowboy who gunned down the badman in the showdown in mainstreet to win the rancher's daughter.

Armor

To be invulnerable is the understandable desire of every fighting man. Mythical heroes such as Achilles and Siegfried could achieve invulnerability by supernatural means, but ordinary warriors who did not have access to the necessary ingredients—dragon's blood or water from the river Styx—had to make do with armor.

The oldest and most widely used element of protective armor is the shield; its invention must go back to the Paleolithic Age, even before the invention of the bow. This can be deduced from the fact that the Australian aborigines use shields though they do not know the bow, which means that they became separated from the mainstream of technical development at that early stage.

The purpose of the shield—held in the left hand, while the right wielded spear or sword—was to catch missiles and to break the shock of blows. Significantly, even invulnerable heroes with impenetrable skins, like Achilles and Siegfried, carried shields against bone-crushing blows.

In the Dark Ages shields were circular or oval, made of wooden boards about half an inch thick and covered with tough leather to hold the shield together even after the wood had split under a heavy blow. In the center of the shield was a circular cutout bridged by the handgrip on the back and covered with the hollow iron shieldboss (umbo) in front. Iron or bronze mountings around the rim or on the board gave additional strength.

Shortly before the year 1000, the oval shield was lengthened, and it acquired a sharp lower point which covered the left knee of a mounted horseman. The rounded top of the shield came up to his eyes, thus covering his entire left side. To keep the shield braced and to hold it more easily in this position, a sling for the underarm and a carrying strap slung around the neck were added. The braced shield and the helmet covered so much of the warrior's face that he was practically unrecognizable, so to tell friend from foe, bold figures and striking patterns were painted on the shields'

surfaces. In time these symbols became canonized and hereditary—the beginning of heraldry.

The drawback of the shield was that it nearly immobilized the warrior's left arm. Gradually the shield was decreased in size and weight, but this was only possible by improving the resilience of the body armor. During the thirteenth and the first half of the fourteenth centuries shields were triangular; the point was kept though it no longer reached to the knight's knee, but the three corners of the shield were seen now, in the spirit of the Crusades, as symbols of the Holy Trinity. Around 1350 there appeared a second type of shield, almost square with a cutout for the couched lance in the upper dexter corner; this was the targe, a shield designed for the tournament. Fashion-conscious knights of the 1380s to the early 1400s had their squires carry two matching shields for them: a triangular traditional battle shield with family arms as "shield for War" and a tournament targe with the personal badge as "shield for Peace," as we know it from the Black Prince.

Medieval body armor was dependent on contemporary technology. In the Dark Ages after the Fall of Rome and during the early Middle Ages up to the time of Charlemagne, body armor was a mixture of surviving Roman techniques and styles introduced by barbarian warriors who had set up their own kingdoms on the ruins of ancient Rome.

Mail, body protection formed by interlinked and riveted rings of steel, had been one of the standard protective materials in Roman times. There were enough master craftsmen left to supply mail to at least the upper class of barbarians. By the time of the Norman Conquest of England and the First Crusade, mail was common enough, though still very expensive; the price of a mail shirt was the same as that for a well-trained battle charger: 12 solidi (the solidus was a gold coin equivalent to the value of a cow, or a month's wages of a soldatus, a soldier). A mail shirt from the period of the Crusades was constructed much like a modern sweater, with rings in rows as in knitting, each ring linked with four others, and with increases and decreases in those rows to shape rounded shoulders, elbows, etc. It even had to be pulled on or off over the head just like a sweater. It took a master craftsman about six months to create such a mail shirt out of up to a quarter million rings, and it weighed about twenty-two pounds. In the thirteenth century, mail shirts had long sleeves, even with mittens (with an inset of leather for the palm) and a mail hood *(coif)* all in one piece.

Mail was flexible and therefore relatively comfortable to wear and was also good protection against sword cuts, but that same flexibility rendered it ineffective against a crushing blow. As a bolster against the chafing of the rings, and as a shock absorber, a padded undergarment, the *acton* (from Arabic *al coton,* cotton), had to be worn, which made it very hot. During the Crusades, under the burning sun of the Holy Land, the metal rings themselves grew almost too hot to touch. As protection against the sun, crusader knights took to wearing over their armor a sleeveless surcoat which they eventually decorated with the heraldic charges of their shield, thus creating the "coat of arms."

The warrior's head was protected by his helmet. In the Dark Ages helmets were constructed of a framework of bronze or iron straps, the interspaces filled with triangular iron plates. These so-called *Spangenhelms* were of barbarian origin, their construction a metal version of the felt caps of the steppe nomads of the Migration Period. By the time of the Norman Conquest, helmets were still constructed out of framework and filling plates, or they could be beaten out of a single sheet of iron in a conical shape, with an attached strip as a nose guard. Later, around 1200, plates were added to cover the face, and with the addition of a neck plate, the helmet achieved the inverted bucket shape of the *great heaume.* This heaume or helm covered the head entirely and thus effectively hid the face; for identification, a *crest* had to be attached on the top of the helm. Both painted shield and crested helm became the basic elements of knightly heraldic arms.

Mail shirt and mail *chausses* (leggins), crested helm, and shield were the armor of the Crusades and of the period of the troubadours and minnesingers, when knighthood was in flower. It was not until the fourteenth century that the "knight in shining armor" made his appearance.

Ironically, it was the crossbowman, one of the despised foot soldiers, who brought forth the armor of plates which we visualize when we think of knights. The mail shirt, so

Fig. 5.
Tomb effigy of Jacquelin de Ferrierre. North French, late 13th century. The Bashford Dean Memorial Collection (29.158.761). Sieur Jacquelin is represented in full mail armor; he has his hands slipped through slits in the wrists of the sleeves, letting his mail mittens dangle. His large knightly shield bears a canting device, horseshoes (fers-de-cheval) as a pun on Ferrierre.

effective against sword cuts, was easily pierced by arrows, and the bolts shot from a crossbow (which was three or four times as powerful as a longbow) could be stopped by neither shield nor mail. The only effective protection would be a surface that the bolts would glance off without doing

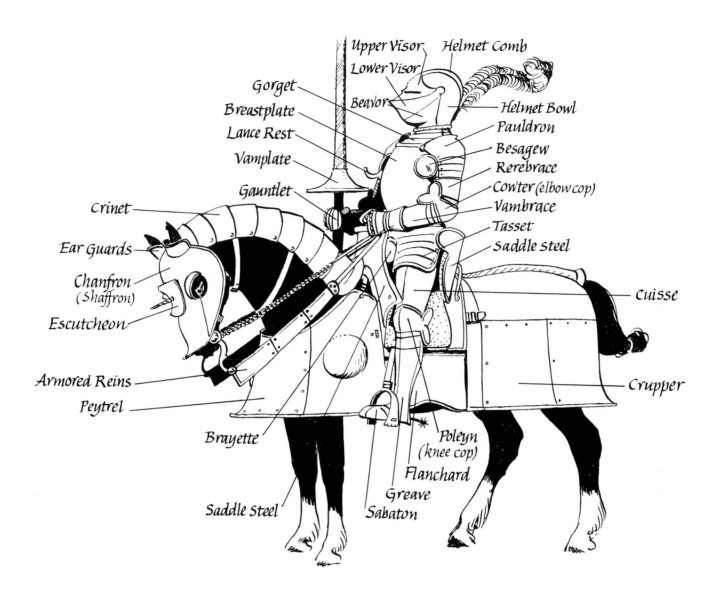

Upper Visor
Lower Visor
Beavor
Gorget
Breastplate
Lance Rest
Vamplate
Gauntlet
Crinet
Ear Guards
Chanfron (Shaffron)
Escutcheon
Armored Reins
Peytrel
Brayette
Saddle Steel
Sabaton
Greave
Flanchard
Poleyn (knee cop)
Helmet Comb
Helmet Bowl
Pauldron
Besagew
Rerebrace
Cow'ter (elbow cop)
Vambrace
Tasset
Saddle Steel
Cuisse
Crupper

much damage, and this deflective surface was offered by plate armor. Elements of plate armor existed in the thirteenth century: they were *poleyns* (knee cops) encasing the knee joint, and *greaves* protecting the lower legs, both parts of the body much exposed to being crushed in the press of a battle on horseback. Next, around 1350, armorers constructed similar defenses for the arms and shoulders, and also for the body itself. With the arms encased in steel

vambraces and steel *gauntlets,* it became difficult, if not impossible, to slip into the shield grips, and therefore, by the end of the fourteenth century, shields went gradually out of use. Furthermore, the improved body armor made the shield unnecessary as a shock breaker.

Interestingly, it took almost a century for knights to adapt to solid plate armor for the body, probably for psychological reasons – claustrophobia. At first the surcoat, which was

Fig. 6.
Knights in mid-15th century Italian armor.
Detail from TRIUMPH OF FAME, *probably the "birthplate" of Lorenzo de' Medici, by the Master of the Adimari Cassone, Italian (Florence), ca. 1449. On loan to The Metropolitan Museum of Art from the New-York Historical Society (The Bryan Collection).*

worn over the mail shirt, was reinforced with horizontal rows of small steel plates riveted in as a sort of lining. This gave enough protection but left plenty of mobility. However, the plate-lined surcoat had to fit very tightly so the plates would not shift and possibly bruise ribs and hips. So tight a fit meant that the surcoat could not slip over the head like the mail shirt, but instead it had to open in front to be put on like a vest. Usually there were two large plates riveted on in front, which would form one breastplate when the vest was closed (medieval English inventories list these as "pairs of plates"). To insure that an enemy's lance point would not slip between the plates, they overlapped from left to right, since it was standard fighting practice that the left side, protected by the shield, was turned toward the enemy. Thus, men's jackets button left to right even to the present day!

In the first half of the fifteenth century, the armorers of Milan in northern Italy, then the leading industrial center, succeeded in constructing the full suit of armor which included a *cuirass* for the body consisting of breastplate and backplate, each fitted with a skirt of plates to protect the lower abdominal and back regions. The first cuirasses, inci-

dentally, were made with breast and backplates in two horizontal sections, loosely connected by straps or sliding rivets for greater mobility. In order to bridge the gap between the skirt and the *cuisses* (thigh defenses), armorers introduced *tassets,* little shield-shaped plates attached at the lower rim of the skirt.

The leading armorer's shops in Milan were those of the Missaglia and the Negroli families; at times there were up to five hundred employees in a shop. The workmen were highly specialized, working only on a single element such as helmet, gauntlets, or leg defenses, but they were supervised by the master who coordinated their efforts to create a full armor as a unit. For this reason, there are sometimes half a dozen different armorers' marks on an otherwise quite homogeneous Milanese armor; these would be, in addition to the workshop mark, the individual specialists' marks stamped as a personal guarantee and presumably also as a way of accounting for their work done.

Besides Milan, there were important armor-making centers in Brescia and Belluno, in northern Italy. In countries beyond the Alps there were Innsbruck in the Austrian

Fig. 7.
The young Emperor Maximilian visiting his court armor shop in Innsbruck. Woodcut by Hans Burgkmair the Elder, German, ca. 1515. Illustration to Maximilian's autobiography DER WEISSKUNIG.

Shield. Italian, ca. 1560-70 (cat. no. 17)

Tyrol; Augsburg, Nürnberg, and Landshut in southern Germany; Antwerp and Brussels in the Netherlands; Paris and Tours in France. In the early sixteenth century, Henry VIII of England established a court workshop in Greenwich (1514); it was staffed with Flemish and German craftsmen (for this reason it was called the Almayn Workshop), and it produced battle and tournament armor in deluxe editions for the king's court and for diplomatic presents.

The German shops worked under entirely different conditions. Their local guild regulations permitted only a small number of helpers per shop, usually not more than five, in order to spread the workload evenly. The head of the shop stamped his mark on the finished armor, which was then checked and counterstamped by the guild.

Armor was subject not only to technical innovations, but also to fashion changes; sometimes there are minute stylistic differences that permit dating of an armor within five years.

During the fifteenth century, especially in Germany, armor elements had a slender, streamlined look, with sharp edges and with elements such as elbow cops and shoulders coming to points, reminiscent of features of Gothic architecture. Therefore this style is called "Gothic" armor. After 1500, the style changed radically; all shapes became more rounded with an emphasis on the horizontal, according to the upcoming Renaissance taste. A special feature which developed at this time was the fluting of armor plates, sometimes called "Maximilian" armor after Emperor Maximilian I (reigned 1493-1519). One of the reasons for this attractive style was the armorer's desire to maximize protection and minimize weight. A fluted armor plate gained strength through this "corrugated-iron" effect and could thus be made slightly thinner and appreciably lighter than a smooth plate.

Though it has been said over and over that the days of the armored knight ended when the stalwart longbowmen of Crécy (1346) and Agincourt (1415) defeated the flower of French chivalry, the plain truth is that ninety-five percent of surviving armor is of the period *after* Agincourt. The armored horseman even adapted to the new menace of the firearm, again brought to bear against him by the foot soldier, and with the development of reliable gunlocks the knight took up pistols instead of the old lance. Elite cavalry regiments wore armor, at least cuirass and helmet, up to World War I; though their breastplates were not proof against the missiles of high-powered rifles, they were still useful against sword cuts, and gave cuirassiers the edge over unarmored dragoons or hussars. Even today armor has its place, as we see when riot squads advance with bulletproof vests (very much like the old "pairs of plates"), with visored helmets, and behind shields, where street fighting leaves modern technology aside and goes back to clubs and thrown rocks.

Fig. 8.
"The Armorer." Woodcut by Jost Amman, from his STÄNDEBUCH *(Frankfurt/Main, 1568), illustrating all crafts and trades.*

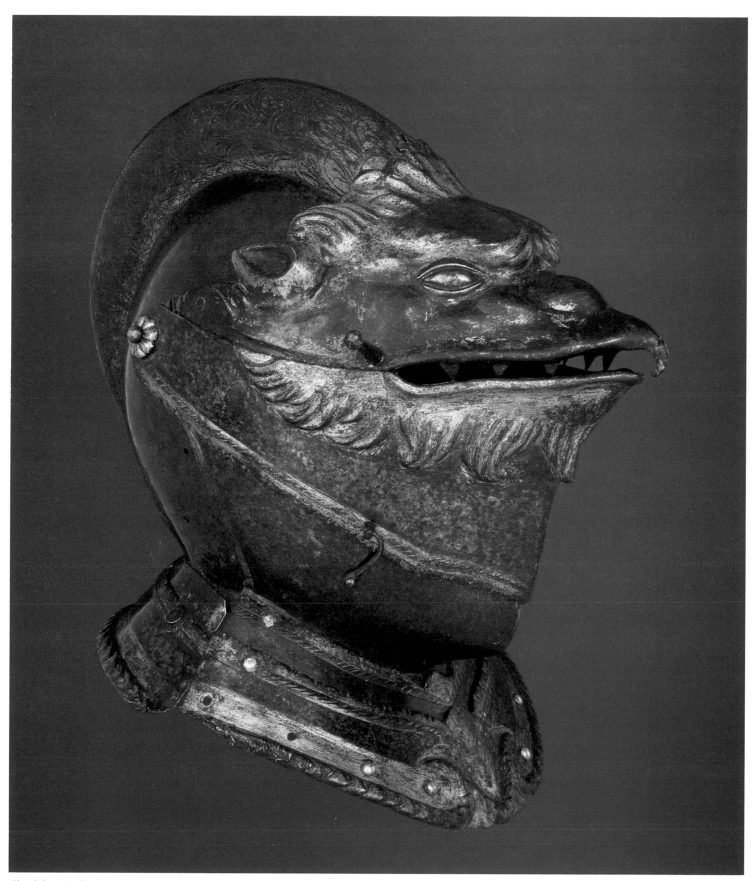

Close helmet. Italian, ca. 1590 (cat. no. 26)

I

Barbut

North Italian (Milan), ca. 1450-60
Steel
Height 11½ in. (29.2 cm.)
Weight 7 lb. 4 oz. (3.28 kg.)
Ex collection: Count Gino Cittadella,
Villa Saonara, near Padua; Luigi Grassi,
Florence; Julius Böhler, Munich; Samuel
J. Whawell, London; Sir Guy F. Laking,
London; Clarence H. Mackay, Roslyn,
Long Island; Stephen V. Grancsay, New
York
Gift of Stephen V. Grancsay, 1942 (42.50.15)

The English term barbut (from the Italian, *barbuta*) denotes a characteristically tall form of visorless helmet with narrow T- or Y-shaped face opening that was worn almost exclusively in Italy in the third quarter of the fifteenth century. This barbut is forged from a single plate of steel, its hemispherical skull rising to a sharp comb at the top and descending at the sides and back almost to the tops of the shoulders; the back of the helmet has an elegant profile that curves inward to follow the nape of the neck, then turns outward to form a short tail. The face opening is T-shaped and is reinforced by an applied band of iron held by decorative rosette rivets. The series of rivets encircling the middle of the bowl formerly secured a strap on the inside, to which was sewn a padded lining; below this, on either side, is a pair of rivets to secure the chin straps, now also lost.

Perhaps no other object in this exhibition better demonstrates the virtuoso talent of the armorer than this simple but elegantly proportioned and gracefully shaped barbut. It should be kept in mind that the armorer forged the barbut from a single plate of steel, hammering the metal into shape while maintaining the protective thickness of the plate and smooth rounded glancing surfaces. Its beauty is thus integral with its protective function. Like most helmets of the fifteenth century, it was originally polished mirror bright, though a number of paintings and other works of art—such as the "birthplate" of Lorenzo de' Medici (fig. 6) or the intarsia panels from Federigo da Montefeltro's study from Gubbio (fig. 9)—show barbuts covered with fabric, mounted at the edges with decorative borders, and surmounted by heraldic crests. Helmets decorated in this manner (cat. no. 3) are referred to in documents as *alla Veneziana* (in the Venetian manner) to denote the preference in Venice for colorfully decorated helmets such as these. This barbut has no holes for the attachment of such ornaments or crest, but nevertheless can be associated with Venice by the presence of a tiny mark in the form of the Lion of Saint Mark stamped on the left cheek. A total of six barbuts in the Metropolitan Museum are stamped with this mark,

Cat. no. 1

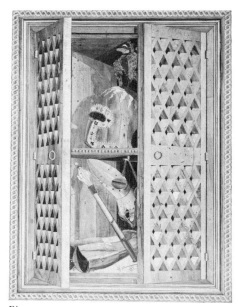

Fig. 9.
Crested barbut on intarsia panel from wainscoting of the studiolo of Duke Federigo da Montefeltro at Gubbio, now at the Metropolitan Museum. Italian, 1480-85. Rogers Fund (39.153).

which is variously thought to be the ownership mark of the Venetian arsenal, or a
customs control mark used in Venetian
territory. This barbut is one of seven or
eight, each bearing various armorers'
marks, but all with the Lion of Saint Mark,
that are said to have been discovered early
in this century in Venetian territory, in the
possession of Count Gino Cittadella, at
Villa Saonara, near Padua.

Three armorer's marks are stamped into
the metal at the rear of the helmet. The
upper mark is formed of the letters XPO
surmounted by an open crown, and a pair
of marks below, each composed of the
letters S Y beneath a split cross.

The marks are apparently unrecorded
but are of a type generally recognized as
Milanese. The letters incorporated into
the marks are usually abbreviations of
the armorer's Christian or family name.
The master's mark on this barbut probably
refers to a Christoforo (the Greek chi-rho
monogram – X P – stands for Christ, so
that X P O can be read Christoforo). Many
armorers with the name Christoforo are
recorded in Milanese documents of the
fifteenth century, including one Christoforo dei Seroni, mentioned in 1483.
Whereas the last name of this armorer
agrees with the second set of marks (the
letters SY beneath a cross could plausibly

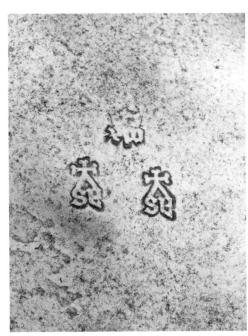

Detail of cat. no. 1. Armorers' marks

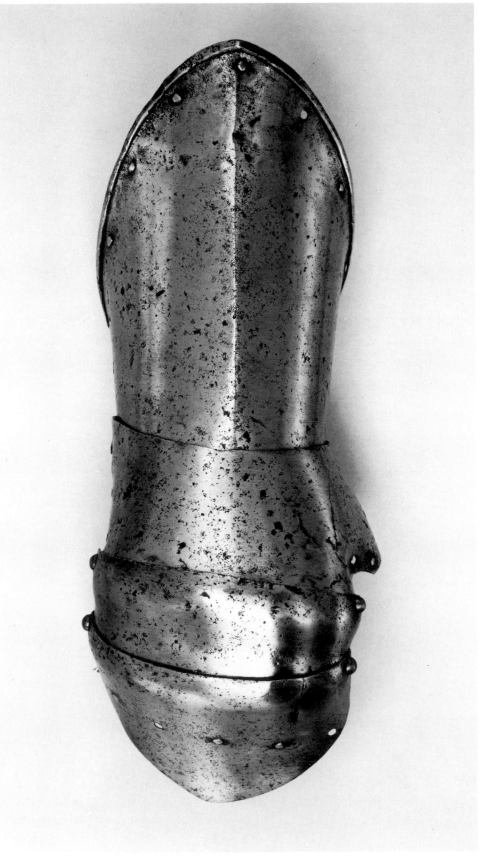

Cat. no. 2

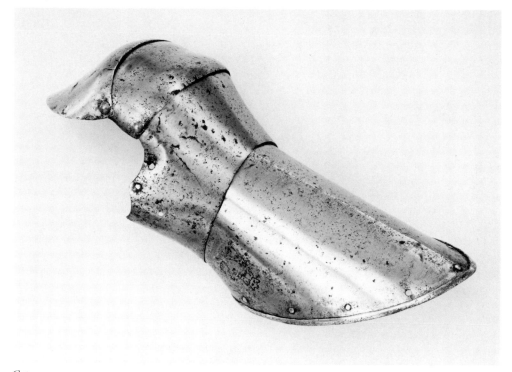

Cat. no. 2

Detail of cat. no. 2. Armorers' marks

be an abbreviation for Seroni), the recorded date for this armorer is considerably later than the dating of this barbut. Whether or not this helmet is an early work by Seroni or is by another armorer named Christoforo is subject for further speculation.

References: Laking sale, 1920, no. 40; Laking, 1920-22, II, pp. 6-7, fig. 340; Grancsay, 1931, no. 57; Grancsay, 1963, p. 183.

2
GAUNTLET FOR THE RIGHT HAND
Antonio Missaglia and workshop, active in the second half of the 15th century
North Italian (Milan), ca. 1452-60
Steel
Length 12³/16 in. (31 cm.)
Weight 15 oz. (.425 kg.)
Ex collection: Bashford Dean, New York
The Bashford Dean Memorial Collection, 1929 (29.158.228)

The gauntlet of mitten type is constructed of four plates held together by dome-headed iron rivets (modern) and com-prises a long pointed cuff plate with sharp medial ridge, the edge turned over outward and flattened, with lining rivets below; a single metacarpal plate extended at one side to accommodate the thumb (the thumb plates are lost); and two plates covering the fingers, embossed slightly to accommodate the knuckles, the lowermost plate pointed and fitted with lining rivets. This gauntlet would originally have been fitted with a leather glove (perhaps covered with mail or thin plates of steel to protect the exposed ends of the fingers) sewn to the lining straps. Stamped at the base of the cuff plate on the inner side just above the thumb are three armorer's marks: (above) the letters MY beneath a crown, and (below) the letter M beneath a split cross, twice repeated.

The marks on this gauntlet identify it as a product of the Missaglia workshop, the most famous Milanese armorers in the fifteenth century, and are of the type believed to have been used by the shop under the direction of Antonio Missaglia and his brothers from 1452 until at least the end of the century. The shape of the gauntlet, with its long pointed cuff, medial ridge, and turned edge, suggests a date early in this period, probably before 1460, and can be compared to gauntlets associated with armors dating from the period about 1450-60 in the Church of Santa Maria delle Grazie, at Curatone near Mantua.

Reference: Boccia and Coelho, 1967, pp. 142-143.

3
SALLET
North Italian (Milan), ca. 1470, with later additions
Steel, gilt copper, velvet
Height 9¹/2 in. (24.2 cm.)
Weight 8 lb. (3.63 kg.)
Ex collection: Richard Zschille, Grossenhain, Saxony; Morgan S. Williams, Glamorgan, Scotland; Bashford Dean, New York
The Bashford Dean Memorial Collection, 1929 (29.158.15)

Italian paintings of the fifteenth century provide ample evidence that color played an important role in the appearance of the

Cat. no. 3

armored knight. The metal plates themselves were often colored by heat to a blue or black finish, and the edges were sometimes enriched with gilt metal borders; rich brocades and velvets frequently covered the armor, and huge crests composed of gilt metal, leather, parchment, and feathers surmounted the helmet. Helmets decorated in this way appear to have had great popularity in Venice, so much so that helmets covered with velvet are generally referred to as *alla Veneziana* (in the Venetian manner). Decoration of this sort is ephemeral, however, and seldom survives in its original condition, though the present example preserves some hints of the brilliant effect such armor must have made.

The helmet belongs to a type known as a sallet (from the Italian *celata*), an open-faced helmet formed of a single plate shaped to the skull. The face opening is wide for ease of vision and breathing, and the sides sweep back in an arc from the face to the short tail. Each side of the skull is covered by a piece of velvet, once red but now mostly rubbed smooth and oxidized to a golden brown color; to the edges of the sallet are applied two bands of gilt copper embossed in the center with an ornamental pattern of threaded buttons, with a repeated pierced leaf pattern along their upper edge; a luxuriant branch of acanthus sweeps over the arched comb. Riveted to the front of the helmet is a decoratively cut cartouche-shaped shield of gilt copper engraved with the arms of the Capello family of Venice: a broad brimmed hat with crossed chin straps, as a "canting device" or pun on the family name (*capello,* "hat" in Italian).

Recent restoration of the sallet necessitated the removal and cleaning of the fabric and metal mounts, a process in which the iron surface of the skull was revealed for the first time in many decades. At the rear of the bowl, to either side of the comb, are faint traces of two armorer's marks. One of these is apparently surmounted by an open crown, a type of mark used by Milanese armorers, though the rest of the mark is indecipherable. The skull, which probably dates about 1470, is pierced with numerous holes; those around the brow are for lining straps, and the rest for securing the decorative mounts. The hole found at the center of each side of the skull provides evidence that additional mounts at one time decorated this helmet, though the lack of corresponding holes in the present velvet indicates that this fabric is a later addition, perhaps of the eighteenth or nineteenth century. The gilt-copper mounts, on the other hand, are much older and may date from the early sixteenth century, when the threaded-button motif was an ornamental device commonly utilized in the etched decoration of armors (for example, cat. no. 9). Many sallets and barbuts of the fifteenth century are today preserved with mounts of much later date (seventeenth century and later), these usually of flat copper or brass sheet cut to the shape of the helmet and gilt. The mounts on this helmet are much better designed and are boldly embossed in relief, which suggests that they are of Renaissance origin. The decoratively shaped shield at the front of the helmet also follows a late sixteenth-century pattern, and so may date somewhat later than the rest of the mounts. The appearance of this helmet was once augmented by a salmon-colored paint, of which faint traces are still preserved in the crevices of the mounts. This sallet has clearly had a long and useful life, and perhaps served in Venetian pageant and parade over several centuries.

References: Forrer, no. 60, pl. 8; Demmin, fig. 74 E; Williams sale, 1921, no. 67; Grancsay, 1930, p. 88.

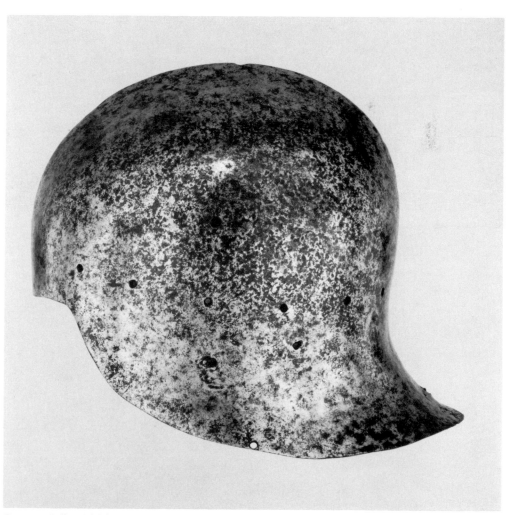

Cat. no. 3. Sallet with fabric and metal mounts removed

Cat. no. 4

Detail of cat. no. 4. Armorer's mark

4

SALLET
Austrian (Innsbruck), ca. 1480
Steel
Height 9³/₄ in. (24.8 cm.)
Weight 6 lb. 2 oz. (2.73 kg.)
Ex collection: Constantin Ressman, Florence; Maurice de Talleyrand-Périgord, Duc de Dino, Paris
Rogers Fund, 1904 (04.3.229)

The high-domed helmet bowl has a sharp central ridge; in front the eyeslit is cut into the recess above the protruding rim; in back this rim is swept into a sharp point. Nine large star-shaped rivets and two small ones secure the lining of the helmet. An armorer's mark (shield with a horseshoe and a crescent) is stamped at the front of the helmet to the left and right of the central ridge.

Sallets were one of the two basic types of helmets in use during the fifteenth century. They were less confining than the other type, the armet (cat. no. 7), which enclosed the head completely, and for this reason they were preferred by light cavalrymen and even foot soldiers. When the man-at-arms was not in action, he wore his sallet pushed back, which left his face entirely free and allowed him better ventilation and easier breathing. The sallet

Fig. 10.
KNIGHT, DEATH, AND THE DEVIL. *Engraving by Albrecht Dürer, German, 1513 (42.160.2).*

worn in fighting position was pulled down over the face, with the fighter peering through the eye slit. However, the rim of the sallet covered the face only partially, and for the protection of chin and neck a special defense element, the bevor, was attached to the upper part of the breastplate and kept in position by a strap around the knight's neck. Some sallets have movable visors, which could be raised instead of pushing the entire helmet back; probably the most famous representation of such a visored sallet is Albrecht Dürer's engraving *Knight, Death, and the Devil*, 1513 (fig. 10).

The shield-shaped armorer's mark with a horseshoe and a small crescent is attributed by Bruno Thomas to Adrian Treytz the Elder of Innsbruck in the Tyrol. The Innsbruck master Jörg Treytz (active 1466-99) had a very similar mark with a horseshoe enclosing a Gothic letter I (for *Jörg*, George). The horseshoe was a popular shop sign for all workers in iron, such as blacksmiths and farriers.

References: Cosson, 1901, no. B. 10, pl. 7; Dean, 1905, fig. 50E; Grancsay, 1953, no. 15, ill.

5

BREASTPLATE
German, ca. 1480
Steel
Height 17¹/₄ in. (43.8 cm.)
Weight 5 lb. 12 oz. (2.6 kg.)
Ex collection: Sir Guy F. Laking, London; Henry G. Keasbey, Eastbourne, England
Bequest of George D. Pratt, 1935 (48.149.32)

This breastplate is made from two parts, held together by four star-shaped rivets. The deeply scooped neckline and the armholes have outward-turned borders; the lower part of the breast is sharply ridged and sweeps up into a central squared-off point with twin cutouts at the top. The edges of the lower plate are paralleled by two shallow embossed ridges, the armholes with triple ridges. The waist lames are missing, but holes indicate they were once attached. In the upper part of the upper breast, two star-shaped rivets indicate where shoulder straps were once attached.

Throughout the fifteenth century breastplates were made in two parts,

loosely riveted together in the German fashion or attached to one another by straps and buckles in the Italian fashion, to allow extra mobility of the body. The cuirass—breastplate and backplate—was the last element of body armor added to the complete "knight in shining armor." This was not for lack of technical dexterity on the part of the armorers, because skillfully articulated and jointed arm and leg defenses of plates were fully developed by the middle of the fourteenth century, but it seems to have been a reluctance of the knights to encase their torsos in unyielding plates. It was not before the beginning of the fifteenth century that knights were willing to accept the confining cuirass. The loose connection between the two sections of the breastplate was a compromise which made it more acceptable by permitting a small amount of movement.

Reference: Keasbey sale, 1924, no. 287, pl. XXXI.

6

ELBOW GAUNTLET
FOR THE LEFT HAND
South German or Austrian (Innsbruck), ca. 1490
Steel
Length 14¹/₂ in. (36.8 cm.)
Weight 1 lb. (.45 kg.)
Ex collection: Bashford Dean, New York
The Bashford Dean Memorial Collection, 1929 (29.158.255 b)

The long, slender cuff is semicircular in section and has a low medial ridge; its upper edge is obliquely cut on the inner side, with turned edge, to facilitate the bending of the elbow. A plate to cover the inside of the lower arm was formerly attached to the cuff by hinges and a strap and buckle (one of the hinges and the buckle remain). The two holes at the top of the cuff allowed the gauntlet to be attached directly to the cowter (elbow cop). The back of the hand is covered by five metacarpal plates, the upper two embossed over the ulna, and an embossed knuckleplate connects the metacarpal lames to the five finger lames of mitten type. The base of the cuff is decorated with V-shaped flutes radiating upward, the area between them filled with a diamond-shaped panel embossed in low relief;

Cat. no. 5

V-shaped flutes radiate in a downward direction across the back of the hand and fingers. The points of the knuckles are outlined with engraved diamond shapes.

This unusual type of gauntlet covered the lower arm up to the elbow and was secured to the cowter by a "point" (lace), and consequently eliminated the need for the lower vambrace. Elbow gauntlets of this type were worn in Germany and Austria at the very end of the fifteenth century, and one of this type is illustrated in Dürer's famous engraving *Knight, Death, and the Devil,* which is dated 1513 but which illustrates an armor of about 1490 (fig. 10). Though unmarked, this gauntlet is similar to several other elbow gauntlets stamped with the marks of Innsbruck armorers that are preserved in the Waffensammlung, Vienna, and Churburg Castle, Sluderno (Italy). The long, slender proportions of this gauntlet and the linear emphasis created by its radiating fluted surfaces are features typical of late fifteenth-century German armor and are quite distinct from the fuller, more rounded forms of contemporary Italian armor.

Reference: Trapp and Mann, 1929, nos. 51, 52, pl. XL, figs. b, c; Innsbruck, 1954, nos. 33, 34, 38.

7
ARMET
Italian, ca. 1490
Steel
Height 10⅝ in. (27 cm.)
Weight 7 lb. 3 oz. (3.26 kg.)
Ex collection: C. A. de Cosson, Florence; Rutherfurd Stuyvesant, Paris; Alan Rutherfurd Stuyvesant, Allamuchy, New Jersey
Gift of Alan Rutherfurd Stuyvesant, 1949 (49.163.4)

The term armet is generally used to denote a visored helmet of particular construction, one in which large cheekpieces are hinged to the base of the bowl just above the ears and close in front of the chin. The face opening is formed in the space between the rim of the bowl and the edges of the cheekpieces, an area closed and protected by a short, pointed visor hinged to pivots on either side of the bowl. The right side of the visor is pierced with a slot and

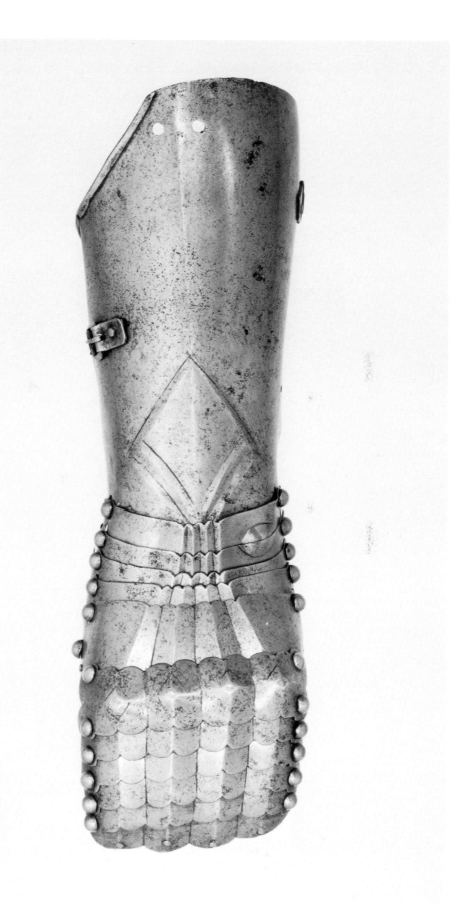

Cat. no. 6

Cat. no. 7. Visor raised

holes for ventilation, and has a lifting peg. A cusped brow reinforce riveted to the front of the bowl, and a circular plate (rondel) attached by a short stem to the base of the bowl at the rear of the helmet are two other features common to the armet. Apart from the rondel and stem, which are restorations, this armet is entirely homogeneous. Its original appearance would have included a protective curtain-like mail fringe attached by rivets to the lowermost edge of the helmet, and several plates known as a bevor, or wrapper, which fit over the front of the armet to reinforce the lower face and neck regions. The bevor was attached by straps reaching around the armet and buckling at the back, just above the stem of the rondel which held the strap securely in place. The keyhole-shaped slot at the top of the comb originally held the support for a decorative or heraldic crest which once surmounted the helmet.

The armet was the typical head piece of the fully armored equestrian knight throughout most of the fifteenth century, and its smooth, compact, rounded form typifies the streamlined appearance of fifteenth-century Italian armor in general. The armet's close-fitting form necessitated its highly practical and ingenious construction, with cheekpieces hinged to the bowl that opened to admit the head. The vulnerable areas that resulted where plates overlapped, particularly at the front of the chin and along the edge of the visor (which, incidentally, was not fastened closed to the cheekpieces but was merely held down by its own weight), were protected by the addition of the bevor that fit over the lower front half of the helmet. The bevor also protected the front of the neck, which was otherwise covered by the collar of a mail shirt worn underneath the armor and by the mail fringe suspended from the edge of the armet. The ventilation holes in the visor are only on the right side, so that the more exposed left side, which usually bore the brunt of blows, was not weakened.

Throughout its long use, the armet underwent gradual changes in design, and this particular example can be dated toward the end of this development, about 1490. Features which distinguish this armet as a late example include the pronounced comb; the large cusped brow reinforce which covers more than half the skull, its lower edges turned out to cover the hinges of the cheekpieces and its front edge turned out over the eyes; the shape of the visor; and the large inverted semicircular face opening.

The pierced ventilation openings on the right side of the visor are unusual for Italian armets but are found on armets believed to be of Flemish origin and on a group of armets found in English churches, such as those at Beverley Minster, Yorkshire, at Isleham, Cambridgeshire, and Hawstead, Suffolk. Apart from the visors, these armets are so similar to their Italian counterparts that it is impossible to determine if they were made in Italy for export to the north, or if they were made locally in England or Flanders, closely copied from Italian models.

References: Cosson sale, 1893, no. 235; Dean, 1911, no. 56, pl. XXIX; Dean, 1914, no. 18, pl. XIII; Laking, 1920-22, II, p. 86, fig. 439.

Cat. no. 7. Back, opened

Cat. no. 7. Profile, visor closed

8

FOOT-COMBAT HELM
English or Burgundian, ca. 1500
Steel, brass
Height 17¼ in. (44 cm.)
Weight 10 lb. 6 oz. (4.7 kg.)
*Ex collection: Adalbert von Kolasinski,
Warsaw; Bashford Dean, New York
The Bashford Dean Memorial Collection,
1929 (29.158.38)*

This helmet consists of only three plates: bowl, visor, and chin defense. All three are connected by a pivoting hinge in the region of the temples; the pivot itself is hidden by a flange of the detachable visor, and a small cutout at the upper edge of this flange permits insertion of the fastening pin. The visor is of the "bellows" type, with twenty-four slits of differing lengths for seeing and breathing; it is secured against accidental opening by a spring-activated peg and push button on the right side of the chin. A brass plume holder is mounted in the center at the back of the bowl.

On the bowl, to the right of the rear end of the comb, are faint traces of the maker's mark: the two horns of a half moon. These are almost certainly parts of a well-known mark, "M under Crescent," that appears on a fragmentary armor in the Hungarian National Museum, Budapest, on several horse armors, two of them in the Real Armeria, Madrid, and two in the Tower of London, and also on two other helmets and one cowter in the Metropolitan Museum. The two horse armors in the Tower were made for Henry VIII, and all elements marked with the "M under Crescent" share features that characterize the very distinctive style of the so-called Greenwich School, the English Royal Workshops at Greenwich, established by Henry VIII in 1514. Its first master armorer in charge was Martin van Royne, who is still mentioned in 1540 as "Old Martin," apparently in an advisory capacity. As his name indicates, Martin van Royne was from the Netherlands, which were part of Burgundy at that time. The elements marked with "M under Crescent" link the few surviving pieces from the Burgundian court workshop with those of the much better known Greenwich School. The most logical explanation for this would be to assume that

the mark "M under Crescent" was that of Martin van Royne, that he was trained in the Burgundian court workshop and later worked for the English court, and that he stopped using his personal mark, when he became official head of the Royal Workshops in 1514. The mark itself could be easily explained as Martin's initial combined with an element from the van Royne family coat of arms, *a half-moon between three stars.*

One of the three basic categories of tournament of the fifteenth and sixteenth centuries was the foot combat: two contestants fought on foot with a variety of weapons, such as swords, pikes, clubs, or poleaxes. Armor designed for foot combat had special features to meet the demands of this technique. For instance, on horseback the inner side of the thighs, the seat, and the crotch of the knight were protected by the body of the horse itself and by the saddle rather than by body armor. In foot-combat armor, on the other hand, the thighs and backs of the knees were completely encased in articulated lames against hamstringing cuts, and the crotch was protected by either a flaring knee-length skirt or by tightly molded plates known as a hoguine. The helmets for foot combat were of two types: those for fighting with pikes had closed visors with narrow eye slits, but those for sparring with swords, quarterstaves, or poleaxes, where thrusting was strictly against the rules, could have visors with multiple perforations for better sight and, especially, much easier breathing. In order to avoid neck injuries, foot-combat helmets had nonflexible neck parts, firmly attached to the cuirass.

References: Kolasinski sale, 1917, no. 1471, pl. 30; Grancsay, 1933, no. 45; Grancsay, 1953, no. 22, ill.

9
ARMOR
North Italian (Milan), ca. 1510
Steel, partly gilt
Weight 19 lb. 13 oz. (8.70 kg.)
*Ex collection: Ambrogio Uboldo, Milan;
C. A. de Cosson, London; William H.
Riggs, Paris
Gift of William H. Riggs, 1913 (14.25.716)*

This armor comprises a gorget (upper three lames restored), a globose breast-

plate with waist lame and three skirt lames (gussets at the armholes restored), a backplate with waist lame and three skirt lames, and complete pauldrons and vambraces. Originally this armor would have had a matching helmet (perhaps originally a visored sallet or an open-faced helmet with peak at the front), gauntlets, and long articulated tassets reaching to the top of the knees. A harness of this type, which has narrow "spaudler"-type pauldrons (those covering only the outer portions of the arms and not overlapping the breast and backplates) and no lance rest on the breastplate, seems to have been intended for an officer in infantry or light cavalry service. The surface of the armor is fluted with a series of shallow concave channels, alternately plain and etched and gilt. The etched decoration includes a number of motifs taken from antique and Renaissance ornament, such as acanthus scrolls, threaded buttons, zigzag, and strapwork interlace, as well as trophies of antique arms and armor, set against an obliquely hatched background. The decoration also includes religious imagery and pious inscriptions: the Trinity at the front of the gorget; a frieze composed of three compartments across the top of the breastplate, with the Virgin and Child in the center, Saint Paul on the right, Saint George on the left, with an inscription below, CHRISTVS RES VENIT IN PACE ET DEVS HOMO FACTVS ES (Christ the King came in peace and God was made man); and another Biblical inscription across the top of the backplate, JESUS AVTEM TRANSIENS PERMEDIVM ILORVM EST (But Jesus passing through the midst of them went His way).

This armor is an extremely rare Italian example of the fluted style of armor commonly known as "Maximilian" (see cat. no. 10), which enjoyed great vogue in Europe—and especially in Germany—during the first three decades of the sixteenth century. A number of innovations in construction, shape, and decoration distinguish this harness from Italian armors of the fifteenth century. One notes, for instance, the appearance of the gorget (or collar) of articulated plates, which was worn beneath the cuirass and protected the vulnerable neck region far better than the collar of a mail shirt. The breast and

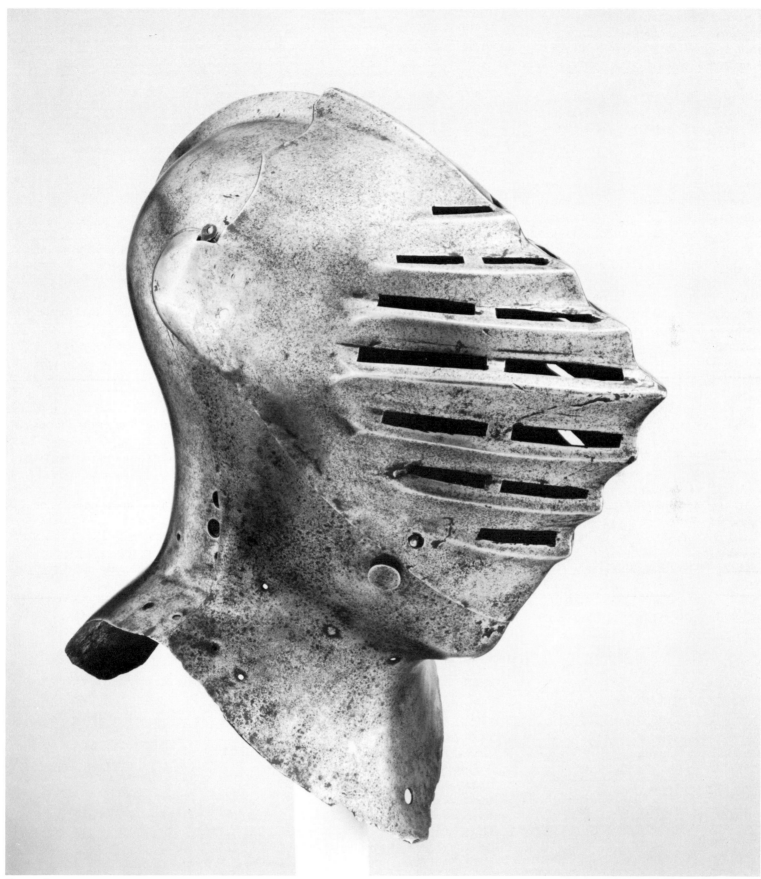

Cat. no. 9

backplates are now constructed as large single plates of steel, rather than formed of two or more overlapping plates connected to one another by rivets or straps as had been the practice of the fifteenth century (for example, cat. no. 5). The years around 1500 also witnessed the cross influence of armor design north and south of the Alps. This exchange of ideas is exemplified here by the adaptation of parallel-fluted surfaces of the native German Maximilian-style armor to the rounded forms typical of Italian armor. This Italian type of fluted harness, referred to in contemporary documents as *armatura alla tedesca* (armor in the German style), differs from a German Maximilian armor in that its channeled surfaces are generally shallower and flatter. The etched decoration of this armor is unmistakably Italian in character, and its pictorial and ornamental vocabulary, its sketchy graphic style, even the hatched treatment of the background, all derive from the example of contemporary Italian prints.

The technique of etching iron or steel with a mild acid (such as warm vinegar) is known from late medieval recipes, but it does not appear to have been used as a decorative medium until the last quarter of the fifteenth century. Its earliest application seems to have been the decoration of armor and sword and dagger blades,

Cat. no. 9

though it was not extensively used in arms decoration until the first decade of the sixteenth century. Two different methods of etching armor should be noted. In the first, plate or blade is completely coated with an acid-proof substance, such as wax or paint, through which the design is scratched with a needle. When the acid is applied, it bites only the exposed metal. The result is a pronouncedly linear design, which was usually blackened or gilt for added contrast with the bright steel. In the second technique, the design is painted directly onto the surface with a brush dipped in wax, leaving the unpainted background areas exposed to the acid; this technique produced a design raised very slightly above its background, which was also blackened or gilt for contrast. The first technique was used primarily in Italy and is represented on this armor, whereas the second technique was preferred in Germany, an example of which can be seen on the German armor in catalogue number 18.

Early etched decoration on Italian armor reflects the eclectic nature of Renaissance art and often combines ornamental motifs derived from classical antiquity (such as portraits of the Caesars and Roman warriors, as well as military trophies), Christian imagery, and personal badges or mottoes. The religious motifs usually include figures of Saint George (the patron saint of knights) or Saint Barbara (patron of armorers and artillery men); pious inscriptions, as on this armor, presumably had a talismanic significance appropriate to the soldier facing battle.

This armor has on several occasions been published as having belonged to Charles de Bourbon, Constable of France (1489-1527). This attribution, first proposed by Cosson in 1893, was based upon the similarity of decoration between this armor and a helmet and shield believed to be the constable's that are preserved in the Waffensammlung, Vienna (inv. nos. A. 328 and A. 328a). The similarity of these pieces is, however, only a general one, so that this attribution need no longer be maintained.

References: Biorci, 1839, p. 14; Uboldo sale, 1869, no. 30; Cosson sale, 1893, no. 121; Dean, 1915, p. 61, pl. XXVII; Laking, 1920-22, III, pp. 248-250, fig. 1035; Mann, 1929, p. 225, pl. LXX, fig. 1.

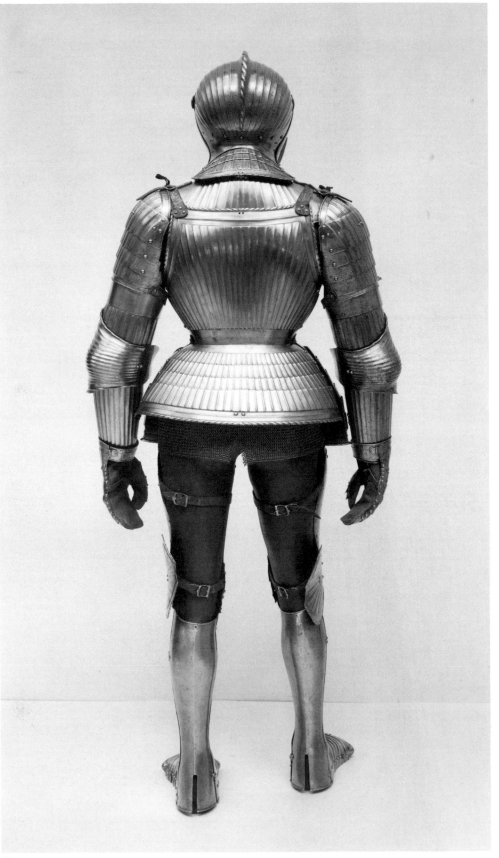

Cat. no. 10

ARMOR, SO-CALLED
"MAXIMILIAN" ARMOR
German (Nürnberg), ca. 1525
Steel, leather
Weight 49 lbs. (22.2 kg.)
Ex collection: Raoul Richards, Rome;
Maurice de Talleyrand-Périgord, Duc de
Dino, Paris
Rogers Fund, 1904 (04.3.289 a-q)

This armor cap-à-pie represents plate armor to its fullest extent. Unfortunately, due to the ravages of time, complete armors, homogeneous in all parts, are of extreme rarity. For this reason, this armor contains several elements – for instance, its helmet and the shoulders – that were not part of the original set. However, they are so closely related in style that only careful examination of minor details, such as the fluting and roping of the borders, confirms that these elements were parts of a different harness, though quite possibly from the same workshop. The left arm defenses – vambrace, cowter (elbow cop), and rerebrace – are modern restorations in place of a lost original; the besagews are also restorations and were added in 1923 by the Metropolitan Museum's armorer, Raymond Bartel. They demonstrate how completely skillful restorations can blend with the original elements that served as models, but how careful observation can tell the difference.

Six of the original elements are stamped with marks: the shoulders are marked with the city arms of Nürnberg, the helmet bears the letter N in a pearly circle stamped on the inside of its chin defense, similar marks – a Gothic N – are on the inside of the upper lames of the thigh defenses, and finally a rather indistinct maker's mark – probably representing a helmet with a plume of three feathers – is stamped on the cuff of the right gauntlet. The arms of Nürnberg, *divided per pale, or, a halved eagle sable, and bendy of six, argent and gules,* are the proof mark of the armorers' guild; the letters N were stamped by officials of the Nürnberg hammermill. A helmet with a triple plume flanked by the letters V and S was the mark of the celebrated armorer Valentin Siebenbürger (died 1564); whether the mark on this armor, which lacks these letters, might be an early form of this mark is not certain,

Cat. no. 10

though it has to be considered that these punches were subject to much wear and had to be replaced fairly frequently.

The pauldrons of this armor show additional punch marks, six dots on the right, and five dots on the left shoulder. These dots were assembly marks for suits of one pattern, in order to prevent their elements from becoming mixed up in the arsenal—which is, of course, exactly what has happened here. Other assembly marks are the Roman numerals I-X with which the consecutive lames of the sabatons—the steel shoes—are marked on the inside.

This fluted armor is most striking in appearance, with the play of light on the rippling surface greatly enhancing its functional beauty. The flutings presumably originated as imitations of the pleatings of late fifteenth-century fabric tunics, but it soon became apparent that they actually strengthened the plates in a "corrugated-iron" effect. As a result the thickness of the plates could be diminished and the total weight decreased. However, probably because of the additional labor necessary for this very exacting fluting and the resulting price increase, this attractive style went out of fashion after a generation or so.

The often used term "Maximilian" for this fluted armor refers to Emperor Maximilian I (reigned 1493-1519) during whose reign this style was introduced. Maximilian—surnamed *der letzte Ritter,* "the Last of the Knights"—was a great enthusiast of knightly prowess, of tournaments, and of fine armor (fig. 11). In 1478 he had married Mary of Burgundy, heiress to the most sophisticated court in Europe, which sported even a court armor workshop at Arbois, set up by Mary's father, Charles the Bold. Unfortunately, Duke Charles had been killed in battle the previous year, 1477, and most of his lands, including Arbois, had been annexed by the French king. Therefore, Maximilian decided to install a court workshop of his own, at Innsbruck in the Tyrol, where there was an established center of armor manufacture. This Innsbruck workshop seems to have been influential in the spreading of the Maximilian style in German lands, particularly to Nürnberg, which became the principal center of production for armors of this type. Interestingly, this fashion did not become popular in western Europe.

References: Richards sale, 1890, no. 1028, pl. XXV; Cosson, 1901, no. A.5; Laking, 1920-22, III, pp. 251, 253, fig. 1037; Grancsay, 1964, p. 15, no. 2, fig. 19.

Fig. 11.
EMPEROR MAXIMILIAN ON HORSEBACK. *Woodcut by Hans Burgkmair, German, 1518.*

11
MAIL CAPE ("BISHOP'S MANTLE")
German, ca. 1530
Steel, brass, leather
Length 25 in. (63.5 cm.)
Weight 14 lb. 13 oz. (6.7 kg.)
Ex collection: William H. Riggs, Paris
Gift of William H. Riggs, 1913 (14.25.1534)

Constructed out of interlinked steel rings of three different sizes, with the thickest rings in thirteen rows forming the standing collar, this cape is composed of triangular gussets to give it its full flaring shape. Around the lower edge are triangular points composed of latten rings for decorative effect. A slit in the collar in front is closed by a strap and buckle at the throat.

These "bishop's mantles" were popular with German mercenary foot soldiers in the first half of the sixteenth century (fig. 12), and were often worn as the only element of armor.

Reference: Nickel, 1974, ill. p. 62.

12
CLOSE-GAUNTLET
(OR LOCKING GAUNTLET)
South German (Augsburg), ca. 1540-45
Steel, partly gilt
Length (open) 15¾ in. (40 cm.);
(closed) 8½ in. (21.6 cm.)
Weight 1 lb. 10 oz. (0.737 kg.)
Ex collection: Richard Zschille, Grossenhain, Saxony; Samuel Austin, Philadelphia; Frank G. Macomber, Boston
Gift of Christian A. Zabriskie, 1936 (36.145.13)

This mitten-type gauntlet is constructed with a circular cuff, to which are attached five metacarpal plates—the fourth covering the base of the thumb and with two thumb lames riveted to it—and four broad finger lames (each extending laterally across four fingers) with embossed and roped knuckle ridges. The lowermost finger lame is unusually long and extends to the back of the cuff, to which it is attachable by means of a keyhole-shaped slot and turning pin. The edge of the cuff is turned over inward and roped, and is followed by a series of brass-covered lining rivets; it retains portions of the original lining strap, which once held a leather glove. The decoration consists of a wide recessed band around the cuff, and narrow bands extending the length of the gauntlet, which are etched with trophies of arms and foliage on the dotted background, completely gilt; between the narrow bands is a series of reversed S-shaped ornaments, etched with foliage, and gilt.

The close-gauntlet (or locking gauntlet) is a special form of mitten gauntlet for the right hand which can be locked in a closed position so the sword cannot be dislodged from the grip. The close-gauntlet appeared at the turn of the sixteenth century, when new and more specialized forms of armor were being developed for the joust and tournament. It was designed exclusively for use with a sword in foot combat, in a closed arena or over a barrier, or in a mock battle with a group of knights on horseback. Though numerous tournament regulations prohibited its use ("He that shall have a close gauntlett, or any thing to fasten his sword to his hand, shall have no prize"), a sufficient number of examples survive to prove that it enjoyed considerable popularity. A very

Cat. no. 11

Fig. 12.
FIVE LANDSKNECHTE. *Etching by Daniel Hopfer, German, ca. 1525. Hopfer was a much sought-after etcher of armor.*

early example of the close-gauntlet is associated with the foot-combat armor of Claude de Vaudrey, made in Milan about 1495 (Vienna Waffensammlung, inv. no. B. 33), which suggests that it may have been an Italian invention. Another early example is the close-gauntlet belonging to the foot-combat armor of Henry VIII of England, about 1520 (Tower of London, inv. no. II 6), which predates the long series of close-gauntlets that accompany the garnitures of armors made at the Royal Workshops at Greenwich, beginning with the so-called Genouilhac armor of 1527 (Metropolitan Museum, acc. no. 19.131.1).

The reversed S-shaped ornament used to decorate the gauntlet alludes to the "slashed" decoration common in European costume in the first half of the sixteenth century. In garments of this fashion, S-shaped cutouts would be made in the exterior fabric, through which would show the lining of contrasting color. Such decoration was often combined with voluminous puffed and gathered forms, as exemplified by the colorful costume of the *Landsknechte* (the German infantry troops

Cat. no. 12

Cat. no. 12

that served as mercenaries throughout Europe, as in fig. 12). Puffed and slashed costume was occasionally imitated in armor of articulated plates, but this fashion was short-lived and is encountered infrequently after about 1530.

This gauntlet is a late example of armor decorated with "slashes" and probably dates to the late 1530s or 1540s, when numerous narrow bands of ornament were common to armor decoration. An incomplete armor from the Scott Collection in the Glasgow Art Gallery (inv. no. '39-65s), which is decorated with narrow vertical bands and slashes etched and gilt, is very similar to this gauntlet, though there are sufficient differences in the etched motifs to indicate that the armor and gauntlet belong to different garnitures. The Glasgow armor is dated 1545, which provides an approximate date for this gauntlet. Though unmarked, the gauntlet may be attributed to Augsburg manufacture by the similarity of its etched foliate ornament with decoration on documented or marked Augsburg armors (Real Armeria, Madrid, inv. nos. A. 118-A. 138, dated 1538, and A. 157-A.158, dated 1543-44). It is worth noting that the fashion for armor decorated with narrow bands and slashes lasted in England until the 1560s: the Elizabethan courtier Thomas Howard, Earl of Norfolk, possessed such an armor, complete with pieces for the tilt and tournament, including a close-gauntlet, which was made for him at Greenwich about 1560-65.

References: Forrer, no. 153, pl. 53; Zschille sale, 1897, no. 100; Austin sale, 1917, no. 370; Macomber sale, 1936, no. 384; Grancsay, 1937, pp. 188-191.

13
FENCING BUCKLER
Italian, 16th century
Steel
Height 12 in. (30 cm.)
Weight 2 lb. (1.30 kg.)
Ex collection: Ambrogio Uboldo, Milan;
William H. Riggs, Paris
Gift of William H. Riggs, 1913 (14.25.732)

The shield is trapezoidal in outline and longitudinally convex in its median section, with the side edges slightly bent forward. It is reinforced around its edges

with hammered turns and the semiglobular heads of the rivets, which once held the lining. A framework of six steel rods is riveted to the surface to stop and entrap an opponent's blade. The hook in the center could also serve this function, but its main purpose was for carrying the shield attached to a waist belt, with its grip on the outside ready to be grasped. The grip is secured by steel straps bridging the hollow of the median ridge.

Since the thirteenth century, small round bucklers faced with steel had been used in sword fencing; when not in use they were usually hung from the belt or over the sword hilt. The quadrangular shield with a hollow mid-ridge is of eastern European origin, and appeared in the fourteenth century as the Lithuanian targe; originally these targes were of wood covered with leather to prevent splitting. In the sixteenth century, formal fencing was practiced with rapier and parrying dagger, though conservative fencers retained round or square bucklers, enhanced with cunning devices such as the catch hook. Both techniques are illustrated in the woodcuts of the treatise *Opera nova*, 1536, by the Bolognese fencing master Achille Marozzo (fig. 13).

Reference: Uboldo, 1841, pl. IV, fig. A.

Fig. 13.
"A combat between a left-hander and a right-hander."
Woodcut illustration from Achille Marozzo's OPERA
NOVA, *1536, shows the use of fencing bucklers and swords.*

14
BURGONET
Attributed to Desiderius Helmschmid (1513-1578/79), armorer, and Jörg Sigman (ca. 1527-1601), goldsmith
South German (Augsburg), ca. 1550-55
Steel, gold
Height 13 1/4 in. (33.6 cm.)
Weight 4 lb. 11 oz. (2.12 kg.)
Ex collection: Anne Louis Girodet-Trioson, Paris; Dukes de Luynes, Chateau de Daumpierre; William H. Riggs, Paris
Gift of William H. Riggs, Paris (25.135.66)

This open-faced helmet, of a type known as a burgonet, looks to classical antiquity as inspiration for its form and decoration. The hemispherical skull is formed of a single plate of iron, which is drawn up into an arched crest at the top and projects at the front and back in a sharp peak over the eyes and a short tail covering the nape of the neck. The consummate skill of the armorer is demonstrated by the way the figure of the winged triton is raised three dimensionally from the front of the crest. The entire surface is covered with dense relief decoration achieved by means of embossing, a technique in which the design is first worked from the inside with mallet and blunt chisel, with the finer details later chiseled directly onto the exterior surface. The relief decoration has a punched background and is blackened overall; in its original appearance the then dark blue metal surface would have been richly highlighted with gold, almost all of which is now lost. Only the brow plate riveted at the inside of the skull, and the recessed border of the peak, contain traces of delicately engraved foliage and gold-damascened ornament. This helmet once would have had cheekpieces to fasten it beneath the wearer's chin, though their absence makes the sweeping lines of peak and neck guard more prominent.

The decorative motifs comprise an encyclopedic variety of classical imagery — with particular emphasis on the themes of triumph and fame — so beloved in the Renaissance. They include, in a medallion in front, the winged figure of Fame holding her attribute, a trumpet, and on the peak over the eyes, two winged putti with writing tablets and pens — genii of history — flanked on either side by trophies of arms

Cat. no. 13

Cat. no. 14

Cat. no. 14

Detail of cat. no. 14. Medallion on right side

the decorative scheme of the famous Gallery of Francis I at the royal Château of Fontainebleau, outside Paris, completed about 1544. These motifs were disseminated throughout Europe by printmakers at Fontainebleau, Paris, and Antwerp, and were favored by German goldsmiths, including Jörg Sigman of Augsburg.

This helmet bears remarkable similarity in design and workmanship to an armor made in Augsburg in 1549-50 for Prince Philip (later King Philip II of Spain), son of the Emperor Charles V. This well-documented armor (preserved in the Real Armeria, Madrid, inv. no. A. 239-A. 242) was the creation of two of Augsburg's most famous metalworkers, Desiderius Helmschmid, armorer to Charles V, and the goldsmith Jörg Sigman, and is one of the most ambitious works of embossed armor ever undertaken by German armorers. The Metropolitan Museum's burgonet is so close in style to Philip's armor that there can be little doubt that it, too, was the product of the collaboration of Helmschmid and Sigman, and dates from about 1550-55. It is not likely, however, that the burgonet was intended as an exchange piece for Philip's armor, as a second burgonet would have been redundant for such a harness. This burgonet also lacks the double-headed eagles, symbols of the Holy Roman Empire, that are so conspicuous on Philip's armor. As it probably does not belong to the Madrid armor, this helmet's original owner unfortunately remains unidentified.

Reference: Grancsay, "Helmet," 1955, pp. 272-280.

and bound captive warriors dressed in antique armor. At the nape of the neck, a winged female satyr holds two banners and is flanked on either side by tritons blowing horns. Each side of the skull is covered with a complex web of strapwork supporting nude male and female figures, putti, satyrs, harpies, grotesque masks, and oval medallions enclosing warriors in antique armor and a youthful figure of David holding Goliath's head. At the center of each side, a laurel wreath encloses a battle scene (left) and a scene of triumph (right), subjects which Stephen V. Grancsay interpreted as the battle of Pharsalus (Julius Caesar defeated his arch-rival, Pompey) and the triumph of Caesar. This particular type of decoration, in which the figures stand on or are enclosed within the strapwork, originated in

15

GAUNTLET FOR THE RIGHT HAND

North Italian (Milan), ca. 1555-60
Steel, partly gilt
Length overall 11³/4 in. (29.9 cm.)
Weight 1 lb. 13 oz. (.822 kg.)
Ex collection: Bashford Dean, New York
The Bashford Dean Memorial Collection,
1929 (29.158.215)

This gauntlet of large proportions is composed of a pointed cuff ending in a heavy roped turnover with dome-headed steel lining rivets below, four metacarpal lames, and embossed knuckle lame, and small scale-like lames covering the thumb and fingers (the scales of all but the little finger are modern). The decoration consists of gilt bands etched with trophies of antique and Renaissance arms and armor, musical instruments, and foliate scrolls on a granular background; three narrow fillets along the margins of each band act as a frame for the ornament.

This gauntlet belongs to a large group of Italian armors which dates from the middle of the sixteenth century and whose decoration consists of wide bands (typically three each on the breastplate and backplate) of trophy and foliate ornament, usually gilt. The most complete and representative armors of this group are those of Paolo Giordano Orsini, Duke of Bracciano, in the Vienna Waffensammlung (inv. no. A. 690), and an armor made for a member of the Farnese family (Ottavio, Duke of Parma, Piacenza, and Guastalla) in the Museo di Capodimonte, Naples (inv. no. 4010-4011), both dating from the 1550s. A single backplate, dated 1557 and decorated in the same style, is in the Museo Stibbert, Florence (inv. no. 515), and it provides the general date for this group.

The decoration of this gauntlet appears to match exactly that of another backplate in the Museo Stibbert (inv. no. 2634), whose trophy decoration also includes the letter S, possibly the initial of the etcher. This gauntlet and the Stibbert backplate probably belong to the same armor, of which other pieces have not yet been identified.

Reference: Boccia and Coelho, 1967, p. 465.

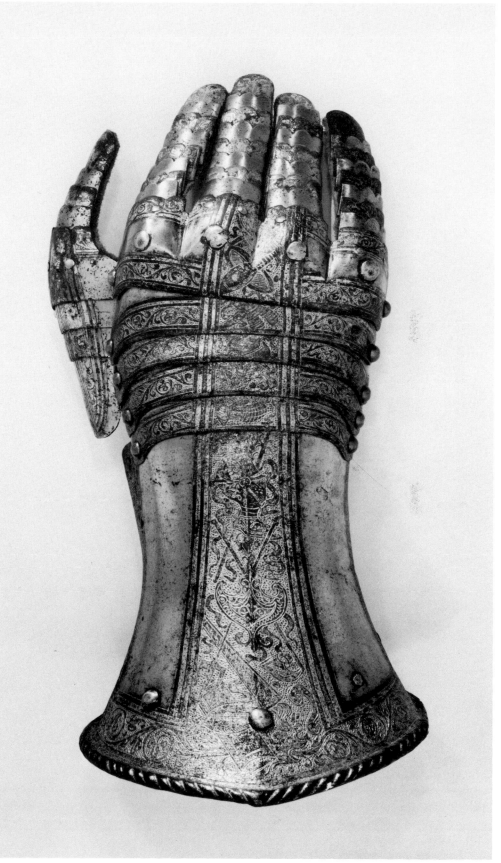

Cat. no. 15

Cat. no. 16

16

CIRCULAR PARADE SHIELD (TARGET)
Italian (possibly Florence), mid-16th century
Wood, leather
Diameter 21⅝ in. (54.9 cm.)
Weight 5 lb. 13 oz. (2.64 kg.)
Ex collection: William H. Riggs, Paris
Gift of William H. Riggs, 1913 (14.25.780)

This shield is formed of a circular base of wood, convex in section, and covered on both sides with black leather embossed in low relief and tooled. The decoration on the front is organized into three fields consisting of two concentric bands enclosing a large circular center, each band framed with a laurel wreath. The center area contains a scene of the hero Perseus rescuing the maiden Andromeda from the dragon (Ovid, *Metamorphoses,* IV). Above Perseus are the letters S L. The wreath surrounding the center field extends out to the next concentric band in four loops which form medallions depicting a satyr holding a trumpet (above), Hercules and the Nemean lion (below), and two bust-length profile figures of a man in armor and a woman (at the right and left sides respectively). Between the medallions and in the outermost band the space is filled with entwined foliate strapwork.

The decoration on the inside of the shield is organized into a large circular field at the center, surrounded by a single concentric band decorated with foliate scrolls, the two fields framed by narrow bands of stylized palmettes. The central field has an undecorated oblong panel, set slightly to right of center, which held the arm pad and straps for the forearm and hand, now lost; six iron rivets in the form of rosettes, which secured the arm pad, are preserved. Within this undecorated area there are random toolmarks, apparently made by the leather worker to test his tools. Above and below this section are horizontally elongated oval medallions framed by scrollwork and enclosing scenes of Hephaestus presenting Thetis with a shield (below), and Thetis presenting the shield to her son Achilles (Homer, *Iliad,* XVIII-XIX); the areas between the medallions and undecorated section are filled with foliate scrolls.

This shield belongs to a large and distinctive group of embossed leather objects made in Italy in the sixteenth century, which includes chests and boxes of various types, as well as shields, helmets, scabbards for swords and daggers, and powder flasks (cat. no. 116). In the process of manufacture (known as *cuir bouilli,* boiled leather in French; *cuoio cotto,* cooked leather in Italian), the leather was first softened and then incised on the exterior with the design, which was raised in low relief by pressure applied from the back. The finer details of the design were added by working again on the front surface, and the background of the decoration was punched for contrast. When the entire surface was then subjected to heat, the leather hardened and preserved the design. The process of working and decorating these leather objects was analogous to the embossing of iron, but was, of course, undertaken by specialized leather workers rather than armorers or goldsmiths. These shields and helmets of embossed leather, like their iron counterparts, were intended for parade rather than for battle.

In spite of their survival in large numbers, surprisingly little is known about the origin of these shields. Their place of manufacture has been ascribed by Gall to Milan, but without documentation, and except for two shields in London and Offenbach inscribed with the initials B P, presumably those of the craftsman, their authorship remains anonymous. (The letters S L found on the front of our shield are too large and conspicuous to be a craftsman's signature and, more likely, refer to the name or motto of the shield's owner, not as yet identified.) L. G. Boccia has recently suggested that an embossed leather shield bearing the portrait of Duke Alessandro de' Medici (Museo Nazionale del Bargello, Florence, inv. no. M. 758) is of Florentine manufacture. If this is indeed the case, the entire group of these

Cat. no. 16. Inner side

shields may also have originated in Florence, a city still renowned for its leatherwork. A shield decorated with identical subject matter and exhibiting the same workmanship as this shield is now also in the Museo Nazionale del Bargello (inv. no. M. 757; formerly in the Medici armory); presumably both were made by the same master.

References: Gall, 1965, pp. 164-187; Florence, 1980, no. 235.

17
Parade shield
Italian (Milan), ca. 1560-70
Steel, gold, silver
Diameter 22¹/₂ in. (57.2 cm.)
Weight 8 lb. 4 oz. (3.73 kg.)
Ex collection: Pierre Moszynski, Cracow
Gift of Henry Walters, 1925 (25.163.1)

The circular shield of blue-black steel is slightly convex in shape and is embossed in relief, chiseled, punched, and richly damascened in gold and silver. The outer edge is rolled over and obliquely striped in gold and silver. A wide band along the outer edge is embossed with four round medallions which are framed by damascened strapwork and contain portrait busts of four Roman emperors. The medallions are connected to one another by ribbons from which are suspended trophies of antique and Renaissance arms, bunches of fruit and flowers, and putti with fluttering striped drapery. The large circular field at the center, framed by a laurel wreath of alternating gold and silver leaves, contains a representation of the Conversion of Saint Paul. The figures are dressed in Roman armor, their flesh silvered, and the details of the costumes and landscape damascened in different patterns. A series of holes around the edge of the shield formerly held rivets to secure the lining, with its arm pad and straps for the forearm and hand, now missing.

The scene depicted on this shield focuses on the most dramatic moment in the life of Saint Paul, his conversion on the road to Damascus: "And as he journeyed, he came near Damascus, and suddenly there shined a light from heaven and he fell to the earth, and heard a voice saying unto him, Saul, Saul, why persecutest

Detail of cat. no. 17

Fig. 14.
CONVERSION OF SAINT PAUL. *Engraving by Mario Cataro, Italian (Rome), 1567 (59.595.16).*

Cat. no. 17

thou me?" (Acts of the Apostles, 9:3-4). Saul (as Saint Paul was known prior to his conversion) is shown thrown to the ground, his horse collapsed under him, with his hands shading his eyes from the blinding apparition. Two of his troopers attempt to assist him, whereas the rest of his band stare in amazement or flee in terror. The deep landscape that opens into the background includes a city of domed buildings, tall pyramids, and statues, and to the left three tiny figures can be seen: Saul, blinded by his vision, is led by two companions to Damascus, where his eyesight will be restored and his new-found Christian faith confirmed.

Circular or oval iron shields embossed in relief with scenes taken from ancient, Biblical, or even contemporary history, or from classical mythology, were a specialty of Milanese armorers and goldsmiths in the second half of the sixteenth century. These shields were often accompanied by open helmets of burgonet or cabasset type decorated to match which, when worn with a fabric costume, mail, or even plate armor modeled upon Roman prototypes, constituted a parade armor in the heroic style. Embossed iron, richly colored and damascened in gold and silver, provided an excellent medium for representing complex, figural scenes which were usually based on engravings issued by Italian and French printmakers. The graphic sources for the decoration of this shield can be identified: the putti and bunches of fruit and flowers suspended from ribbons that decorate the rim appear to be based upon the ornamental border of a print by French engraver Jean Mignon at Fontainebleau, and the scene of the Conversion of Saint Paul derives from a print of that subject by the Parisian engraver Etienne Delaune. Delaune's print is undated, but it must have been issued before 1567 when an exact copy of it was published by Mario Cataro in Rome (fig. 14). In light of the fact that there are no major differences between the Delaune print and the copy by Cataro, there is no way of ascertaining which print served as the model for the armorer. If the print by Cataro was used, the shield must date after 1567.

The Conversion of Saint Paul seems to have been a popular Christian theme for the decoration of these shields (most of which favored ancient history in their subject matter) and is found on two shields in the Musée de l'Armée, Paris (inv. nos. I.65 and I.79), four shields in the Armeria Reale, Turin (inv. nos. F.17, F.19, F.20, and F.21), and on a cabasset in the Wallace Collection, London (inv. no. A.133). The scene on the cabasset also appears to be based upon the same print by Delaune or Cataro.

References: Dean, 1925, p. 291; Grancsay, 1953, no. 33.

18
ARMOR
North German, ca. 1560
Steel
Weight 27 lb. (12.23 kg.)
Ex collection: Prince Peter Soltykoff, Paris; William H. Riggs, Paris
Gift of William H. Riggs, 1913 (14.25.711)

This armor consists of an open burgonet wrought in one piece, rising to a low comb at the top, with short, upturned projections at the front and back, and hinged cheekpieces that tie beneath the chin; an "almain"-type gorget to which spaulders of eight lames each are permanently attached; a breastplate without lance rest, with pronounced medial ridge projecting to a sharp point two-thirds from the top, and mounted with movable gussets, waist lame, and skirt lame; and backplate with attached waist and skirt lames. The decoration consists of bands of etched ornament, white on a blackened dotted ground, found on the principal surfaces and along the edges of the main plates. The ornament includes hunting scenes on the burgonet; satyrs, allegorical figures, masks and other grotesque ornament on the gorget, spaulders, and breastplate; and equestrian figures, horses, and trophies of arms and musical instruments on the backplate. Parallel to the main etched bands are two narrow recessed bands, the outer one etched with a series of "pearls." The main surfaces of the armor between the etched bands are painted black (modern). On the left side of the breastplate is a quatrefoil medallion, etched and silvered, in the center of which is a figure of Daniel in the Lion's Den, and around the edges the inscription (now badly rubbed) ACH GOT BEWA(HR) M(IR NI)CHT MEHR LEIB SELE GVT V(ND) EHR (Oh God, protect no more than my body, soul, property, and honor); below the medallion is etched a badge consisting of clasped hands, the initials H and I, and a heart surmounted by a ducal crown.

This armor is one of a series of similar harnesses generally believed to have been made for the festivities surrounding the wedding of Duke Julius of Brunswick-Luneburg to Hedwig of Brandenburg, which took place in Berlin on February 25, 1560. Each of these "wedding armors" bears the same silvered medallion, with

the lover's device of clasped hands and crowned heart below, together with the initials H (for Hedwig) and I (for Julius). Presumably these armors would have been worn by the duke and his favorite retainers for the tournaments held in celebration of this event. An inventory of 1667 of the duke's arsenal at Wolfenbüttel records the existence of fifteen of these harnesses, of which only five are still found in Brunswick. Long before the dispersal of these armors in the nineteenth century, their parts were inadvertently mixed up and the majority are now incorrectly assembled. Judging from the different types of decoration on this harness, it seems to be composed of at least three different "wedding armors," of which the helmet belongs to one, the gorget and breastplate to another, and the backplate to a third.

The "wedding armors" belong to an even larger group of armors made for the central and northern German courts in Saxony, Schleswig-Holstein, and Hesse, as well as Brunswick. Not a single example bears armorer or guild marks, so that the center of manufacture has not yet been identified (the town of Brunswick is known to have produced foot-soldiers' armors in large numbers, but not necessarily armors of such high quality as these). Though constructed along the lines of the famous black and white infantry armors produced in great numbers in Nürnberg, these north German armors exhibit peculiarities of construction, form, and decoration that distinguishes them from contemporary south German armors. Two of the most obvious characteristics of this northern group are the sharply pointed breastplate and a distinctive etched decoration of high quality, with a marked preference for pictorial scenes and grotesque ornament.

Some of the graphic sources for the decoration of this armor can be identified. The scrolled band across the top of the breastplate is etched with satyrs amid strapwork which derive from the ornamental engravings of Cornelis Bos of Antwerp, as do the figures of Mercy and Justice in the band at the center of the breast; the scenes of boar and bear hunting on the burgonet are taken from a different graphic source, two prints by Virgil Solis of Nürnberg.

Cat. no. 18

Cat. no. 18

The Metropolitan Museum also possesses a number of arms from the duke of Brunswick's arsenal, including a two-hand sword dated 1573 (acc. no. 04.3.60), an all-steel wheellock pistol (acc. no. 14.25.1424), and a cartridge box dated 1571 (acc. no. 14.25.1500), each bearing the monogram of Julius and Hedwig; from a later period comes a partisan bearing the arms of Duke August Wilhelm, dated 1718 (acc. no. 41.146).

References: Bohlmann, 1914, pp. 333-358; Bohlmann, 1935, pp. 40-41; Mann, 1952, pp. 5-7; Grancsay, Allentown, 1964, no. 3; Schele, 1965, nos. 143 and 147; O'Dell-Franke, 1977, nos. g.3 and g.9.

19a
ARMOR
Italian, ca. 1575
Steel, partly gilt, leather, velvet
Ex collection: William H. Riggs, Paris
Gift of William H. Riggs, 1913 (14.25.717 a-r)

This armor cap-à-pie is almost completely intact, though the decoration on its breastplate was re-etched and the gilding on all elements was done in modern times. On the gorget and the gauntlets several minor lames are restorations.

Spanish fashion dominated the style of armor in the second half of the sixteenth century. Backed by the enormous wealth of the newly discovered and conquered Americas, Spain had become the foremost political power in Europe and was able to exert its influence in practically all ways of life. In armor, a direct influence from the fashionable Spanish costume was the decoration with etched stripes on otherwise plain surfaces. It is particularly conspicuous here on breast and backplate where the three stripes — down the center and slanting from the armholes — imitate the seams of a Spanish doublet which would there have been enhanced by fancy stitching or applied ribbons.

The seemingly peculiar "peascod" shape of the breastplate originally had a thoroughly practical function: in fighting with lances it was essential for a knight to safeguard against his opponent's lance slipping in under his own left arm because this could wrench the arm out of its socket or even break it. The best way to avoid such a mishap was to make sure that the

Cat. nos. 19a, b

enemy's lance would snap on impact, which would be possible only if the lance point hit the armor plate at an angle of exactly ninety degrees. In order to withstand the impact of the lance thrust, the knight had to lean forward in his saddle at an angle of thirty degrees, so to present a vertical surface to meet the onrushing lance, the breastplate had to be slanted forward in its lower part, thus creating the peascod shape. Oddly, the dashing peascod shape, so functional in armor, became fashionable in civilian clothes, and doublets with peascods were soon worn by dandies and solid burghers who never would have dreamed of braving a lance thrust in battle or on tournament field.

The lance, incidentally, was braced under the right armpit and against the lance rest on the right side of the breastplate. In order to accommodate the lance shaft, the right pauldron is shaped noticeably smaller than the left and has a cutout in its main lame. The left pauldron has a bolt for attaching a reinforcing element for the joust.

This armor possesses a second helmet designed for the tilt. It was the height of fashion during the sixteenth century for a knight to have a garniture of armor for field and tournament, with exchangeable parts for all eventualities. Since there were three categories of tournament—the tilt, the baston course on horseback, and the foot combat—with about two dozen finer nuances, some of the more comprehensive armor garnitures consisted of more than two hundred elements, though as a rule only a fraction of those survives.

References: Indianapolis, 1970, p. 46, no. 33; Nickel, 1974, ill. p. 127.

19b
ARMOR FOR HORSE
Italian, ca. 1575
Steel, leather, velvet
Ex collection: Counts Collalto, Castle Collalto in Treviso, Italy
Fletcher Fund, 1921 (21.139.2)

The word for "knight" in most European languages—*chevalier, caballero, cavaliere,*

Ritter—reflects the fact that he was a fighter on horseback. To own a horse was a considerable status symbol as well as an investment; a well-trained battle steed was equivalent to a dozen milch cows at least. For this reason it is understandable that a knight took great pains to protect his precious charger.

Though it was unchivalrous to harm the horse of an opponent (in a tournament this meant instant disqualification) because a horse was a valuable trophy meant to be captured, not destroyed, the knights discovered that their steeds were vulnerable by foes such as archers who did not feel compelled to obey the code of chivalry, and who themselves had little use for a war-horse. Horse trappings were introduced during the thirteenth century, mainly as protection against missiles. Made first of fabric—presumably quilted—and later of mail, their development paralleled that of armor for men, solid elements such as chanfrons, crinets, peytrels, and cruppers were gradually added. Many of these early armor elements were not necessarily of steel plates, but were often of hard-boiled leather, *cuir bouilli*. The first armored horses, completely clad in steel, appeared about 1450. The earliest surviving example, by the Master Pier Innocenzo da Faerno in Milan (active about 1450-60), is preserved in the Historisches Museum der Stadt Wien.

The horse armor shown here came originally from the armory of the counts of Collalto, an ancient dynastic family in northern Italy. During World War I the ancestral castle Collalto near Treviso was destroyed; the contents of the armory were packed up and sent to the count's residence in Vienna, but all got lost on the way except one cart carrying two horse armors, and one arm defense of a man's armor with decoration matching one of the horse armors (acc. no. 21.139.1). Shortly after the war they were located in Vienna by the Metropolitan Museum's first curator of arms and armor, Bashford Dean, and acquired for the Museum. Dean published his find in the Museum's *Bulletin*: "horse armor is *rarissima* in collection: indeed, more than one author has noted that the rank of a great armory depends upon its horse panoplies..." The Metropolitan Museum's collection,

incidentally, now has five complete horse armors.

References: Dean, 1922, pp. 190-193, ill.; Indianapolis, 1970, p. 46, no. 33.

20
PARADE ARMOR FOR FERNANDO ALVAREZ DE TOLEDO, DUKE OF ALBA
Luccio Piccinino (active ca. 1575-85)
North Italian (Milan), ca. 1575-80
Steel, gold, silver
Weight 25 lb. 12 oz. (11.66 kg.)
Ex collection: Dukes of Alba and Berwick, Madrid; William H. Riggs, Paris
Gift of William H. Riggs, 1913 (14.25.714)

This fragmentary armor is composed of a close helmet fitted with peak and barred visor, gorget, cuirass with deep peascod-shaped breastplate, pauldrons, and complete vambraces. The entire surface is embossed in high relief with vertical bands divided into architectural niches and medallions enclosing an encyclopedic variety of pagan gods and goddesses (Mars, Cupid, Apollo, Ceres), classical allegorical figures (Victory and Fame), Christian virtues (Fortitude, Justice, and Temperance), Biblical figures (Judith with the head of Holofernes, and David with the head of Goliath), and grotesques. The vertical bands are connected laterally by swags of fruit and flowers and bands of strapwork from which masks and bunches of fruit are suspended. The grotesque element of decoration is repeated in the large, grimacing Medusa, lion, and satyr masks at the top of the breastplate, the front, top, and back of the pauldrons, and on the points of both elbows, which also provide points of focus amid the superabundant and diffuse decoration. Though now patinated to a dark brown color, the iron surfaces retain traces of their original brilliant appearance: the flesh and costumes of the figures were silvered and gilt against a contrasting ground of blued iron, the strapwork bands were damascened in gold and punctuated with encrusted silver beads, and the areas between the vertical bands and garlands were chiseled with silver ribbons set against a ground damascened with gold scrolls. Some of the damascened

Detail of cat. no. 20. Back of left pauldron

1581, at the advanced age of seventy-three. The deep peascod shape of the breastplate and the general similarity between this armor and that of Farnese suggest a date of the late 1570s for the Alba armor. The existence of several other fragments of embossed armor in the distinctive Piccinino style (two gorget plates, a complete left vambrace, and fragments of a right vambrace), still preserved in the Liria Palace, as well as a falling buff (which does not fit the present helmet) in the Metropolitan Museum, suggests that a second armor by this Milanese master was also owned by Alba, or by another member of his illustrious family.

References: Dean, 1915, p. 72 and pl. XXVII; Laking, 1920-22, IV, p. 137, fig. 1223; Grancsay, "Luccio Piccinino," 1964, pp. 257-271; Grancsay, 1977, pp. 47-48.

21
BREASTPLATE
South German, 1580
Steel, leather
Height 17 in. (43 cm.)
Weight 11 lb. 15 oz. (5.4 kg.)
Ex collection: Bertram Arthur Talbot,
17th Earl of Shrewsbury, Alton Towers;
Bashford Dean, New York
The Bashford Dean Memorial Collection,
1929 (29.158.164)

This breastplate is of peascod shape with a sharp mid-ridge; its tassets are missing and the arm gussets are restorations. On either side of its deeply scooped neckline with prominent roped border are remnants of the leather shoulder straps. Its etched decoration is distributed in the typical three-bands arrangement styled after the embroidered seams of a Spanish doublet; an etched band of floral scrolls en suite with the three bands follows the curve of the neckline and is joined to the central band. To the right of the central band is etched a large crucifix with skull and crossbones at its base; on the left side is a kneeling man-at-arms, his hands raised in prayer and his halberd leaning against his shoulder, his open-faced burgonet is set next to his left knee on the ground. He is surmounted by a winding scroll inscribed O GOT ERERCI HOFNONG 1580.

This breastplate is of the so-called *Harnasch* type, designed for a light caval-

decoration is well preserved at the sides of the helmet, and one must imagine that the original chromatic effect was somewhat like that of the embossed iron shield (also of Milanese workmanship) in this exhibition (cat. no. 17).

The ravages of time have left this armor an unfortunate example of the terrible destruction moisture can wreak on steel surfaces. Now damaged and incomplete (the collar plates on the helmet, all but one plate of the gorget, the gussets on the breastplate, the entire right pauldron, and the lower lames of the left pauldron are all modern restorations), this armor nevertheless stands as a representative example of the work of one of Milan's finest armorers, Luccio Piccinino. All that is known about this craftsman, whose talents combined the art of the goldsmith with that of the armorer, is contained in a few sentences written in 1595 by a contemporary Milanese writer, Paolo Morigia, who praised Piccinino for his embossed and damascened decoration and mentioned an

outstanding armor made by Piccinino for Alessandro Farnese, Duke of Parma. An armor that belonged to Alessandro Farnese is preserved in the Vienna Waffensammlung (inv. no. A. 1132) and is presumed to be the very harness to which Morigia refers. Around the Farnese armor can be grouped a half-dozen other armors of very similar form and decoration, including the example illustrated.

This armor is presumed to have been made for Fernando Alvarez de Toledo, Duke of Alba (1508-1583) and was purchased in 1863 by the American collector William H. Riggs from the Alba collection housed in the Liria Palace, Madrid. Alba was one of the most famous generals of his day, a contemporary of Farnese's who served both the Emperor Charles V and his son, King Philip II of Spain. Alba is best known – or infamous – for his iron-fisted subjugation of Protestant forces in the Spanish Netherlands, of which he was military commander in the years 1567-73, as well as for his conquest of Portugal in

ryman or foot soldier. This is suggested by the absence of a lance rest, the pivoted hook on the right side of the breastplate for a full battle armor which would be necessary for the support of the heavy lance of a knight. The armored man portrayed wears the cuirass with long tassets, mail sleeves, and the open-faced burgonet that, together with the halberd, would be the typical equipment of an officer of *Landsknecht,* the celebrated German mercenary foot soldiers of the sixteenth century. It is most likely that this breastplate was part of the armor of just such an officer.

The particularly fine decoration of etched floral arabesques is practically identical to that on a breastplate in the Bayerisches Nationalmuseum, Munich (N 1478/79), which is signed by Hans Holzmann, an etcher documented in Augsburg, 1562-68. Surprisingly, however, the Munich breastplate bears the marks of the armorer Stefan Rormoser of Innsbruck in the Tyrol. Other Innsbruck armor with similar decoration and the same distribution of crucifix and praying warrior can be found in Churburg Castle, South Tyrol, where it is still kept in its original armory. It seems either that Hans Holzmann worked occasionally at Innsbruck, or that Innsbruck armor was sent to him when special decoration was desired.

References: Shrewsbury sale, 1857, no. 838; Stöcklein, 1908, pp. 382-387; Grancsay and Kienbusch, 1933, p. 145, no. 65, pl. XXXVI; Grancsay, 1953, no. 15, ill.

22
Jousting armor (Rennzeug)
German (Saxony), ca. 1580-90
Steel, leather
Weight 100 lb. (45.36 kg.)
Ex collection: Royal Saxon Armory, Dresden
Gift of Henry G. Keasbey, 1926 (26.92.3)

In addition to the jousting styles practiced all over Europe, there was a special joust – the *Rennen* – popular only in Germany and countries immediately adjacent to the east, such as Hungary. For the *Rennen* the lance was tipped not with a blunt or multiple-pronged coronel, but with a sharp point. *Rennen* armor differed from the other styles insofar as it used not a helm or a visored close helmet, but a *Rennhut,* a late version of the sallet. This *Rennhut* covered only the upper part of the face and had to be supplemented by a large molded shield, the *Renntartsche,* which covered upper arm, breast, shoulder, and chin up to the eye slit of the *Rennhut.*

At the court of the Prince Electors of Saxony, jousting was a favorite sport, enthusiastically shared by the electors themselves, particularly during the reigns of Moritz (1521-53), Augustus (1553-86), Christian I (1586-91), and Christian II (1601-11). The Saxon court armorers – Wolf and Peter von Speier and Wolf Beppighorn – designed a *Rennen* armor with special safety features, such as the bevor screwed and bolted together with breastplate, *Rennhut,* and shoulder guard, and a special brace bolted to the backplate and to the comb of the *Rennhut,* in order to keep neck and head of the jouster secure against whiplash. The large shoulder guard extending down to the left elbow like a one-sided cape was designed to prevent an opponent's lance from slipping in between body and arm, an accident which could easily result in a broken arm. The jouster's left arm was protected by an elbow reinforcement (missing on this example) and a special tilting gauntlet with a stiff cuff, while the right gauntlet has multiple lames in its cuff for greater mobility.

The *Rennen* was practiced in two basic varieties: the *Ballienturnier* and the *Freiturnier.* In the *Ballienturnier* the jousters were kept from colliding accidentally by a low lengthwise barrier (*Ballie*), while the *Freiturnier* was held in the open field. As a protection for the rider's legs, which might be crushed against the barrier by a swerving horse, the *Ballienküriss* was equipped with full leg armor, including steel sabatons. *Freiturnier* armor had leg armor only down to the knees.

The greaves mounted with the armor shown here are stamped with the mark of the armorers' guild of Augsburg, and are probably a later addition to make a Saxon-made *Freiturnier* armor suitable for the *Ballien* course. These tilting armors were stored in large numbers at the Dresden armory; besides "white" ones with polished surfaces, such as this one, there

Cat. no. 22

Cat. no. 23

were also many black ones for contrast. The Metropolitan Museum's armor has the name *He(rr) von Breitenbach* painted on the inside of its backplate; this means that at one time it must have been reserved for this gentleman. The Breitenbach family was of local Saxon nobility, with many of their members holding offices at the court throughout several centuries. In 1588 a knight Wolf von Breitenbach was steward (*Truchsess*) at the Dresden court, but he was not necessarily the one who had a claim on this armor. Jousts were held in Dresden as popular festivals even in the seventeenth and eighteenth centuries, long after this sport had become obsolete elsewhere, and it may have been a later member of this family who wore this harness. The very last of these jousts were romantic revivals held in 1938 and 1939!

There are at least six similar armors from the Dresden armory in this country: two in the Metropolitan Museum (one white, one black), two in the Philadelphia Museum of Art, and two in the John Woodman Higgins Armory in Worcester, Massachusetts.

Reference: Haenel, 1933, p. 18, pl. 9.

23
MORION
German (Nürnberg), ca. 1580-91
Steel, blackened, partly gilt, brass, leather
Height 10¹/2 in. (26.8 cm.)
Weight 4 lb. 1 oz. (1.84 kg.)
Ex collection: Royal Saxon Armory, Dresden;
Maurice de Talleyrand-Périgord, Duc de Dino, Paris
Rogers Fund, 1904 (04.3.224)

Forged in one piece this helmet has a high comb across its rounded bowl and an elegantly swept brim rising to sharp points at the front and back. Cheekpieces with chin straps are built up from three overlapping plates. The decorative heads of the rivets securing the lining are lion's masks holding rings in their mouths; the rivet heads on the cheekpieces are brass rosettes. A brass plume holder in the shape of a winged female half-figurine is attached to the rear end of the comb. The entire surface is blackened except for etched and gilt bands of arabesques along the edges of brim and comb and circular medallions on

bowl and comb. The smaller medallions on the comb show the arms of the Dukes of Saxony, *barry of ten, or and sable, a crancelin vert in bend overall,* on one side, and on the other those of the archmarshalship of the empire, *per fess sable and argent, two swords gules in saltire overall.* The large medallions on either side of the bowl show figural scenes from classical Roman history: the self-sacrifices of Marcus Curtius and of Mucius Scaevola.

Morions like this were once equipment of the personal guard – *Trabantenleibgarde* – of the Prince Electors of Saxony at Dresden, probably Christian I (reigned 1586-91). The colors black and gold were the livery colors of the Electors, taken from the arms of Saxony. The uniform of the guard was also black and yellow: black doublets and yellow trunk hose and stockings. The *Trabantenleibgarde* consisted of two companies, one mounted (on black horses) and one on foot, each about a hundred men strong. Great numbers of these morions were kept in the Dresden armory until the 1830s when a progressive-minded monarch ordered them to be sent to the opera house as stage props in an attempt to rid the armory of too much clutter. Alert dealers rescued them from the ignominious fate of slowly perishing in the obscurity of backstage shelves, and today they are prized collector's objects,

Detail of cat. no. 23. Mucius Scaevola

no self-respecting armor collection being without one.

This morion is stamped with the proofmark of the armorers' guild of Nürnberg and a master's mark, M R, probably the mark of Martin Rothschmied (died 1597).

References: Cosson, 1901, no. B. 39; Haenel, 1923, p. 68, pl. 34; Schöbel, 1975, no. 39.

Fig. 15.
"Squires of the Guard" (Spiessjungen). Woodcut by Jost Amman, from his STAMMBÜCHLEIN *(Nürnberg, 1589).*

24
MORION
German, ca. 1586-91
Steel, partly silvered, brass, glass, leather
Height 12⁹/16 in. (32 cm.)
Weight 4 lb. 11 oz. (2.12 kg.)
Ex collection: Royal Saxon Armory, Dresden;
Prince Peter Soltykoff, Paris; William H. Riggs, Paris
Gift of William H. Riggs, 1913 (14.25.650)

Forged in one piece with an extraordinarily high comb (4³/4 inches) rising from the rounded bowl, the strongly curved wide brim of this morion comes to sharp points at the front and back. Each cheekpiece is formed of three overlapping scales. Silvering over the entire surface covers intricately interwoven etched strapwork with a different design on each side. Large gilt

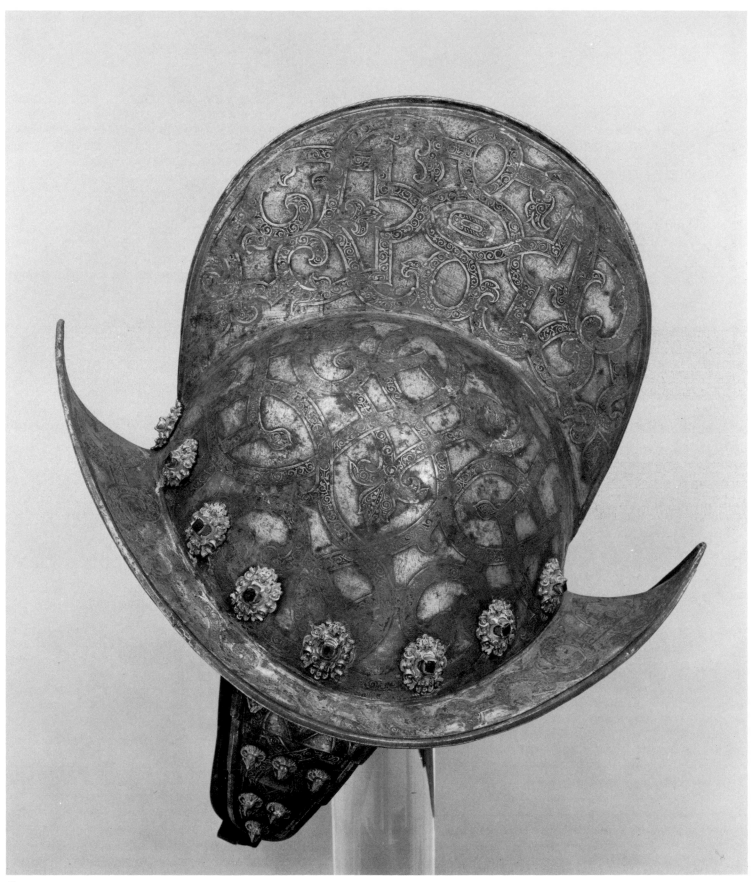

Cat. no. 24

Cat. no. 25

brass rosettes act as rivet heads securing
the inner lining, and each rosette contains
a square-cut glass "jewel," alternately red,
green, and blue. The rivet heads on the
cheekpieces are in the shape of ram's
masks.

Black morions with gilt strapwork and
medallions were part of the equipment of
the *Trabantenleibgarde* of the Prince Electors of Saxony in Dresden; these silvered
helmets seem to have been worn by officers of the guard.

Reference: Haenel, 1923, p. 70, pl. 35.

25
CABASSET
Flemish, ca. 1580-90
Steel, partly gilt, brass-capped iron rivets
Height 10 in. (25.4 cm.)
Weight 3 lb. 12 oz. (1.70 kg.)
Ex collection: Maurice de Talleyrand-
Périgord, Duc de Dino, Paris
Rogers Fund, 1904 (04.3.200)

Of typical cabasset form, this helmet has a
tall almond-shaped skull forged in one
piece, with a small backward-turned point
at the apex, and a short brim. The entire

surface is etched with a complex grid of
strapwork which supports architectural
elements, baldachins and canopies, swags
of drapery and fruit, and masks. This
framework is inhabited by a variety of
humans, animals, and fantastic creatures,
including warriors in Roman armor holding flaming torches, winged putti, winged
stags, snails, and dragonflies. At the center
of each side, standing beneath a canopy, is
a female figure personifying Astronomy
(right) and Rhetoric (left). The decoration is lightly etched onto the surface and

was once gilt. Brass-headed rivets around the base of the skull and edge of the brim retain on the inside fragments of the original lining straps, which also held the now-missing cheekpieces. The present plume holder at the back of the skull is etched with trophies of arms in a different manner from the rest of the helmet and is probably an old replacement. Etched in the strapwork along the left side of the brim is the number 1503 (for 1583 or 1593?) and *Laol...*, graffiti whose meaning is not clear.

This cabasset belongs to a small but distinctive group of Flemish armor which can be distinguished by the ornament which covers the entire surface. Some of the armors in this group are decorated with heraldic arms of some Netherlandish provinces, and one bears the arms of Antwerp, reputedly a major center for the production of armor; another piece is inscribed with the date 1585, which is also the approximate date of this cabasset. The decoration of this Flemish group shows a manneriest preference for dense, space-fitting ornament of complex design, and some of the finest decoration is actually adapted from prints published in Paris

or Antwerp. In the case of this cabasset, the figures of Astronomy and Rhetoric (fig. 16) are copied after two prints of the same title by the Parisian goldsmith and engraver Etienne Delaune. The seated Roman warriors and part of the complicated strapwork comes from prints of a very different nature, the Passions of Christ series designed by the Flemish engraver Marcus Gheeraerts the Elder and engraved by his co-patriot Jan Sadeler of Antwerp. The identification of the graphic sources utilized in the decoration serves to demonstrate, on the one hand, the eclecticism of sixteenth-century ornamental design, and on the other, the decorator's inventiveness in creating from diverse sources a new ornamental composition that is so well adapted to the irregular shape of this cabasset.

References: Robert-Dumesnil, 1865, IX, p. 103, nos. 340 and 344; Cosson, 1901, no. B. 38; Dean, 1905, p. 114, fig. 51 J; Mann, 1961, p. 22, fig. 13; Hodnett, 1971, pp. 60-61.

26
CLOSE HELMET
North Italian (Brescia?), ca. 1590
Steel, blued, silvered, and gilt
Height 11 3/4 in. (29.8 cm.)
Weight 6 lb. 10 oz. (3.00 kg.)
Ex collection: Della Scala family, Verona;
Lodovico Moscardo, Verona; Counts Erizo,
Verona
Fletcher Fund, 1929 (29.17)

The extraordinary appearance of this helmet is the result of its having been conceived as a fantastic dragon's head, the two-part visor embossed with fierce, penetrating eyes, a sharply arched beak, and a mouth full of menacing teeth, through which the wearer can peer. Bold, too, is the conceit of the crest as the body or tail of the beast draped over the skull, embossed in the round and engraved with a pattern of scales. The scale pattern is repeated along the embossed edges of the skull and collar lames. The surfaces were once brightly colored, the principal surfaces blued (now oxidized to a rich brown color) and the embossed areas silvered and gilt, of which some traces remain. Though intended for pageant rather than battle, the construction of this helmet follows conventional close-helmet form, with

visor and bevor pivoted together at the sides. A lifting peg fitted to the left side of the visor allows the upper half to be raised for ventilation, while a hook and pierced stud, also on the right side, secure the lower visor to the bevor. A strap and buckle originally fastened the bevor closed to the skull, and a plume holder was attached at the base of the skull, fixtures which are now missing. Five tiny holes between the scroll volutes at the center of the lowermost front collar lame indicate that something like a medallion or plaque (perhaps containing the arms or badge of the original owner?) was formerly riveted to this spot.

This helmet belongs to the Renaissance tradition of pageant armor made in imitation of antique Roman armor, or of more fantastic types which combined human, animal, and vegetable forms to create a grotesque appearance. Armor of this type was used for pageant and theatrical purposes from the fifteenth through the eighteenth century, but most sixteenth-century examples, including this helmet, owe their inspiration to the imaginative and exquisitely worked armors *alla romana*, or *alla grotesca*, created in em-

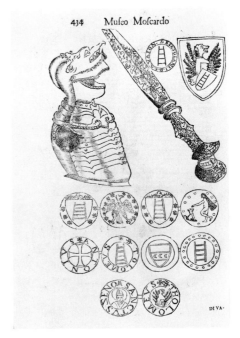

bossed, chiseled, and damascened iron by the Negroli family of armorers in Milan. Helmets formed into grimacing human masks, or shaped into lion, dragon, or dolphin heads, and shields emblazoned with Medusa heads (in ancient legend reputed to turn into stone anyone who gazed into her face) were said by contemporary Renaissance writers to have the power to strike terror into the heart of the beholder. Naive as this may sound to modern ears, the quality of *terribilità*, usually associated with the awe-inspiring art and personality of Michelangelo, was a cherished concept in sixteenth-century thought. As a consequence, this spectacular helmet may have been appreciated by

contemporaries not only as a demonstration of the virtuoso metalworking skills of the armorer, but of the intellect, fantasy, and sense of humor of the patron who owned and wore it.

This helmet is first recorded in a woodcut illustration from the catalogue of the "museum" of Lodovico Moscardo of Verona, published in 1672 (fig. 17). The woodcut illustrates together this helmet, a cuirass of "anime" construction (that is, composed of horizontal plates vertically articulated by means of straps and sliding rivets), and an ear dagger bearing the arms of the della Scala (or Scaligeri) family of Verona, all of which Moscardo asserted once belonged to the famous fourteenth-

century lord of Verona, Cangrande I della Scala (1291-1329). This romantic attribution is not supported by the obvious sixteenth-century date of the three pieces, though there may be some truth to the statement that the armor originally belonged to the della Scala family (which was extinct by 1598). In spite of the crudeness of the woodcut, both helmet and cuirass show the same borders of overlapping scale pattern and so probably belong to the same parade armor. The shape of the breastplate and the embossed border of overlapping scales, which terminate in volutes, are very similar to an incomplete armor, possibly of Brescian manufacture and dating to about 1590, which is known to have belonged to the soldier Giovanni Battista Bourbon del Monte (Metropolitan Museum, acc. no. 14.25.710). The cuirass illustrated in the woodcut of 1672 has unfortunately not been located.

References: Moscardo, 1672, p. 434; Erizo sale, 1929, no. 239; Grancsay, "Helmet," 1929, pp. 209-210.

Cat. no. 26

27
WAR HAT (CHAPEL-DE-FER)
Italian (Milan), ca. 1590
Steel, gold
Height 6½ in. (16.5 cm.)
Weight 3 lb. 9 oz. (1.61 kg.)
Ex collection: Prince Thurn and Taxis
Rogers Fund, 1967 (67.194)

The hemispherical bowl is traversed by a heavy, cabled median ridge, the straight brim is slightly downward turned, and bowl and brim are encircled by rows of semiglobular rivet heads in two different sizes for the attachment of the inner lining. In back is a tubular plume holder. The entire surface of the bowl is subdivided into ten sections which converge toward the top and which are filled with medallions of trophies and of figural scenes from classical Roman history (Horatius at the bridge, Marcus Curtius leaping into the chasm, Mucius Scaevola holding his hand into the fire, etc.). The background areas are damascened in gold with closely set scrollwork.

The German name of such a war hat, *Schützenhäubel* or "shooters' little hat," indicates its use by men needing an un-

Cat. no. 27

obstructed field of vision for handling a firearm; its straight rim was convenient for bracing the gun butt against the cheek. Helmets of this type, therefore, were the standard equipment of light mounted troops, such as arquebusiers and dragoons, as well as light infantry, such as musketeers, who fought in open formation flanking the solid squares of pikemen.

A war hat was often among the exchange pieces of an armor garniture for field and tournament; as the least confining type of helmet it would be worn with the most abbreviated form of armor such as cuirass alone or just a colletin and leather jerkin. It would have been the proper equipment if its owner were to have to serve as a captain of arquebusiers or musketeers.

The workmanship of this war hat is similar to that of an armor in the Metropolitan Museum (acc. no. 38.148.1) and to a helmet in the George F. Harding Museum, Chicago. In turn they are stylistically close to a foot-combat armor, probably made for Emperor Ferdinand II (1578-1637), in the Waffensammlung, Vienna (inv. no. A.1712); this armor is signed by the anonymous master IO and stamped with the castle mark of Milan.

28
ARMOR
French, ca. 1600
Steel, partly gilt
Weight 77 lb. 11 oz. (35 kg.)
Ex collection: Zeughaus, Giessen; Hessisches Landesmuseum, Darmstadt
Rogers Fund, 1927 (27.177.1,2)

This armor for heavy cavalry service consists of a close helmet with two-part visor, gorget, breastplate with sharp medial ridge ending in a short point below the waist, long tassets of seventeen lames which include the poleyn (now separated

Cat. no. 28. Chanfron

into two sections, but formerly attached), backplate with deep culet of four lames, symmetrical pauldrons, vambraces with closed bracelet cowters, and gauntlets. The surface is etched overall with a delicate pattern of interlaced strapwork and foliage, gilt on a gray background formed of tiny loops; the principal edges are roped and bordered by a narrow recessed band etched with foliate scrolls on an obliquely hatched background. The original helmet lining covered with yellow silk and many straps of red leather sewn with silver thread are preserved. The white doeskin boots mounted with the harness are modern. This armor for man is accompanied by a chanfron; the matching saddle is preserved in the Musée de l'Armée, Paris (inv. no. G.557).

This armor dates from the turn of the seventeenth century, a period in which changing military armament and tactics led to the gradual disappearance of the

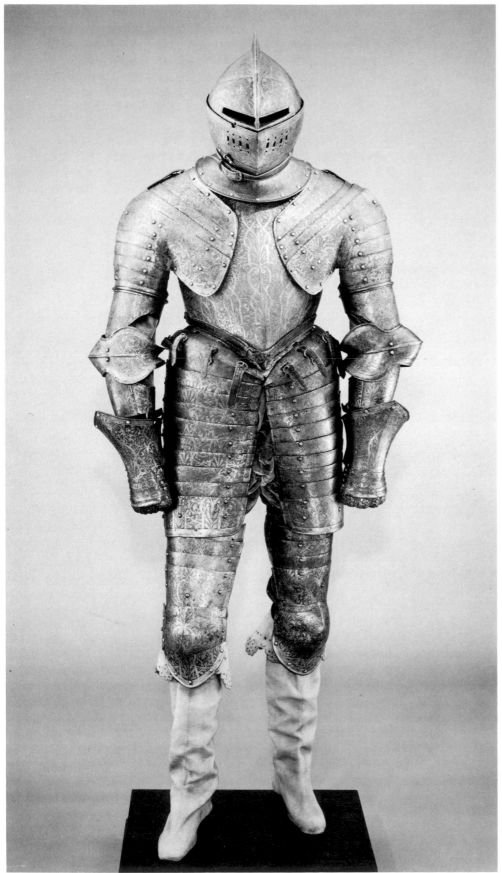

Cat. no. 28

fully armored knight on horseback that had dominated European warfare since the Middle Ages. The increasing use, and accuracy, of firearms required armor of thicker plates, and the resulting increment in weight made the full harness, from head to toe, too heavy and cumbersome. Armor was gradually discarded piece by piece, starting with the greaves and sabatons, a stage of evolution represented by this armor. The devastating effectiveness of firearms also gave rise to the practice of wearing a second breastplate that fit over the first for additional protection, and most armors were furnished with a deep culet attached to the backplate for protection of the rump and upper thighs not always covered by the saddle. A bullet dent on the right side of this breastplate testifies that this armor actually was "proof" against firearms. The symmetrical pauldrons and absence of a lance rest on the breastplate reflect yet another change in tactics, the abandonment of the heavy cavalry lance (which had to be supported by the lance rest) in preference for lighter lances, cut and thrust swords, and pistols.

This armor is one of the most complete examples dating from the reign of King Henry IV of France (1589-1610) and displays many characteristic features of French armor. The construction of the helmet, whose skull is formed in two halves joined along the comb, is common to most French helmets, and can be documented as early as 1567 (armor, inv. no. G. 79, in the Musée de l'Armée, Paris); this construction was used throughout in Europe in the seventeenth century as an effort-saving measure by armorers. Other French features of construction include the large, symmetrical pauldrons, cowters of closed "bracelet" type, the attachment of the tassets directly to the flange at the base of the breastplate, and long, articulated tassets terminating with poleyns, which can be shortened if desired. The decoration reflects French taste in its delicacy and preciousness of design, and in the distribution of ornament over all of the armor's surface. This decoration also succeeds in lessening the appearance of the mass and weight of the plates. The mixture of two different backgrounds for the decoration, circles and hatched lines, is a mannerism peculiar to French armor and

Cat. no. 28

is not found on German or Italian examples.

The excellent state of preservation and relative completeness of the armor is owed to the fact that it was maintained for several centuries in the huge Zeughaus (arsenal) at Giessen, near Darmstadt, in the old German state of Hesse. First mentioned in a letter of 1805, this harness and its horse armor was described (with some skepticism) as having belonged to Landgrave Philipp (the Magnanimous) of Hesse (1504–1567), a romantic association which cannot be reconciled with the late form of the armor. In 1811 the contents of the arsenal were removed from Giessen to Darmstadt, and this harness remained in the Landesmuseum until sold in the 1920s. No doubt the saddle, now in Paris, was stolen by French troops during the Napoleonic invasion of Germany in the first years of the nineteenth century. There is no documentary evidence to indicate when this French armor came to Germany, though it may have been a diplomatic gift to a landgrave of Hesse made sometime in the seventeenth century. A contemporary French armor of similar build and quality of etched decoration,

Fig. 18.
Pikeman at attention. Engraving by Jacob de Gheyn, one of a series illustrating the military manual WAF-FENHANDLUNG VON DEN RÖREN, MUSQUETTEN, UNDT SPIESSEN *(Amsterdam, 1608).*

Cat. no. 29

also preserved with its chanfron and saddle, is now in the Badisches Landesmuseum, Karlsruhe.

References: Müller, 1904, pp. 155-160; Müller-Hickler, 1923, p. 5; Dean, 1928, pp. 18-22; Stöcklein, 1928, pp. 269, 274.

29
PIKEMAN'S ARMOR
English, early 17th century
Steel, blackened, brass, leather
Weight 19 lb. (8.6 kg.)
Rogers Fund, 1919 (19.129a-f)

A high-combed helmet ("pott"), gorget, breast and backplate with tassets make up this pikeman's armor. The breastplate of vestigial peascod shape is embossed with three scalloped stripes in imitation of the converging seams of a contemporary doublet, and backplate with three matching stripes, pott, gorget, and tassets are decorated en suite. All elements are blackened and profusely studded with decorative brass rivets, and tasset hinges and shoulder-strap reinforcements are of bright steel. The pott is constructed in two halves and riveted together along its comb.

Pikemen were the backbone of infantry tactics up to the middle of the seventeenth century because the rate of fire of musketeers was too slow to hold their own against cavalry charges. Pikemen, wearing armor against lance thrusts and sword cuts, stood in massed squares to back up the unarmored musketeers, who were deployed on the flanks and retreated behind the pikemen when the cavalry attacked. Against bullets the usefulness of the pikemen's armor was rather limited; shot-proof plates had to be of such a thickness—and therefore weight—that they became unpractical for men on foot. The wide-brimmed potts were designed as defense against arrows, for in England the longbow was still used long after it had become obsolete in Continental warfare. The wide tassets were adaptations of the contemporary dress with wide-skirted doublets and bulky trousers.

Pikemen's armor like this was even brought to America by the early colonists

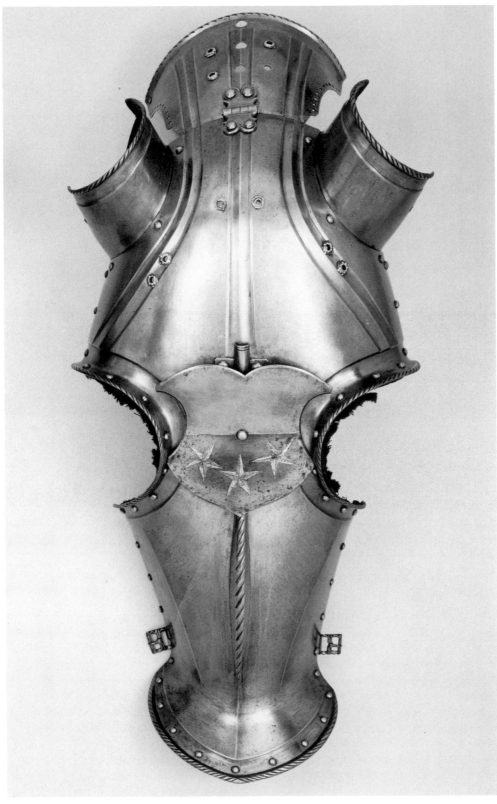

Cat. no. 30

in anticipation of fights against Indians armed with bows and arrows. However, as the Spanish conquistadores had found out earlier in Mexico and Peru, steel plates were not a good defense against arrows tipped with flint or obsidian, which shattered on impact into a spray of splinters. Steel armor was soon replaced by quilted fabric or deerskin coats after the example of the Indians.

References: Laking, 1920-22, V, p. 50, fig. 1457A; Grancsay, Hagerstown-Newark, 1955, no. 6, ill.; Nickel, 1969, pp. 196-203, fig. 15; Nickel, 1974, ill. p. 125.

30
CHANFRON
South German, 1530-40
Steel, partly blued and gilt
Height 24 1/8 in. (71.5 cm.)
Weight 5 lb. 2 oz. (2.32 kg.)
Ex collection: Counts von Freyberg-Preysing, Schloss Hohenaschau, Upper Bavaria; Winter, Munich; William H. Riggs, Paris
Gift of William H. Riggs, 1913 (14.25.1644)

This chanfron – armor for a horse's head – was constructed from seven plates: front plate with eye flanges, two small side plates, two ear plates, hinged neck plate, and an armorial escutcheon plate set between the eyes. All edges and the central ridge are cabled, the plates have sunken borders, and there are three faceted sunken bands on the upper part of central plate, lower part boxed. The upper part of the central plate has three sets of double eyelets for attaching an inner lining; protruding from behind the escutcheon plate is a tubular plume holder.

The coat of arms shown on the frontal shield, *per fess argent and azure, in base three stars or,* is that of the family von Freyberg auf Hohenaschau. The original arms of the family had three golden balls (in folklore called "egg yolks") which were changed to stars by the branch settling in Hohenaschau. The Swabian branch of the family still bears the "egg yolks." The ancient armory of the von Freyberg family in Castle Hohenaschau was sold and dispersed in 1861.

References: Grancsay, 1964, no. 34; Reitzenstein, 1962, pp. 34-50, fig. 17.

31

HORSE MUZZLE
German, dated 1567
Steel, gilt
Height 10½ in. (26.5 cm.)
Weight 2 lb. 2 oz. (0.96 kg.)
Ex collection: Frédéric Spitzer, Paris;
William H. Riggs, Paris
Gift of William H. Riggs, 1913 (14.25.1683)

Six plates, each of them richly pierced in openwork floral scrolls, make up this completely gilt horse muzzle, dated 1567 at the front. In back, three inverted-V shaped bars are connected by short lengths of chain. Two large oval openings for the nostrils are in front, and at the bottom is a rosette with central geometric pattern.

Horse muzzles like this were particularly popular in central and northern Germany during the second half of the sixteenth century. Contemporary representations of such muzzles are found in paintings by the court artist of the Prince Electors of Saxony, Lucas Cranach the Younger, or woodcuts by Jost Amman, one even titled *A Horseman from Brunswick* (fig. 19). They probably served the double purpose of discouraging an evil-tempered stallion from biting, and a placid gelding from stopping at every convenient bush for a snack.

References: Spitzer collection, 1892, VI, no. 505, ill. p. 98; Spitzer sale, 1895, no. 462, fig. 47; Grancsay, Hagerstown-Newark, 1955, no. 44, pl. 44; Grancsay, 1967, no. 33.

Cat. no. 31

Fig. 19.
"A Horseman from Brunswick." Woodcut by Jost Amman, from his STAMMBÜCHLEIN *(Nürnberg, 1589).*

Cat. no. 32

32

Curb bit
Western European, late 16th century
Steel, bronze
Length 12⅝ in. (32 cm.)
Weight 1 lb. 11 oz. (.765 kg.)
Ex collection: Theodore Offerman, New York
Gift of Christian A. Zabriskie, 1937
(37.189.11)

The mouthpiece of this curb bit consists of two cylindrical sections linked in the center. The S-shaped shanks of the branches are of russeted steel, with traces of gilding, and are decorated with delicately pierced scrolls along their edges and two large pierced rosettes.

The battle steed of a knight was a stallion, and so a bit with extraordinarily long shanks like these was necessary to keep this powerful animal under control.

References: Grancsay, 1931, no. 118; Offerman sale, 1937, no. 214; Grancsay, 1953, no. 50; Grancsay, Louisville, 1955, no. 31, ill.

33
Stirrup
German, ca. 1520
Steel, brass
Height 6⅝ in. (16.8 cm.)
Width 7½ in. (19.1 cm.)
Weight 1 lb. 12 oz. (0.79 kg.)
Ex collection: Count d'Arlincourt, Paris;
Count Hector Economos, Paris; William
Randolph Hearst, New York
Rogers Fund, 1955 (55.185.3)

The unusual width of this stirrup is to accommodate the wide and blunt-toed "bear-paw" sabatons of German "Maximilian" armor (cat. no. 10). The arch and suspension loop are decorated with brass appliqués; those on the shoulders of the arch are in shape of cockle shells, probably a reference to the badge or heraldic device of the unknown owner. Two of the three parallel bars of the footrest are cabled, one of them is dentated for better holding the foot. On top of the arch, to one side of the suspension loop, there is a master's mark, a hawk's bell. Hawk's bells were popular symbols in Germany: among other things they are one of the four suit signs of German-style playing cards (the others are acorns, linden leaves, and hearts).

Reference: Grancsay, Allentown, 1964, no. 23.

Cat. nos. 33 (top), 34 (bottom), 35 (left), and 36 (right)

34

STIRRUP (*one of a pair*)
Western European, 16th century
Steel, gilt
Height of arch 3³/₄ in. (8.7 cm.)
Weight 13 oz. (0.36 kg.)
Ex collection: William H. Riggs, Paris
Gift of William H. Riggs, 1913 (14.25.1744a)

These stirrups of strongly curved, almost
circular form are entirely gilt; the arch is
fluted on its outer sides. The suspension
loop is sculpted in front as a scallop shell.
The footrest consists of three bars, the
anterior one dentated for a better hold of
the foot.

References: Grancsay, 1933, no. 56; Grancsay, Louisville, 1955, no. 137, ill.; Grancsay, Allentown, 1964,
no. 25.

35

STIRRUP
German (Munich), 17th century
Steel, tinned
Height of arch 4³/₄ in. (12 cm.)
Weight 13 oz. (0.31 kg.)
*Ex collection: Richard Zschille, Grossenhain,
Saxony; Oliver H. P. Belmont, New York;
Clarence H. Mackay, Roslyn, Long Island*
Gift of Stephen V. Grancsay, 1942 (42.50.423)

Forged of steel, this stirrup is tinned as a
rust-proofing device. All parts—arch,
footrest, and suspension loop—are richly
pierced in openwork; on one side of the
tread is spelled in cutout letters IACOB
CLAS (presumably the name of the
owner). On either side of the arch are
stamped marks with the city arms of

Munich: *a monk with upraised arms, holding a book in one hand.* The suspension
loop is attached by a swivel joint.

References: Zschille and Forrer, 1896, pl. XIII, no. 2;
Grancsay, Louisville, 1955, no. 148, ill.; Grancsay,
Allentown, 1964, no. 26.

36

STIRRUP (*one of a pair*)
Western European, ca. 1730-40
Bronze, gilt
Height of arch 4⁷/₁₆ in. (11.6 cm.)
Weight 27 oz. (0.75 kg.)
Ex collection: William H. Riggs, Paris
Gift of William H. Riggs, 1913 (14.25.1747a)

Cast in bronze and gilt, these stirrups of
exceptionally highly arched shape are

Cat. no. 37

richly decorated with baroque scrollwork. The suspension loops are attached in swivels; the footrests are almost circular and are pierced with a geometric design.

Reference: Grancsay, Louisville, 1955, no. 155.

37
PAIR OF ROWEL SPURS
Western European, second half of the 15th century
Bronze, gilt
Length 6³/4 in. (17.2 cm.)
Width 2¹/4 in. (5.8 cm.)
Weight 4 oz. (.113 kg.) each
Ex collection: Maurice de Talleyrand-Périgord, Duc de Dino, Paris
Rogers Fund, 1904 (04.3.172-173)

Each spur comprises a U-shaped heel plate formed of two downward arched branches of flattened rectangular section, which rise to a small outward-turned beak above the neck, and narrow toward the ends and terminate in a pair of obliquely set rings; a circular buckle attached to a ring on the outer branch of each spur and strap hooks with decoratively lobed faces attached through the other rings; and a neck of irregular pentagonal section, arched slightly downward, forked at the end and terminating in raised lobes, to

which is attached a rowel of eight branches.

Gilt or golden spurs were the very symbol of knighthood and were ceremoniously buckled to the heels of a novice at his investiture to knighthood. The precious metal distinguished the knight's spurs from those of the squire, the knight-in-training, who was allowed only silvered spurs.

The great length of these spurs was necessary because the armored knight sat in the saddle with legs extended, unlike modern bent-leg riding. He thus required extra-long spurs to reach the horse's flank.

References: Cosson, 1901, p. 51, no. E.11; Grancsay, Louisville, 1955, no. 82.

38
ROWEL SPUR
German, ca. 1490-1500
Steel, brass
Length 9³/4 in. (24.7 cm.)
Weight 6¹/2 oz. (.182 kg.)
Ex collection: Richard Zschille, Grossenhain, Saxony; Clarence H. Mackay, Roslyn, Long Island
Gift of Stephen V. Grancsay, 1942 (42.50.279)

This single spur for the right foot comprises a U-shaped heel plate formed of

two straight-edged branches of flattened semicircular section, the end of each stepped and cut square; pierced slots for straps at the end of each branch, the upper one obliquely set, the lower two horizontal and set side by side; a long straight neck of flattened elliptical section, tapering slightly toward the forked end, with a raised boss on each side, and through which a brass rowel of six points is secured. The faces of the heel plate and neck are inlaid with a wide strip of brass, and the branches of the heel plate are also engraved with a herringbone pattern. Three circles are stamped in the face of the outer branch at the end of the brass strip.

Long, straight spurs of this type appear to have been used in Germany and Austria at the end of the fifteenth century. A number of similar examples, some of them of great length, are preserved in the Waffensammlung in Vienna, where they are associated with the jousting armors of the Emperor Maximilian I. Brass was a favorite medium for the decoration of arms and armor in this period, and a number of these iron spurs are completely covered with decoratively engraved sheets of brass.

References: Zschille and Forrer, 1891-99, pl. XI, no. 3; Grancsay, Louisville, 1955, no. 90.

Cat. no. 38

39

ROWEL SPUR (one of a pair)
French, ca. 1600
Iron, gilt and painted
Length 5³/4 in. (14.6 cm.)
Weight 3¹/2 oz. (.098 kg.)
Ex collection: Maurice de Talleyrand-
Périgord, Duc de Dino, Paris
Rogers Fund, 1904 (04.3.171)

This spur for the left foot, one of a pair, comprises a U-shaped heel plate of flattened semicircular section, each branch terminating in a pair of obliquely set loops; a large buckle attached to the upper loop on the outer side and strap hooks with decoratively lobed faces attached through the remaining loops; a short neck of baluster form, with flat circular collar; and a rowel box set at a slight downward angle to the neck, of recurved form, to which a delicately pierced rowel of twelve points is attached. The exterior surfaces are etched with foliage, entwined strapwork, and trophies of arms on a stippled background, completely gilt, the details picked out in red, green, and white paint. The interior of the heel plate is etched with foliate scrolls on a crosshatched background, with a mask in the center.

The etched, gilt, and painted decoration of this spur indicates its French origin and a date from the reign of Henry IV of France (1589-1610). Examples of polychromed French armor are extremely rare and are preserved in only two harnesses: a complete armor, with chanfron and saddle, in the Badisches Landesmuseum, Karlsruhe (inv. no. D.5), and an incomplete armor from the Pauilhac Collection, now in the Musée de l'Armée, Paris (inv. no. P.O. 547). Even closer to the decoration of this spur is a well-preserved gorget in the Musée de Condé, Chantilly, which is etched with trophies of arms, foliage, and a monogram, heavily gilt and painted red and green. Presumably these spurs were decorated to match an armor like that in Karlsruhe or Paris.

References: Cosson, 1901, p. 51, no. E.13; Grancsay, 1953, no. 40; Grancsay, Louisville, 1955, no. 97.

40

SPUR
Western European, ca. 1600-25
Iron, silver
Length 7¹/4 in. (18.4 cm.)
Weight 5 oz. (.141 kg.)
Ex collection: William H. Riggs, Paris
Gift of William H. Riggs, 1913 (14.25.1734)

The U-shaped heel band of flattened semicircular section, each branch tapering toward the ends, terminates in a pair of loops set at an oblique angle. The single remaining strap hook is attached in reversed position to one of the lower loops, and the short upturned neck is of triangular section. Attached to the neck at a slightly down-turned angle is a rowel box with a rowel of seven points. The outer surfaces are punched with a series of circles of various sizes, arranged to form a foliate scroll, the petals of which are encrusted with silver (some missing). The iron surface, now gray, was probably originally blackened. The symmetrical form of this spur and the absence of all but one strap hook make it impossible to identify on which foot this spur was to be worn.

Encrustation was a decorative technique which left the gold or silver inlay standing in slight relief above the iron surface. It appeared on Italian arms and armor in the last quarter of the sixteenth century (for example, cat. no. 27), and by the early seventeenth century seems to have been utilized all over Europe. A sword hilt decorated in this manner is included in this exhibition (cat. no. 53).

References: Blair, 1974, pp. 67-68, 83-86; Norman and Barne, 1980, pp. 360-362.

41

ROWEL SPUR (one of a pair)
Italian, second quarter of the 17th century
Iron, gold
Length 6¹/4 in. (15.8 cm.)
Weight 3 oz. (.085 kg.)
Ex collection: Prince Peter Soltykoff, Paris;
William H. Riggs, Paris
Gift of William H. Riggs, 1913 (14.25.1730b)

This spur for the right foot is one of a pair and comprises a U-shaped heel plate with branches of flattened triangular section narrowing toward the tips, which are recurved and pierced with a pair of loops. The upper loop on the outer branch contains a large scrolled buckle, and the outer loops contain strap hooks with lobed faces. A short neck of irregular hexagonal section rises at an oblique angle from the heel plate and is joined to the heel plate by a scroll molding. The sharply turned-down rowel box is joined to the neck by a scroll molding and terminates in a lobed molding through which a rowel of five points is attached.

The exterior surfaces are damascened with fine gold wire in the form of foliate scrolls, strapwork, and vases on a blackened ground; on the inner surfaces of the heel plate, buckle, and strap loops are traces of gold. The fine decoration combines in an unusual and complex way traditional Renaissance candelabra ornament composed of vases and flowers, and complicated pierced strapwork cartouches of a type found in the late sixteenth century. However, the form of the spur, with its elaborate buckle and sharply down-turned rowel box suggests a date in the second quarter of the seventeenth century, and the quality of the damascening points to Italy as the country of origin.

References: Grancsay, 1953, no. 41; Grancsay, Louisville, 1955, cat. no. 100.

Cat. nos. 39 (bottom), 40 (middle), and 41 (top)

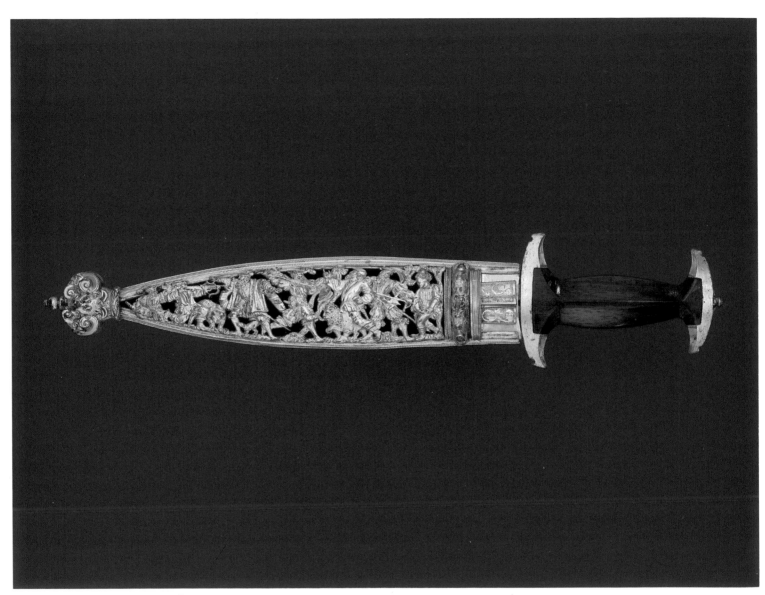

Swiss dagger. Swiss, ca. 1570 (cat. no. 49)

Small-sword. French, 1768-69 (cat. no. 63)

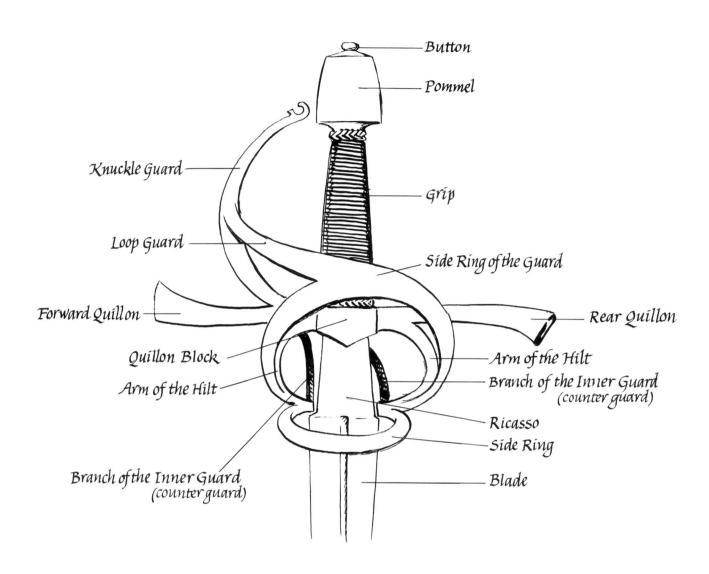

Button

Pommel

Knuckle Guard

Grip

Loop Guard

Side Ring of the Guard

Forward Quillon

Rear Quillon

Quillon Block

Arm of the Hilt

Arm of the Hilt

Branch of the Inner Guard
(counter guard)

Ricasso

Side Ring

Branch of the Inner Guard
(counter guard)

Blade

Edged Weapons

Most edged weapons developed from tools, basically the knife and the axe whose origins are lost in the dawn of man's history. From the knife developed the dagger and the sword; even the spear is in principle a knife on a long shaft. From the axe developed, in addition to the obvious battle-axe, the halberd, bill, and glaive.

The sword, however, is the first true weapon. It was designed purely to kill men and is useless as a tool or a hunting arm. Probably for this sinister reason the sword is regarded as the most noble of weapons; in the Middle Ages it was a status symbol of the knightly class, carried long after the introduction of impenetrable plate armor made it ineffective. Swords of state are still regalia of ceremony, swords continued to be worn in cavalry regiments up to World War II, and in the same way that medieval epics of chivalry ended in a blaze of glory around Roland's Durendal or King Arthur's Excalibur, today's *Star Wars* climaxed in a cosmic duel with laserbeam swords.

The sword was difficult to fashion with Dark Age technology; a good sword had to both keep a keen edge and have enough toughness to withstand the stress of a heavy blow. Unfortunately, the material properties of iron and steel are such that these qualities are mutually exclusive. Hardened steel, which would keep the edge, becomes brittle as glass, and softer iron would be tough but would lose the edge. As a compromise, the ancient bladesmiths laboriously hammer-welded together a core of strips of steel of varying hardnesses, and added separate edges of very hard steel. The core strips—often twisted and braided for extra cohesiveness—showed on the polished surface of the finished blade as the much-prized "dragon-skin pattern" of light and dark spots. In order to produce these blades, a strict temperature control of the steel was essential; this could only be achieved by close observation of the changing colors of the heated metal from dark red to white hot, and this was best done in the dark of night. This secretive working at night, of course, added to the mystique sur-

rounding the smith and made it seem as though magic was involved.

Good swords were rare, and they were much prized possessions of a champion; they were expensive enough to put them out of reach of the rank and file of common warriors. The famous swords had names—a custom familiar to us from the Arthurian Excalibur—and were often traceable through generations.

Steel for swords had to have different qualities from that used for armor; thus the important centers of bladesmithing are usually different from the armor-producing places. The three most famous centers for sword manufacture—all three of them going back at least to Roman times—were Toledo in Spain, Passau on the Danube at the border between Austria and Germany, and Solingen in the Rhinelands, near Cologne. The blades of Toledo were highly prized for their superb quality, but presumably also because they came from such a far distance (for northern Europeans), and the Passau blades had an almost equal reputation. Their distinguishing mark was the image of a wolf inlaid in the blade; through skillfully propagated rumors, doubtlessly launched by the smiths themselves, Passau blades came to be considered to have magical properties and to be bearers of good luck. The Solingen blades did not have such an enhanced reputation, but their smiths were perfectly willing to put wolf marks on their products if the customer insisted (they did the same with Toledo marks). In spite of these somewhat nonchalant business practices, Solingen blades were of high quality, and to this day Solingen remains the most important European center for cutlery.

Ore for the blades was usually found near the production centers. It was mined in the north Spanish hills, and in the Austrian Alps (a fourth important center for sword manufacture was Graz, the capital of the Austrian province of Styria), but in Solingen, bog iron was used. This bog iron was called *Brock,* and it is interesting that one of the old swordsmith families of Solingen was named Brach, and the goblin smith in Germanic mythology who fashioned Thor's hammer was called Brock.

During the High Middle Ages, improved technology made obsolete the laborious technique of pattern-welding blades from strips of steel, and the long knightly swords could be fashioned in one piece, though now it was their hardening process that became the workshop secret. Particular care had to be taken with the selection of the quenching fluid in which the heated blade was dipped for tempering. If dragon blood was unavailable, the urine of a red-haired boy or of a billy goat fed on fern leaves was highly recommended. If one had to do with water, one could not be too careful; one smith in the Norse Edda searched through nine kingdoms until he found the right water to steel the magic sword Ekkisax. The strange recipes reported for production of a superior sword blade nevertheless had a great deal of practical value based on experience and imaginative observation. Of the legendary smith Wieland (Wayland, Völund), it is told that he made a special sword which he tested by letting a piece of felt drift against it when he held it in the Rhine (he seems to have been an early Solingen smith). The sword cut the felt in two, but Wieland filed the sword to dust, mixed the iron filings with dough, and fed these cakes to chickens. Collecting their droppings, he smelted the iron out again and this time fashioned a superfine blade which cut a flock of wool. The feeding and smelting process was actually a clever device to free the iron of slag by the stomach acid of the chickens and to enrich it with nitrogen through the ammonia in their dung.

The fighting knights of the early Middle Ages took care to block their enemies' sword strokes with their shields; they did not clash swords Errol Flynn-style because this would have damaged their precious edges unnecessarily. During the period of full suits of armor—the fifteenth and sixteenth centuries—swords were worn with armor (the sword was *the* knightly weapon after all), but for hand-to-hand combat with an armored opponent, the mace or the war hammer was more efficient. Against a lightly armored or even unarmored fighter, the sword was of course the preferred arm. By the late fifteenth century, regular fencing academies had been established in places like Bologna, Frankfurt, and Paris, where skills with sword, dagger, but also polearms were taught.

The trained fencer prefers the thrust over the cut because the out-held blade is always in a position to parry if necessary, while a sword raised for the cut leaves a wide opening. In order to have a cross-hilted sword firmly in grip for a thrust, it was found to be convenient to hook the forefinger over the quillon of the guard for extra leverage. However, this put the finger in grave danger of being sliced off in a parry, so a single forward-curling extension, the arm of the hilt, was added to the guard, to protect the forefinger. Later these arms were doubled to make the hilt symmetrical again.

With increasing refinement of fencing techniques, additional rings and branches were gradually added to the guard to protect the entire fist, a process completed shortly before the middle of the sixteenth century with the so-called swept hilt. It is significant that the swept hilt appeared at exactly the same time as pistols for cavalry use. The old-fashioned cross-hilted sword hilt had served well as long as the hand was protected by a steel gauntlet (in addition, the cross shape was of deep spiritual significance to the Christian knight), but when the use of pistols made steel gauntlets

Fig. 20.
"The Bladesmith." Woodcut by Jost Amman, from his STÄNDEBUCH *(Frankfurt/Main, 1568).*

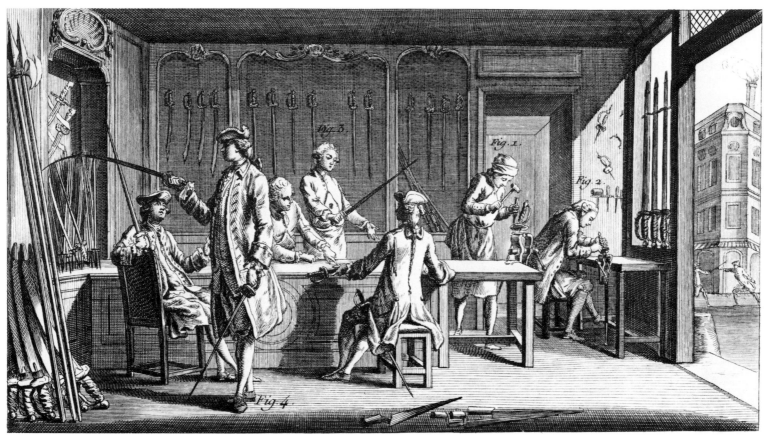

Fig. 21.
A swordsmith's shop. Engraving from Denis Diderot's ENCYCLOPÉDIE, *vol. IV (Paris, 1765).*

impossible, the sword hilt had to be enlarged and improved regardless of spirituality.

The hand freed from the steel gauntlet was, too, much more mobile, and fencing technique took advantage of this. In 1536, the Bolognese fencing master Achille Marozzo published a textbook, *Opera nova,* in which he advised the use of a specially designed dagger held in one hand to parry and deflect the opponent's blade, while the attack was carried on by the long, light sword of new style, the *rapier,* held in the other hand. This fencing with both hands, a logical development from the old-style fencing with sword and shield, was the regular method until the late seventeenth century, when it was superseded by the modern technique of fencing with the small-sword alone, using the same blade for attack as well as for parry.

A particularly impressive type of fencing with both hands was that with the two-handed sword, the *Bidenhander* or *Flamberg,* as it was called in German lands, where it was

highly respected as the most difficult achievement in sword fencing. The German fencing academies gave out special diplomas for *Meister vom langen Schwerte* (Masters of the Long Sword), and mercenary soldiers trained with the *Bidenhander* could claim double pay. However, these giant swords (the longest one in the Metropolitan Museum's collection, dated 1573, is 77 inches long) were strictly for foot soldiers, though all too often they can be seen exhibited in the hands of knightly suits of armor.

The secondary weapon of the knight was the lance. It derived from the ten-foot-long *kontus* introduced into western Europe during the Migration Period by the Alani and Sarmatians, the armored horsemen from the eastern steppes. These long lances could be used for stabbing only; for greater impact they were tucked under the right armpit and angled slightly across the horse's neck toward the left. A shorter form, which could double as a throwing spear, was used at the time of Charlemagne and the Norman Conquest. These spears had a short crossbar or toggle at the socket of the point, to stop the blade from penetrating too deeply and to enable its quick recovery. This toggle survived in hunting spears for boar and bear until the eighteenth century.

"A lance" was also a term used for a military unit: one knight and his immediate followers, i.e., one or two mounted men-at-arms and one or two archers or crossbowmen. The composition of such a "lance" was not consistent, and varied from army to army, and possibly even from campaign to campaign.

The knightly lance from about 1300 onward was equipped with a special handguard, the *vamplate*. Otherwise it changed little in appearance over the next three centuries. For tournaments, the points of lances were blunted, usually split into three or four short prongs; these were called *coronels* because the multiple prongs vaguely resembled a crown. Tournament lances were often gaily decorated with bright paint or ribbons wound around them; battle lances, like the pikes of the foot soldiers, were considered expendable because they were usually shattered on impact, and therefore were left "plain as a pikestaff."

Other staff weapons used by foot soldiers were the *halberd,* the *bill,* and the *poleaxe,* versatile instruments for hacking, hewing, or stabbing; the *partizan,* with its subtypes *runka, korseke,* and *spontoon,* which were all distinguished by wide triangular blades with paired parrying hooks; the long-bladed *glaive* and *guisarme.* Some of these were of quite bizarre shapes and therefore were very popular for the martial pomp of palace guards.

42
SWORD

Western European, ca. 1450
Steel, copper, wood, leather
Length 37¹/₈ in. (94.3 cm.)
Weight 2 lb. 8 oz. (1.13 kg.)
Ex collection: William H. Riggs, Paris
Gift of William H. Riggs, 1913 (14.25.1096)

With its simple cruciform hilt, this sword is representative of the knightly sword of the Middle Ages; its basic shape did not change significantly between 1200 and 1500. The large discoidal pommel served as a counterweight to the double-edged blade and gave the fighter full mastery of a perfectly balanced weapon. The slightly down-curved quillons of the guard not only made the blocking of an enemy's blow easier, they were particularly important for greater ease of handling the sword on horseback; they came into fashion about 1300. The double-edged blade has a rounded tip, indicating that it was designed primarily for slashing, though it could be used for a thrust.

The "running wolf" mark inlaid with copper on one side of the blade was the guild mark of the renowned swordsmiths of Passau, a small town situated on the Danube at its confluence with the river Inn, on the border between Austria and Germany. The town's name derives from a unit of the Roman army, the *IX cohors Batavorum,* which was garrisoned there for almost three hundred years, and the wolf in the city's arms is thus probably descended from the she-wolf, emblem of Rome. Mines in the Austrian Alps not far from Passau yield an iron ore of such quality that Passau swords became widely famous, and the "running wolf" was a much coveted (and occasionally pirated) mark. The Passau swordsmiths, in a remarkable feat of public relations, managed to convince their customers that their wolf blades had magical properties—they were even thought to make their owners bulletproof! The other mark on this blade is the personal mark of an unknown armorer; because of its shape it is called "the mill-rind," the metal mounting in the center of a millstone or a grinding wheel. (In the Metropolitan Museum's collection there is a second blade with the same marks—"mill-rind" and "running

Cat. no. 42

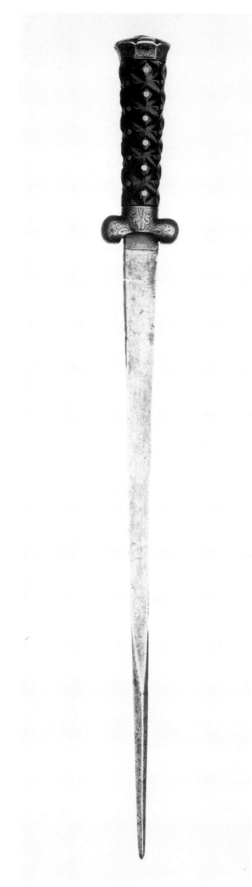

wolf"– that has been fitted into a North African hilt, and was picked up on the battlefield of Omdurman, during the Mahdi uprising in 1898, an indication of how much a fine sword blade could have been treasured, and for how long it could have been in active use.)

Though this sword is said to have been found in the river Vendée in France (the deep corrosion marks on pommel and guard testify to its excavated condition; the grip would have disintegrated and is therefore replaced by a modern restoration), there is an almost identical sword shown in a portrait of Federigo da Montefeltro, Duke of Urbino, about 1475, by Pedro Berruguete, in the Ducal Palace in Urbino. This indicates how universally widespread this simple hilt shape must have been.

References: Belous, 1969, pp. 12, 118, no. 76, ill. pp. 12, 14, 15; Tulsa, 1979, no. 2.

43
DAGGER
Western European (Burgundy?),
second half of the 15th century
Steel, brass, wood
Length 18¹/8 in. (46 cm.)
Weight 11 oz. (0.31 kg.)
Ex collection: Jean Jacques Reubell, Paris
Gift of Jean Jacques Reubell, 1926, in memory
of his mother, Julia C. Coster, and of his wife,
Adeline E. Post, both of New York City
(26.145.19)

The long, slender blade is triangular in section for most of its length, with a cutting edge throughout its entire length. The tip, however, is square in section for about one quarter of the total length, as a reinforcement of the almost needle-like point. On the back of the blade near the hilt are inlaid five small decorative panels of brass. The hilt has a slightly conical grip widening toward the pommel, its surface carved into a pattern of lozenges, each bearing a brass nail in its center. The double-lobed guard and the octagonal, flat pommel cap are of brass, engraved with stylized foliate or feather ornament. The top of the pommel cap is carved with eight swirling grooves radiating from a central stylized flower.

These long daggers were part of every man's daily attire (according to records of feudal lords such as the Earl of Warwick, any man was welcome to take from the communal cauldron in the castle kitchen as much meat as he could spear on his dagger), but they were also designed for self-defense. The reinforced point of this dagger was for piercing mail.

Because these daggers were worn hanging from the belt in front of the body, and because of the lobed guard combined with the upright grip, they were called "ballock knives," a term changed by Victorian antiquaries to "kidney daggers."

Reference: Dean, *Daggers*, 1929, no. 50, pl. XII.

44
HUNTING SWORD
Austrian, ca. 1500
Steel, brass, horn, bone
Length 49¹/2 in. (125.7 cm.)
Weight 3 lb. 8 oz. (1.58 kg.)
Ex collection: Bashford Dean, New York
The Bashford Dean Memorial Collection,
1929 (29.158.704)

The brass hilt is composed of four elements: a quillon block with two straight quillons slightly widening toward their ends, two grip plaques inlaid with double rectangles of dark horn and separated by long strips of pale yellowish horn, and finally an elongated pommel with a stylized bird's-head finial. The pommel and the grip plaques are delicately engraved with late Gothic foliate scrollwork. One of the quillons is slightly bent. A small shell guard (now missing) was once attached to the obverse of the quillon block. The single-edged stiff blade with short back edge bears an unidentified armorer's mark and has traces of punched decoration along the top.

This sword is very close in style to the *Hirschfänger* (hunting sword) in the Waffensammlung, Vienna, which belonged to the Emperor Maximilian (1493-1519) and was made by the swordsmith Hans Sumersperger in Hall in the Tyrol, in 1496. A pair of serving knives, documented as having belonged to Maximilian's father, Emperor Frederick III (1440-93), now in the Wallace Collection,

Cat. no. 44

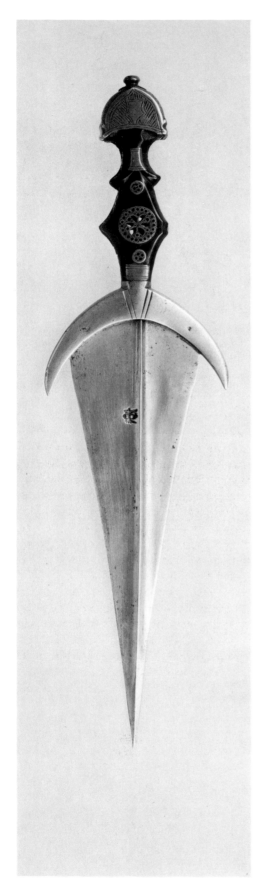

London, bears the same mark as our sword. Thus it can be safely assumed that this sword was also made for the Imperial household, presumably by a Tyrolean master, either in Hall or in Innsbruck.

These swords were designed as defense against dangerous game such as bear and boar, as shown in illustrations to Emperor Maximilian's autobiographical romance, *Thewerdanck*. They were also popular in civilian use, as light sidearm in traveling or about town. However, oversize specimens such as this sword suggest that it was made for use with one hand as well as with both; number 38 in Hans Burgkmair's woodcut series *The Triumph of Maximilian* (about 1515) illustrates swordsmen with oversize single-edged swords like this, called *Kriegsmesser* (battle knives). Two-handed *Kriegsmesser* seem to have been part of the equipment of the Imperial guard in Vienna, under the emperors Frederick III and Maximilian I.

Reference: Grancsay, 1933, no. 139.

45

DAGGER

Italian, ca. 1500
Steel, brass, horn
Length overall 11 ¹⁵/₁₆ in. (30.3 cm.)
Length of blade 7⁵/₈ in. (19.4 cm.)
Weight 8 oz. (.226 kg.)
Ex collection: William H. Riggs, Paris
Gift of William H. Riggs, 1913 (14.35.1264)

The flat, arched pommel of sheet brass has raised moldings at the base of the sides and is engraved on either face with a pointed polygonal shield of Italian type against a background of oblique lines, and at sides with zigzag ornament. The flat grip is formed of two plaques of dark brown horn, swelling at the center, and riveted to either side of the tang of the blade; the plaques are pierced with three circular rosettes of brass filigree. Brass shims, molded in a zigzag pattern and engraved, are fitted at the sides between the grip plaques and tang. The flat quillons are of bright steel, arched toward the blade, and tapering to points at the tips. The short, double-edged blade of triangular shape has a raised rib down the center of both sides. On either side of the blade is a deeply punched cutler's mark.

This dagger is an extremely short version of a type of dagger or short-sword popularly (but probably incorrectly) known as a "cinquedea." The blades of cinquedeas are generally quite wide at the hilt (supposedly five fingers—*cinque diti*—wide, hence the supposed origin of the name) and are often decorated with scenes from ancient history or mythology, with portrait busts or coats of arms and mottoes, etched in the same manner as in early Italian prints. These daggers seem to have been an exclusively Italian type and were worn by the civilian population from the late fifteenth century through the first quarter of the sixteenth. Contemporary paintings usually illustrate such weapons worn on the right hip, or sometimes against the flat of the back, ready for a quick draw with the right hand.

The places of origin of this type of dagger are not known, though they have been attributed to different centers in Italy (Bologna and Ferrara). An almost identical dagger of comparable size, proportion, and decoration, also in the Metropolitan Museum (acc. no. 04.3.226), bears the mark identified as that used by members of the Biscotti family of cutlers in the little town of Villa Basilica, north of the city of Lucca, in Tuscany. The similarity of these two daggers has led Boccia and Coelho to suggest that the illustrated example may also have originated in Villa Basilica. A third, unmarked dagger of this group is in Waddesdon Manor, Aylesbire, England.

References: Viollet-le-Duc, 1858-75, VI, p. 205, fig. 1; Dean, *Daggers*, 1929, no. 75; Grancsay, Allentown, 1964, no. 38; Reid, 1965, pp. 6-9; Blair, 1974, no. 58, fig. 66; Boccia and Coelho, 1975, p. 348, fig. 185.

46
EAR DAGGER
French, ca. 1540
Steel, gold, bone
Length overall 17 in. (43.2 cm.)
Length of blade 10⁷/16 in. (26.6 cm.)
Weight 17 oz. (.476 kg.)
Ex collection: Giovanni P. Morosini, New York
The collection of Giovanni P. Morosini, presented by his daughter Giulia, 1932 (32.75.99)

The grip is characterized by the large circular "ears" at the end of the tang. To these ears and to the sides of the tang are riveted plaques of bone which form the ears, grips, and spindle-shaped guard. These plaques are carved with foliage, with one ear inscribed AVDA FORTVNA the other FIDES FICIT. The ears are attached through shims to the tang by rivets secured by large buttons of gilt steel in the form of pine cones, with engraved and gilt rosette washers. The straight blade is double edged, with edges of unequal length; the base of the blade is of thickened rectangular section and extends asymmetrically toward the upper edge. The tang, the base of the blade, and the shims are deeply blued and damascened in gold with a variety of hunting scenes set against a dense foliate background.

The exotic-looking ear dagger appears to have been introduced into Europe through Spain and is apparently of Moorish origin. One of the earliest documented examples, now preserved in the Real Armería in Madrid, belonged to Boabdil, the last Moorish king of Granada, whose reign ended in 1492. Diego de Çaias, a cutler and damascener of iron of presumed Spanish origin who worked both for Francis I of France and Henry VIII of England, is known to have made several daggers of this type. One of these may be the *dague à oreilles* (ear dagger) which is recorded among the French royal arms in an inventory of 1561, and another may be the one that appears in a portrait of young Edward VI of England as Prince of Wales, about 1546. An ear dagger of similar appearance, signed by Diego, is in the Metropolitan Museum (acc. no. 39.159.1), but is decorated in a style quite different from the one illustrated here.

Hunting scenes of distinctly French style decorate this ear dagger. The scenes of huntsmen blowing horns and carrying boar-spears and of hounds chasing stags are based upon woodcut illustrations decorating a series of Books of Hours published by Simon Vostre in Paris in the 1490s and first two decades of the sixteenth century. The artist responsible for designing those illustrations is anonymous, but he has most recently been identified by Souchal as the author of the famous *Hunt of the Unicorn* tapestries at The Cloisters in New York.

Though the woodcut sources for the damascened decoration of this dagger date from the late fifteenth century and early years of the sixteenth, the dagger itself was probably made in the years around 1540. The prominent metal button and washers attached to the ears appear to be late features and are found on a masterpiece drawing submitted on May 7, 1538, to the goldsmith's guild in Barcelona by Cristofol Joan, and on the dagger in the portrait of about 1546 of Edward VI mentioned above.

References: Grancsay, 1939, p. 16, fig. 6; Grancsay, Hagerstown-Newark, 1955, no. 73; Blair, 1970, pp. 149-156; Souchal, 1973, pp. 22-49.

47
SWORD
Italian, ca. 1550-60
Steel, wood
Length overall 43¼ in. (110 cm.)
Length of blade 37 in. (94 cm.)
Weight 2 lb. 6 oz. (1.17 kg.)
Ex collection: William H. Riggs, Paris
Gift of William H. Riggs, 1913 (14.25.987)

The hilt of blackened iron is constructed of the following elements: a pommel of flattened conical form cut with four deep grooves diverging from the button and chiseled with stylized acanthus leaves; a wooden grip of hexagonal section bound with elaborately twisted iron wire; a guard consisting of a rectangular quillon block, with flat, ribbon-like quillons, countercurved and expanding toward the tightly scrolled tips; arms of the hilt; a diagonal side-ring; and an upward curving prong emerging from the end of the forward arm of the hilt. The inner guard consists of two curved branches. The elements of the outer guard are engraved with a double line along their margins and are chiseled with stylized acanthus leaves.

The wide, double-edged blade of flattened elliptical section is chiseled on each side with three narrow grooves of different lengths which extend from the flat, rectangular ricasso to one-third of the blade's length. Each of the grooves is inscribed MAESTRE (reverse) DOMINGO (obverse), now almost illegible.

Francisco Palomares's list of the famous blade makers of Toledo, Spain, published

in 1762, lists two "Maestre Domingo," the elder and the younger, and reproduces their marks. Neither mark is found on this blade. The fact that the inscription is etched, rather than punched as was customary, suggests that the blade may be of nineteenth-century manufacture.

Hilts of similar construction and compact form, having flat ribbon-like guards with tightly scrolled ends, appear to be Italian in origin and date from the middle of the sixteenth century. The decoration of this hilt with chiseled acanthus leaves is simple but elegant, and the hilt has a robust sturdiness which reflects a functional purpose. Not all hilts of this period were as practical, however, and many of them aspired to miniature works of art, the quillons and guards transformed into human figures, animals, or serpents.

References: Seitz, 1968, II, fig. 259; Norman and Barne, 1980, pp. 90-92.

48
RAPIER
European, ca. 1570
Steel, partly gilt, copper, wood
Length overall 46^1/8 in.(117.2 cm.)
Length of blade 39^7/8 in. (100.13 cm.)
Weight 2 lb. 9 oz. (1.162 kg.)
Ex collection: Maurice de Talleyrand-Périgord, Duc de Dino, Paris
Rogers Fund, 1904 (04.3.281)

Hilt of iron is chiseled with a continuous pattern of raised rosettes separated by crisscross bands, and is gilt. The pommel (possibly a modern replacement) is fig shaped and is surmounted by a flattened globular button. The grooved wooden grip is of octagonal section and bound with fine, twisted copper wire. The guard is formed of branches of circular section and consists of long, straight quillons terminating in bulbous, fig-shaped knobs, arms of the hilt with a knob in the center of each, and two parallel side rings, the larger, upper one emerging from the quillons, the smaller, lower one emerging from the base of the arms, each with a bulbous knob in the center. The inner guard is composed of two curved branches. Hilts of this construction were worn throughout Europe over a very long period, from the middle of the sixteenth century to the early seventeenth. The proportion of this hilt has an elegance quite different in character from the more robust and compact hilt of catalogue number 47.

The blade is double-edged, of flattened hexagonal section, and has a rectangular ricasso. A wide groove on either side of the blade extends two-fifths of its length and each is inscribed SA·HA·GVM. This name refers to the famous clan of swordsmiths in Toledo, Spain. Francisco Palomare's list of Toledo bladesmiths, published in 1762, illustrates the Sahagun mark as an S surmounted by a cross. The absence of this mark, the misspelling of the Sahagun name, and the form of the letters with which it is spelled suggest that this blade is a German imitation of a Toledo blade. The name Sahagun was often copied (and misspelled) outside of Spain, so much so that the name seems to have become accepted as a mark of quality, even though it was not made by the Toledo master himself. On the reverse side of the ricasso is a partially obliterated mark, apparently a crowned letter S, which suggests that the blade may be south German, probably one of the Ständler family of bladesmiths in Munich.

References: Cosson, 1901, no. F.12, pl. 4; Stöcklein, 1918-20, pp. 204-205.

49
SWISS DAGGER (SCHWEIZERDOLCH)
Swiss, ca. 1570
Steel, gilt bronze, wood, black velvet
Length 17 1/2 in. (44.5 cm.)
Weight 1 lb. 6 oz. (.623 kg.)
Ex collection: Louis Carrand, Paris; Frédéric Spitzer, Paris; Maurice de Talleyrand-Périgord, Duc de Dino, Paris
Rogers Fund, 1904 (04.3.130-132)

Broad, double-edged blade has a narrow groove on either side running down about three-quarters of its length. An armorer's mark—a letter R—is stamped on one side next to the groove. The hilt is I-shaped with wooden grip mounted in crescent-shaped bronze-gilt pommel- and guard-bar. The wide scabbard has heavy gilt-bronze mounts with figural decoration in relief. In separate compartments are a small by-knife and a bodkin en suite. On

Cat. no. 48

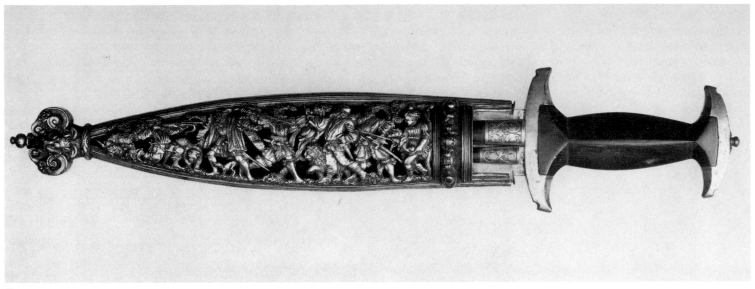

Cat. no. 49

the reverse side of the scabbard are two spaced belt loops, and the back is covered with black velvet.

The figural decoration on the scabbard represents the story of William Tell, told in a still medieval manner, with two events incorporated into the same scene. In the center, the huntsman William Tell is arrested for failing to make proper reverence to the hat of the wicked *Landvogt* (governor) Gessler, which had been set upon a pole in the marketplace of Altdorf as a sign of authority and a symbol of Austrian subjugation of the Swiss. Gessler gives Tell a choice: either be executed or show his famous marksmanship by shooting an apple set on his son's head. The boy with the apple on his head is on the far right, near the scabbard mouth; Tell, kneeling and aiming his crossbow, is on the left, near the scabbard tip. Next to him are one of the henchmen of the *Landvogt* and the *Landvogt* himself in a sumptuous cloak with flowing sleeves. Observe the second arrow stuck in the back of Tell's collar. When asked by the irate *Landvogt* the purpose of this extra arrow, Tell answered that he would have used it to shoot Gessler in case he hurt his son—and this time he would not have missed! Infuriated, Gessler had Tell arrested again, but Tell escaped and managed to shoot the *Landvogt* later in the day with that arrow. The death

of the hated *Landvogt* was the signal for a general uprising that led to Switzerland's enduring freedom.

The two animals which seem incongrously incorporated into the composition next to Tell are symbols for the two major towns in Switzerland, the bear for Berne and the lion for Zurich.

These daggers with I-shaped grip were known as basilards, after the city of Basel, and were considered a national arm of the Swiss. Splendidly decorated specimens such as this one were worn by officers and wealthy burghers, who usually also held high-ranking positions in the militia. William Tell, in the scabbard relief, wears just such a basilard dagger to identify him as the Swiss national hero.

References: Spitzer collection, 1892, V, no. 219, pl. XXXVII; Spitzer sale, 1895, no. 282; Dean, *Daggers,* 1929, no. 15, pl. VII; Grancsay, 1956, p. 232, ill.; Bosson, 1964, pp. 167-198, ill.; Schneider, 1977, p. 160, no. 104, ill.

50
RAPIER
German, ca. 1610
Steel, iron, wood
Length 48 in. (121.9 cm.)
Weight 3 lb. 3 oz. (1.58 kg.)
Ex collection: Royal Saxon Armory, Dresden
Gift of Prince Albrecht Radziwill, 1928
(28.100.3)

51
PARRYING DAGGER
German (Saxony), ca. 1610
Steel, iron, wood
Length 18 in. (45.7 cm.)
Weight 1 lb. 6 oz. (.623 kg.)
Ex collection: Royal Saxon Armory, Dresden
Arthur O. Sulzberger Fund, 1981 (1981.2)

The simple, but elegant swept rapier hilt is deeply blued. It has a fig-shaped pommel with eight facets, and a guard consisting of a knuckle guard, split branch, strongly curved quillon, side rings, and arms of the hilt, and an inner guard of three branches; the grip is wrapped with iron wire over a wooden core. The long double-edged blade is inscribed IN VALIN TIA on its short groove and stamped with an indistinct swordsmith's mark (probably the moor's-head mark of Andreas Munsten, Solingen) and the letter T on its ricasso. The inscription is supposed to give the impression of a Valencia-made Spanish blade, but the blade was certainly made in Solingen. Though Solingen blades were of the highest quality and much sought after, the swordsmiths of Solingen obligingly stamped spurious Spanish or Italian inscriptions, as well as the Passau "wolf" mark, on their products if a customer desired something seemingly exotic and prestigious (see cat. no. 42).

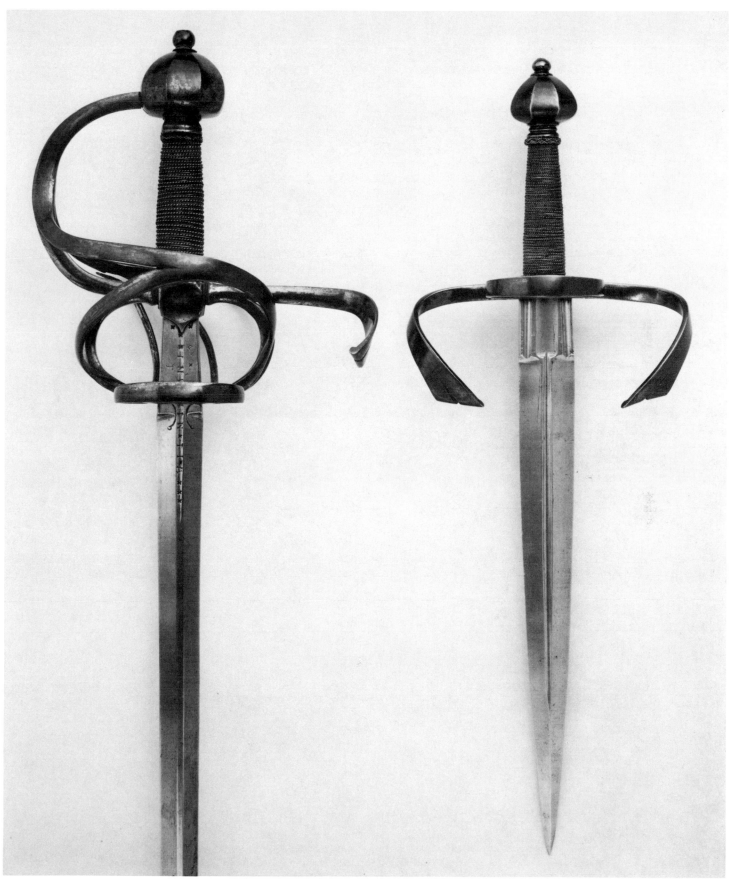

Cat. nos. 50, 51

The dagger's hilt of blue-black steel, with its octagonal fig-shaped pommel and perforated guard ring, is so close to the hilt of the rapier that these were certainly complementary weapons. The dagger is of the type intended to be held in the left hand for parrying the cuts and thrusts of an opponent's rapier in formal fencing, according to rules established in the early sixteenth century and followed by conservative fencers until well into the eighteenth.

This rapier and dagger were equipment for the *Trabantenleibgarde* (bodyguard) of the Prince Electors Christian II (reigned 1601-11) and Johann Georg I (reigned 1611-56) of Saxony, a unit which guarded the palace and the ducal family in Dresden. A large number of practically identical swords and daggers was in the ducal (after 1806, royal) armory at Dresden, from which some were sold during the nineteenth century, and particularly after the abdication of the last king in 1918 and the nationalization of the royal collections.

References for rapier: Weyersberg, 1926, p. 35 ff, pl. II; Grancsay, "Swords," 1929, pp. 56-58, fig. 2; *for dagger:* Anonymous sale, 1980, no. 471, ill.

52
RAPIER

German, ca. 1600-10
Iron, partially gilt, wood
Length overall 47¹/₁₆ in. (119.5 cm.)
Length of blade 40¹/₂ in. (102.9 cm.)
Weight 2 lb. 10 oz. (1.19 kg.)
Ex collection: Medici Armory, Florence;
R. von Kaunitz, Schloss Neuschloss;
Wickliffe P. Draper, New York
Bequest of Colonel Wickliffe P. Draper, 1973
(1973.27.3)

The hilt is of blackened iron and consists of an ovoid pommel surmounted by a flattened button, a knuckle guard, two quillons slightly expanding toward rounded tips, arms of the hilt, and two side rings, the upper one connected to the knuckle guard by a short diagonal branch. The wooden grip of oval section is bound with twisted and braided iron wire. The branches of the guard are chiseled in high relief with a multitude of tiny battling warriors, forty-two on horseback and forty-four on foot, some of them dressed in Roman armor, others nude. In some areas faint landscape details are present in the background behind the figures and, judging from the traces of gold that re-

main, the entire background was apparently once gilt. The pommel is chiseled with cavalry and infantry figures against a monumental architectural background of columns and arches. Large stylized acanthus leaves decorate the bases of the arms and side rings, and the backs of the knuckle guard, quillons, and arms are chiseled with stylized fruit and foliage. The inner guard, formed of three branches of circular section, is plain.

The double-edged blade of diamond-shaped section is chiseled on each side with four deep grooves extending almost to the tip. These grooves are pierced with a series of over six hundred circular holes and slits in a decorative repeat pattern. The flat ricasso of rectangular section is inscribed on the inner side PIETRO DE, and on the outer side FORMICANO, in decoratively engraved letters. On the narrow front edge of the ricasso is a partially obliterated mark, a rectangle enclosing what appears to be a complex monogram formed of the letters F.G.D.T. and surmounted by the crown of the grand dukes of Tuscany.

The hilt of this rapier is one of a conspicuous group of late sixteenth- and early seventeenth-century hilts chiseled with numerous minute figures on the pommels and guards. Some of the finest examples are preserved in the former Royal Saxon Armory (now the Historisches Museum) in Dresden, where they are called Italian. In the absence of any documentation to support this attribution, it may be pointed out to the contrary that the stylized foliage on the rear of the guards is very similar to motifs found on German swords, particularly one made by the iron-chiseler Othmar Wetter in Dresden in the last decade of the sixteenth century (Historisches Museum, formerly inv. no. E.228). A German—and possibly Saxon—attribution is thus suggested here for this hilt.

The inscription on the ricasso of the blade refers to Pietro de Formicano, one of the famous bladesmiths working in Belluno, north of Venice, at the turn of the seventeenth century. A sword from the Odescalchi Collection, now in the Palazzo Venezia, Rome, has a blade inscribed with this smith's name in almost identical lettering, and bears the date 1603. The crowned

Fig. 22.
Fencing with rapier and parrying dagger. Woodcut illustration for Jacob Sutor's fencing manual (FECHTBUCH), 1612.

Cat. no. 52

formed of elements of flattened oval section, and consists of a knuckle guard, quillons, arms of the hilt, and two oval side rings; the inner guard is formed of three branches. The pommel and outer sides of the guards are heavily encrusted with silver which stands in slight relief above the punched and blackened iron surface. The motifs consist primarily of a dense pattern of scrolling foliage containing a variety of blossoms, as well as animal masks, winged cherub heads, and several full-length human figures: Venus and Cupid on the outer side of the pommel, with Mars on the inner side, a standing nude female on the knuckle guard, and two reclining nudes on the side rings. The silver encrustation is quite massive, as can be seen from the deep, undercut grooves left by inlays missing from the broken area near the end of the knuckle guard. The inner surfaces of the side rings and inner guard are crosshatched and damascened in silver with strapwork and foliate motifs.

The narrow, double-edged blade is of flattened hexagonal section, with flattened rectangular ricasso; a shallow groove on either side extends through the ricasso and down the center of the blade for one-third its length. Each groove is inscribed IOHANES. On either side of the ricasso is stamped an oval mark with pearled border enclosing a stag, the mark of Meves Bernes, a member of a famous family of Solingen bladesmiths, who is recorded working about 1610-40. This particular form of Bernes's mark is said to be found on a rapier dated 1613 in the Vienna Waffensammlung.

The rapier shown here belongs to a distinctive group of early seventeenth-century sword hilts of blackened or russet iron heavily encrusted with silver, a type of iron decoration recently discussed in depth by Blair and Norman and also represented in the exhibition by a spur (cat. no. 40). Hilts decorated this way were used throughout Europe in the years about 1600 to about 1640 and, except for a clearly defined English group, are not easily identifiable by nationality. However, certain elements of the decoration suggest that this hilt may be of German origin. The figures of Venus and Cupid (fig. 23), and Mars on the pommel are copied from the ornamental engravings of the Parisian

monogram on the ricasso has been identified by Boccia and Coelho as the ownership mark of Ferdinando de' Medici, Grand Duke of Tuscany (reigned 1621-70), which is also found on other arms from the former Medici armory now preserved in the Bargello, Florence. This sword, or at least its blade, apparently once formed part of the famous Medici armory which was housed in the Uffizi until its dispersal in the 1780s.

References: Kaunitz sale, 1935, no. 9; Boccia and Coelho, 1975, p. 410, nos. 680-682; Schöbel, 1975, figs. 82 b, 90, 97, 98; Norman and Barne, 1980, p. 371.

53
RAPIER
South German, ca. 1610-20
Iron, silver, wood
Length overall 47⁵/₁₆ in. (120.2 cm.)
Length of blade 41 in. (104 cm.)
Weight 2 lb. 3 oz. (.99 kg.)
Ex collection: Theodore Offerman, New York; Wickliffe P. Draper, New York
Bequest of Colonel Wickliffe P. Draper, 1973
(1973.27.5)

The swept hilt of blackened iron is of similar form and construction to the preceding example. The wooden grip of rectangular section is bound with twisted and cabled copper wire (modern). The guard is

printmaker Etienne Delaune (1518/19-1583). These engravings also served as models for the mythological and allegorical figures found on a series of hilts decorated completely in chiseled iron, rather than in silver encrustation, which were made by Daniel Sadeler, recorded as having worked as an iron chiseler in the court of the Emperor Rudolf II at Prague, about 1600-10, and subsequently in the court of Duke Albrecht VI of Bavaria in Munich for the period about 1610-32. The similarities in the decoration of the Sadeler hilts and this example, and particularly the placement on the pommels and guards, of figures derived from Delaune engravings is very striking and may be more than coincidental. For this reason the hilt shown here is tentatively attributed to an unspecified south German center and dated to about 1610-20.

References: Robert-Dumesnil, 1865, IX, no. 4; Weyersberg, 1926, pp. 11-12; Grancsay, 1931, no. 156; Weyersberg, 1932-34, pp. 137-138; Grancsay, 1933, no. 80; Blair, 1974, pp. 84-86; Norman and Barne, 1980, pp. 129-131, 222-223.

Fig. 23.
Ornamental engraving by Etienne Delaune, Paris, third quarter of the 16th century (47.139.120).

54
CUP-HILT RAPIER
Italian, middle of the 17th century
Steel, iron, wood
Length overall 45³/₄ in. (116.2 cm.)
Length of blade 41 in. (104.1 cm.)
Weight 2 lb. 3 oz. (1.00 kg.)
Ex collection: Bashford Dean, New York
Gift of Mary Alice Dyckman Dean, 1949, in memory of Alexander McMillan Welch (49.120.10)

55
PARRYING DAGGER
Italian, middle of the 17th century
Steel, iron, wood
Length overall 21³/₈ in. (54.3 cm.)
Length of blade 16⁷/₈ in. (42.8 cm.)
Weight 1 lb. 3 oz. (.682 kg.)
Ex collection: Maurice de Talleyrand-Périgord, Duc de Dino, Paris
Rogers Fund, 1904 (04.3.17)

The hilt of the rapier is composed of a cup-shaped guard pierced with foliate scrolls, and with a down-turned rim, long, spirally twisted quillons, matching knuckle bow, and plain arms of the hilt. Inside the cup, a reinforcing disc (*guarda-polvo*), also pierced with scrolls, is attached with screws. The very short grip of wood is bound with iron wire and is surmounted by a plain flattened pommel. The narrow blade is double edged, with grooves on both sides of the forte; stamped in the grooves is the inscription ENRIQUE COLL ESPADERO EN ALAMANIA / MI SINNAL SANTISMO CRUCIFICIO (Heinrich Coll Swordsmith in Germany / My Mark is the Holiest Crucifix).

The dagger's hilt consists of a wide convex guard of triangular shape, pierced with foliate scrolls, its edges turned over outward, and long quillons chiseled with leaves. Inside the guard is attached a reinforcing plate, also pierced with scrolls. The wooden grip is bound with iron wire and is surmounted by a flattened pommel chiseled with foliate scrolls. The blade is single-edged with a short back edge at the tip, the back indented; at the base are two chiseled scrolls with a bladesmith's mark in the form of a Saint Andrew's Cross between them. The base (ricasso) is square, with an oval depression for the thumb on the reverse.

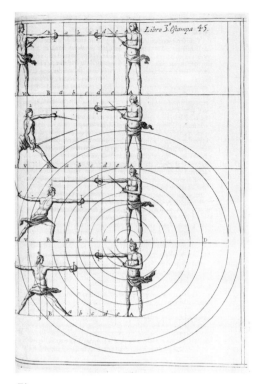

Fig. 24.
Various positions in fencing with cup-hilted rapiers and daggers. Illustration from the Spanish fencing manual NOBLEZA DE LA ESPADA, *by Francisco Lorenzo de Rada, 1705.*

The cup-shaped rapier guard was developed in Spain in the second quarter of the seventeenth century as a highly convenient alternative to the guards built up of bars or shells, or a combination of both. Despite all intricacies of these hand defenses, a skillful opponent's weapon could fairly easily penetrate them, thus disabling the fencer. The cup-shaped guard completely covered the hand, its turned-over edge could stop or even entrap the point of the opponent's weapon, and the long quillons were an excellent device to parry, deflect, or catch the opposing blade. By trapping the blade between a quillon and the forte of his own sword, the fencer even had a chance to break the point off his opponent's rapier. The knuckle guard further protected the fingers from cutting blows. The dagger, with its guard of similar style, served as a parrying weapon that was held in the opposite (usually, but by no means always, the left) hand, with the thumb propped on the base of the blade for leverage. Like the cup of the rapier hilt, the dagger's large triangular guard with

Cat. nos. 54, 55

recurved edges protected the fencer's hand; here, too, the long quillons acted as parrying and trapping devices.

The guards of both weapons are richly decorated with chiseled and pierced arabesques and spirals in the style typical for iron chiselers in northern (especially Brescia) and southern Italy (Naples), who provided not only domestic but also Spanish markets with weapons of Spanish construction but adorned in Italian taste. (This particular rapier and dagger, though similarly decorated, do not match exactly and did not originally form a set.) Such

swords and daggers certainly were spectacular accessories of the nobleman's town or court dress and in an emergency could still serve him well for a fight. However, for a more formal encounter – the duel – the fencer would probably have preferred weapons with solid, polished guards much less susceptible to getting broken and penetrated.

Italian and Spanish schools of fencing with two armed hands dominated Europe from about 1500 to about 1650 when the French style of fencing with small-sword alone took over. In Spain and in the

Spanish-dominated areas of southern Italy, however, fencing (and dueling) with sword and dagger of which the cup-hilted rapier and its matching parrying dagger were the characteristic weapons, continued well into the eighteenth century. The cup-shaped guard proved to be so efficient that it was adopted in the nineteenth century for formal dueling swords all over Europe, and later became a standard feature in all sporting foils and swords (épées), while Italian models have preserved quillons even up to the present time.

Very little is known about Heinrich
Coll (or Kohl) who signed the rapier
blade. Though his name is rendered in
Spanish, he belonged to a bladesmith's
clan of Solingen and probably for a time
worked in Spain, as did many sword makers who desired to improve their skills by
practicing in the highly reputed Spanish
arms-producing centers.

Reference for rapier: Weyersberg, 1926, pp. 16-17; *for
dagger:* Cosson, 1901, no. G.38; Dean, *Daggers,* 1929,
no. 182, pl. LXII; Grancsay, Hagerstown-Newark,
1955, nos. 63, 78.

56
RAPIER

Dutch, ca. 1650-60
Steel, iron, wood
Length overall 42¹/₂ in. (107.9 cm.)
Length of blade 37¹/₂ in. (95.2 cm.)
Weight 1 lb. 5 oz. (.595 kg.)
Ex collection: Rutherfurd Stuyvesant, Paris;
Alan Rutherfurd Stuyvesant, Allamuchy,
New Jersey
Gift of Alan Rutherfurd Stuyvesant, 1953
(53.216.4)

The hilt is of bright steel. The pommel is
chiseled in the round in the form of a lion,
with an intense, grimacing face and an
extremely long tail wrapped around its
body, crouched upon a tree stump. The
wooden grip of oval section is carved with
raised diamond-shaped bosses and bound
with fine twisted iron wire. The guard
consists of a rectangular quillon block
chiseled in the form of two gaping dragon
mouths, from which emerge two grotesque female harpies, recurved in a plane
with the blade (the rear quillon is probably an old replacement). The small side
ring is chiseled as a lion similar to that of
the pommel. The narrow, straight blade is
of hollow diamond shape, with a narrow
groove extending down the rib on either
side of the blade.

This light rapier dates from the middle
of the seventeenth century, a period which
saw the gradual transition from the long,
heavy rapier to the shorter, lighter small-
sword. It belongs to a distinctive group
of hilts whose pommels and guards are
chiseled in the round with lions, unicorns,
serpents, and other animals, often engaged in vigorous combat. Another extremely fine example is in the Metropoli-

tan Museum (acc. no. 53.216.4), whose pommel and side ring are chiseled with a unicorn attacking a serpent, with quillons formed of half-unicorns. This group of hilts has been discussed in detail by Blair and Norman, who suggest that most of these hilts are Dutch in origin, based on the fact that similar hilts appear in Dutch portraits and still-life paintings of the 1650s. A sword belonging to this group, formerly in the Beardmore collection, was mounted with a blade dated 1659.

References: Beardmore, 1844, no. 333, pl. 15; Dean, 1914, no. 57, pl. XXIV; Blair, 1974, pp. 111-115; Norman and Barne, 1980, pp. 185-186, 374.

57
SMALL-SWORD
Dutch, ca. 1650-60
Steel, iron, brass, wood
Length overall 38³/8 in. (97.4 cm.)
Length of blade 31¹⁵/16 in. (81.1 cm.)
Weight 1 lb. 3 oz. (.538 kg.)
Ex collection: Jean Jacques Reubell, Paris
Gift of Jean Jacques Reubell, 1926, in memory of his mother, Julia C. Coster, and of his wife, Adeline E. Post, both of New York City
(26.145.270)

Hilt of blackened iron is of fully developed small-sword form. The ovoid pommel is chiseled in high relief with a cavalry battle of soldiers in contemporary dress and armed with swords and pistols. The wooden grip of hexagonal section is bound with brass wire. The guard consists of a tall quillon block chiseled on either side with the same composition of two battling figures; two quillons, slightly recurved, chiseled in the form of two warriors in classical Roman armor; arms of the hilt; and a separate shell guard formed of two oval lobes of equal size, slightly concave toward the hand, and chiseled on the inside and outside surfaces with battle scenes. The decoration on the inside of the shell is worked in very shallow relief, whereas the chiseling on the outside of the shell is quite high, like that on the pommel, utilizes deep undercutting for its effect. The scene on the outside of the shell is continuous over both lobes, with the larger figures in the foreground on one lobe, and the smaller figures (in the act of storming a city) in the background on the adjacent lobe.

Cat. no. 57

The double-edged blade of flattened elliptical section has three parallel grooves on either side of the forte, each groove pierced with a series of holes and slits in an alternating pattern.

This sword is an early example of the small-sword which developed in the middle of the seventeenth century. A large number of these early hilts are chiseled with battle scenes with warriors in Roman armor, or with soldiers in seventeenth century costume, and some have quillons chiseled in the round as figures, a traditional type of decoration for sword hilts since the sixteenth century. The place of origin of these hilts is not known, though both France and Holland have been suggested. A shell guard (now detached from the hilt) in Waddesdon Manor, Ayleshire, England, is decorated with battle scenes almost identical to the shell guard on this hilt, and may have come from the same workshop.

References: Dean, Swords, 1929, no. 2, pl. II; Carrington-Peirce, 1937, p. 14, fig. 14; Blair, 1974, pp. 127-128.

58
SMALL-SWORD
Western European, ca. 1720
Steel, gold, silver, wood
Length overall 37¹/4 in. (93.9 cm.)
Length of blade 30¹/2 in. (77.5 cm.)
Weight 1 lb. 3 oz. (.538 kg.)
Ex collection: Bashford Dean, New York
The Bashford Dean Memorial Collection, 1929 (29.158.724)

The hilt of russet steel is of typical small-sword construction. The pommel is of inverted egg shape, flattened slightly in a plane with the blade, and is surmounted by a flattened globular button. The wooden grip of oval section is bound with twisted silver wire. The guard comprises the knuckle guard, a rear quillon turned slightly to the outside, two arms of the hilt, and a double-lobed shell. The decoration is encrusted in gold and includes antique gods and goddesses and allegorical figures surrounded by dense foliate scrolls and leafy grotesque masks. Among the recognizable figures are Mars, Fortune, Abundance, Hercules, and two couples, Venus and Cupid, and a nymph and satyr.

The narrow, double-edged blade of flattened hexagonal section has a short groove on either side and is inscribed on the obverse TOMAS, on the reverse AIALE.

The form of this hilt, with its squat, inverted egg-shaped pommel, its stocky oval grip, and its relatively small shell guard with heavy moldings along the edges, points to a date in the early years of the eighteenth century. Russet iron hilts, encrusted with silver or gold, were particularly popular during this period. The motifs employed in the decoration, mythological and allegorical figures amid dense foliate scrolls, reflect a baroque taste without any trace yet of the new rococo style that was to influence small-sword ornament after 1730. One of the figures on this hilt, the armed warrior (Mars) on the inner side of the shell guard, is dressed in Roman armor and incongruously wears a full shoulder-length wig of late seventeenth-century type. A gold-encrusted hilt in the Victoria and Albert Museum, London (reg. no. M.955-1928), is decorated with masks and foliage very similar to those on this hilt, and may have been decorated by the same craftsman. Hilts with this type of decoration have been called English, Dutch, or French, but since no evidence points clearly to their place of origin, the present example is ascribed generally to western Europe.

The inscription on the blade refers to the early seventeenth-century bladesmith of Toledo, Spain, Tomas de Aiala. This name, like that of Sahagun (cat. no. 48), was frequently added to blades of German manufacture, of which this seems to be an example.

References: Dean, Swords, 1929, no. 18, pl. XIII; Grancsay and Kienbusch, 1933, no. 165, pl. LII; Hayward, 1948, p. 88; Blair, 1962, fig. 149.

Detail of cat. no. 58. Inner side of shell guard

59
SMALL-SWORD
German, ca. 1750
Steel, gold, silver, copper
Length 35³/8 in. (89.8 cm.)
Weight 14 oz. (0.4 kg.)
Ex collection: Jean Jacques Reubell, Paris
Gift of Jean Jacques Reubell, 1926, in memory of his mother, Julia C. Coster, and of his wife, Adeline E. Post, both of New York City (26.145.297)

The entire hilt of this small-sword is of steel and chiseled with rocailles and floral sprays in delicate relief. Some elements of the decoration are inlaid in silver and copper for colorful effect against the mat gilded background. The bulbous shape of the handgrip is a typical feature of German small-swords. The upper half of the double-edged blade is etched with rococo ornament, medallions, trophies, and figures in strapwork, and entirely gilt.

The vestigial guard with its seemingly nonfunctional arms of the hilt (it is impossible to put a finger through the loops, in the manner required for the traditional fencing grip) was gripped between thumb and forefinger with the quillons horizontal. This way it allowed for very delicate finger play (*doigté*), thus making this sword—which we today consider a mere accessory to a gentleman's costume—actually an instrument of mortal combat.

Reference: Dean, Swords, 1929, no. 44, pl. XXXIV.

60
SMALL-SWORD
Japanese (for the European market), ca. 1740-50
Shakudo, partly gilt, steel
Length overall 35¹/2 in. (90.1 cm.)
Length of blade 29¹/4 in. (74.3 cm.)
Weight 14 oz. (.396 kg.)
Ex collection: Jean Jacques Reubell, Paris
Gift of Jean Jacques Reubell, 1926, in memory of his mother, Julia C. Coster, and of his wife, Adeline E. Post, both of New York City (26.145.328)

The hilt is made of "shakudo," an alloy of gold and copper, treated with acid to color it bluish black, that was used exclusively in Japan. The bulbous hollow pommel of

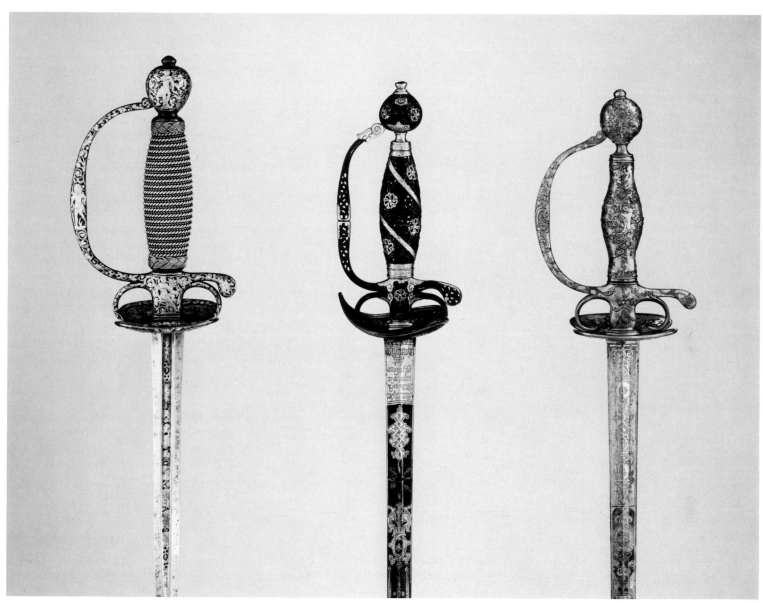

Cat. nos. 58 (left), 60 (center), 59 (right)

squat egg shape rests on a round collar and tall stem, and is surmounted by a flattened globular button. The hollow grip, oval in section, is decorated to match the rest of the hilt. The guard consists of a squared knuckle guard, a hollow quillon block, a rear quillon, arms of the hilt, and a heart-shaped shell, concave toward the hand, with a narrow forked end curved toward the knuckle guard. All parts of the hilt are pierced and chiseled with tight foliate scrolls, with gilt rosettes and leaves. A spi-

ral band, engraved with wavy lines and gilt, wraps around the grip, which has similarly engraved and gilt washers at either end. Another gilt band encircles the edges of the shell.

The narrow, double-edged blade of flattened hexagonal section, elliptical at the forte, is etched with grotesque figures, trophies of arms, a crown, and strapwork, on a blued ground. The forte is inscribed near the hilt: *Jan Hossee Mr. Zwaardveger op de Vygendam tot Amsterdam* (Jan Hos-

see, master cutler in the Vygendam in Amsterdam).

This sword is one of a series of small-swords and hunting swords, of which there are nine in the Metropolitan Museum, believed to have been made in Japan for the European market. The earliest reference to swords of this type is found in an inventory of the Dresden armory of 1728, which describes a short saber or hunting hanger of European design, but of the same distinctive Japanese workmanship,

Edged Weapons 107

as "of Moscow work"; that sword was said to have entered the Dresden collection in 1704. As is evident from this eighteenth-century inventory, the origins of this group were quickly forgotten, and earlier in the twentieth century they were considered to be of Chinese origin ("Tonkin work"). Recently, however, the workmanship of these hilts has been recognized to be the same as that on tea sets, tobacco boxes, and other objects exported from Japan to the West. Hilts of these swords are frequently mounted on blades with the name of Dutch cutlers, which suggests that they entered Europe through Holland. The Dutch East India Company had its trading post at Deshima, one of the few contact points between the West and xenophobic Japan. Since there are no records of the export of these decorated hilts, they may have been products of a "black-market" trade with enterprising employees of the company, who risked circumventing the strict Japanese law against export of weapons and parts thereof.

All Far Eastern objects—especially porcelain, but also apparently these sword hilts—greatly appealed to the European taste for the exotic, as is reflected by the growing eighteenth-century interest in chinoiserie.

Dating these small-swords, which are usually decorated in a native Japanese fashion with plum blossoms and occasionally even landscape scenes, is particularly difficult. The presence of a concave heart-shaped shell on this example points to the period about 1725-60, when hilts of this construction were most common in Europe. The heart-shaped shell is generally considered a manifestation of the rococo taste for asymmetry, and European-made hilts with the shells are often decorated with spiral gadroons and rocaille ornament. The spiral ribbon on the grip may also reflect this rococo spirit. On the other hand, the squarish knuckle guard with its double knobs in the center is of a type found on European small-swords of the late seventeenth century and first decade of the eighteenth century; these earlier features, archaic by the time this sword was made, continued to be employed by the Japanese craftsmen. Since this hilt appears to have been mounted in

Amsterdam by Jan Hosse (or Hossee), recorded working 1731 to 1768, a date around the middle of the eighteenth century is likely. Another of these Japanese small-sword hilts mounted by Hosse is in the Victoria and Albert Museum, London (reg. no. 1736-1888).

References: Dean, *Swords,* 1929, no. 39, pl. XXX; Carrington-Peirce, 1937, p. 43, fig. 28; Blair, 1962, p. 86, fig. 153; Norman and Barne, 1980, pp. 213, 347-348.

61
SMALL-SWORD
French (Strasbourg), 1762
Steel, partly blued and gilt, silver, wood, red felt
Length 38¹/₂ in. (97.7 cm.)
Weight 14 oz. (0.4 kg.)
Gift of Samuel P. Avery, 1912 (12.62)

62
SMALL-SWORD FOR A BOY
French (Paris), 1758-59
Steel, silver, wood
Length 30¹/₈ in. (76.5 cm.)
Weight 7 oz. (0.2 kg.)
Ex collection: Jean Jacques Reubell, Paris
Bequest of Jean Jacques Reubell, 1933, in memory of his mother, Julia C. Coster, of New York (34.57.3)

The hilts of these swords are entirely of silver and practically identical in their decoration of spiral and shell moldings. The blades are triangular in section and etched with floral rococo ornaments; the larger blade is also partly blued and gilt.

The larger sword hilt bears three silversmith's marks: the *poinçon de charge* for Strasbourg for the period 1750-96, the date-letter of the Strasbourg silversmiths' guild for the year 1762, and an illegible maker's mark; stamped on the hilt of the boy's sword are the marks of the *fermier-general* Eloy Brichard (1756-62) and the date-letter of the silversmiths' guild of Paris for the years 1758-59.

In spite of the precious material of such hilts, these swords are entirely functional. The triangular cross section of the blade assures the rigidity and lightness necessary to make these very narrow blades a deadly weapon in the hands of a master swordsman. At the same time they would nor-

mally be worn as the badge of rank of a cavalier, and even by a small boy of a noble family as a status symbol.

63
SMALL-SWORD
French (Paris), hallmarked for 1768-69
Steel, silver-gilt, Meissen porcelain
Length overall 38⁵/₈ in. (98.1 cm.)
Length of blade 32 in. (81.25 cm.)
Weight 1 lb. 2 oz. (.510 kg.)
Ex collection: Jean Jacques Reubell, Paris
Gift of Jean Jacques Reubell, 1926, in memory of his mother, Julia C. Coster, and of his wife, Adeline E. Post, both of New York City (26.145.344)

The hilt is of silver-gilt, cast and chased with trophies of arms and agricultural tools (symbols of war and peacetime activities) on a punched ground. The knuckle guard, quillon, and arms of the hilt are treated as an undulating twisted ribbon. The slightly bulbous grip is formed of a single piece of Meissen porcelain, molded with rocaille scrolls, glazed white, and painted on either side in colors with naturalistic flowers. The hilt bears Paris hallmarks on every element, among them the date-letter E, used on silverwork for the period 1768-69. The double-edged blade of flattened hexagonal section has a wide forte etched with trophies of arms, rocaille scrolls, and a female figure holding a sword and lance and surrounded by trophies of arms at her feet (Bellona).

Small-sword hilts with porcelain grips epitomize the increasingly decorative role played by such weapons. A grip of such delicacy would quickly shatter in the first moments of fencing and render the weapon useless. Though not practical, porcelain grips nevertheless made a striking addition to the already elaborately decorated hilts and no doubt made perfect accessories to the colorful and richly embellished male costume of the period. The majority of porcelain small-sword grips came from Meissen, the factory controlled by the Prince Electors of Saxony, and the source (after 1709) of Europe's first hard-paste porcelain. Meissen porcelain was exported all over Europe, and price lists include sword grips described as having relief decoration painted with natural

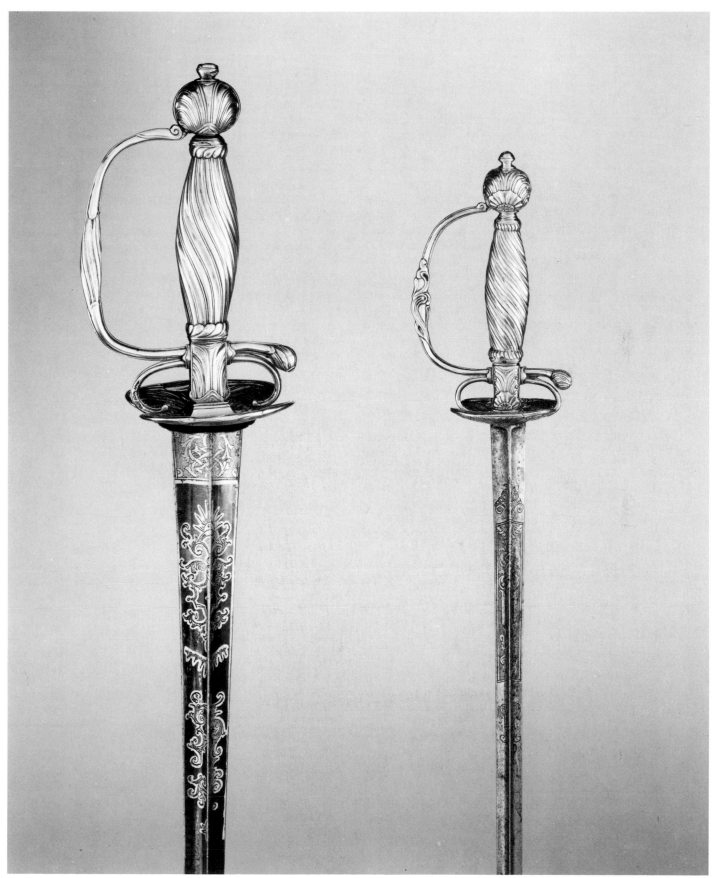

Cat. nos. 61, 62

Cat. no. 63

flowers, exactly as found on this hilt. It is no surprise, then, to find a Meissen grip mounted on a hilt made in Paris. The presence of asymmetrical scrolls and the fanciful treatment of the knuckle guard, quillon, and arms of the hilt as twisted ribbon are a late manifestation of rococo taste.

It is interesting to note that this small-sword is not assembled in the typical European manner, used since the Middle Ages, in which the tang of the blade passed through the hilt and was riveted over the pommel. Instead, the pommel button of this example screws onto the tang of the blade. This construction is usually found on hilts made of delicate materials such as porcelain or paste brilliants (cat. no. 64) and allows the hilt to be taken apart easily for repairs.

References: Dean, *Swords,* 1929, no. 74, pl. LVI; Norman and Barne, 1980, pp. 207, 388.

64

SMALL-SWORD

French (Paris), 1778
Steel, silver-gilt, paste brilliants
Length 37 1/8 in. (94.5 cm.)
Weight 12 oz. (0.33 kg.)
Ex collection: Jean Jacques Reubell, Paris
Gift of Jean Jacques Reubell, 1926, in memory
of his mother, Julia C. Coster, and of his wife,
Adeline E. Post, both of New York City
(26.145.303)

The silver-gilt hilt is richly jeweled with paste brilliants set in rows on pommel and grip, and large star shapes between the two down-curved quillons. In the center of the knuckle guard is a small rosette of brilliants, while the rest of the knuckle guard is studded with rows of silver nail heads. Similar nail heads are on the quillons. The inner side of the oval guard is also set with brilliants; the outer side is plain.

The narrow blade is triangular in section, gilt-etched with scrollwork and the inscription VIVE LE ROY. On the silver hilt are the marks of the inspector Jean-Baptiste Fouchard (1774-80) and the date-letter for 1778 of the Paris silver-smiths' guild.

Reference: Dean, *Swords,* 1929, no. 98, pl. LXXIV.

Cat. no. 64

65

SMALL-SWORD

French, ca. 1780-90

Steel, partly gilt, silver, wood, leather

Length overall (sword alone) 38⅛ in.
(96.8 cm.)

Length of blade 31⅝ in. (80.3 cm.)

Weight 11 oz. (.311 kg.), with scabbard 15 oz.
(.425 kg.)

Ex collection: Jean Jacques Reubell, Paris

Gift of Jean Jacques Reubell, 1926, in memory
of his mother, Julia C. Coster, and of his wife,
Adeline E. Post, both of New York City
(26.145.290)

The steel hilt is chiseled in low relief with
military figures on horse and on foot, variously dressed in antique or contemporary
costume and set in stylized landscapes, as
well as putti in armor, lion masks, strapwork, and foliate ornament; the elements
of the decoration are polished bright
against a punched gold ground. The
wooden grip of rectangular section is
bound with braided and twisted silver
wire of alternate thicknesses. The slender
blade is of hollow triangular section,
without decoration. The scabbard of black
leather has two steel lockets mounted with
carrying rings, and a chape at the tip. The
lockets are decorated to match the hilt, the
upper one chiseled with a dragon, the
lower one with flowers.

Steel hilts chiseled with military figures
in antique or contemporary costume were
popular throughout the seventeenth century (cat. nos. 52 and 57) and remained so
in the eighteenth century. A number of

Detail of cat. no. 65. Outer side of shell guard

small-swords dating from the 1780s, decorated with single figures occupying the pommel, knuckle guard, quillon block, and each lobe of the shell guard, forms a distinctive group which there are four examples in the Metropolitan Museum. Three of these (including the one illustrated) are of chiseled steel, the figures variously blued or bright against a gilt ground, sometimes chiseled in fairly high relief with precise outlines, in other cases (as on this example) in lower relief, with softer, rounder forms. In spite of the similarity of these hilts, there are sufficient differences in workmanship to suggest several craftsmen at work. One hilt of this group (Metropolitan Museum, acc. no. 26.145.323) decorated with military figures is fashioned of silver rather than steel and bears Paris hallmarks for 1786-89, which provide an approximate date for the unmarked steel hilts.

References: Dean, *Swords,* 1929, no. 86, pl. LXIV; Grancsay, 1953, no. 95; Norman and Barne, 1980, p. 388.

66
"MOURNING" SWORD

English, ca. 1790
Steel
Length 30¾ in. (78.1 cm.)
Weight 15 oz. (0.425 kg.)
Ex collection: Jean Jacques Reubell, Paris
Gift of Jean Jacques Reubell, 1926, in memory
of his mother, Julia C. Coster, and of his wife,
Adeline E. Post, both of New York City
(26.145.307)

The entire hilt is of deeply blued steel, with faceted steel beads of different sizes arranged in rows and rosettes to give the impression of a "jeweled" hilt. The neoclassical urn shape of the pommel was very fashionable in England after 1780 up to the end of the century; in most cases the top part of the urn was concavely shaped, and the slightly domed "lid" as in this example is relatively rare.

These deeply blued, almost black, small-swords were said to have been worn with mourning attire.

References: Dean, *Swords,* 1929, no. 109, pl. LXXX; Norman and Barne, 1980, pp. 282-283, pl. 151.

Cat. no. 66

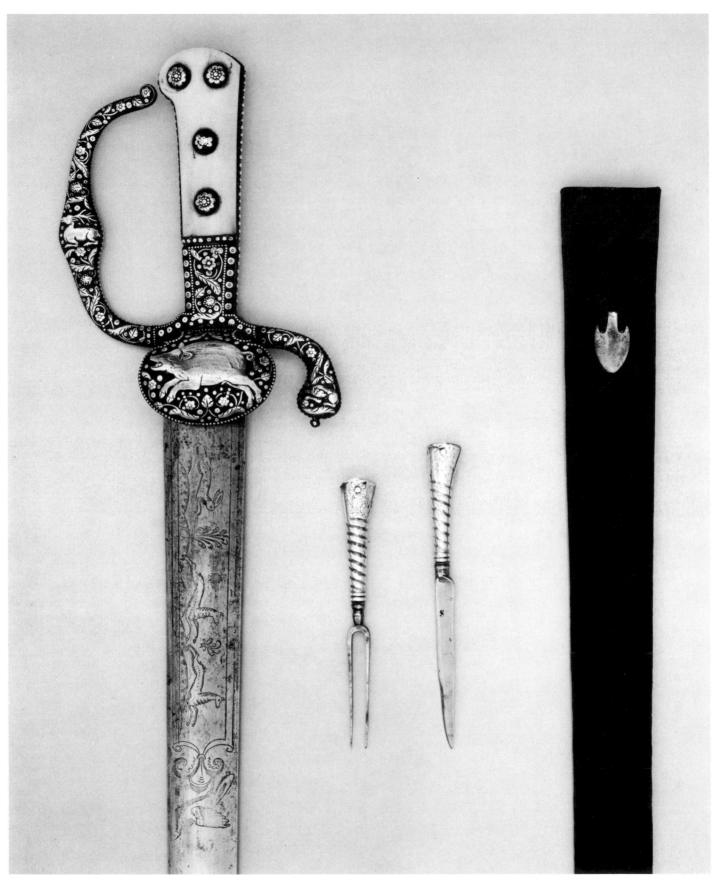

Cat. no. 67

67
Hunting sword (hanger)

German, dated 1656
Steel, iron, silver, ivory, leather
Length overall 25¾ in. (65.4 cm.)
Length of blade 20⅜ in. (51.8 cm.)
Weight 1 lb. 9 oz. (.708 kg.)
Ex collection: Jean Jacques Reubell, Paris
Gift of Jean Jacques Reubell, 1926, in memory
of his mother, Julia C. Coster, and of his wife,
Adeline E. Post, both of New York City
(26.145.256a-d)

The flat grip is formed by two plaques of ivory, held to the tang of the blade by four domed iron rivets encrusted with silver rosettes. There is no separate pommel, but the grip expands slightly toward the end, which is rounded and has a semicircular lobe on one side. The lower third of the grip is covered by iron plaques made in one piece with the guard. The knuckle guard of flattened oval section expands to a diamond-shaped lobe in the middle, its end turned outward in a tight curl just before reaching the grip. The rear quillon turns toward the blade and has a semicircular tip to which a tiny button is attached. An oval shell guard, convex toward the hand, is attached to the outside of the quillon block and turns down toward the blade. The blackened iron surfaces are heavily encrusted with silver, with dots outlining the various elements of the guard and the edges of the tang, and with dense foliate scrolls with leaves, flowers, and berries covering the guard. The decoration also includes hunting related motifs: a reclining stag in the center of the knuckle guard, a crouching dog on the tip of the quillon, and a charging boar on the shell guard. Most of the silver is applied in high relief and has engraved details.

The straight, single-edged blade is hollow-ground at the sides and has a short back edge at its tip. The outer side of the blade is etched with two running deer and a rabbit, framed above and below with double lines which converge toward the point and are closed by a feather-like ornament surmounted by a large bird. The inner side of the blade has large stylized vase-shaped ornaments and includes an oval medallion enclosing the portrait of a bearded man and a rectangular cartouche

with the date 1656. There is no cutler's mark.

The simple scabbard of black leather is mounted with a bright steel chape. Near the top of the scabbard is a pocket, the front of which holds a shield-shaped suspension hook. The pocket now contains a small knife and fork of steel, their handles of spirally twisted silver engraved with flowers, the flat ends engraved with the letters D.A.G.N. (probably the owner's initials) and the date 1685.

Short curved hunting swords, known in England as "hangers" or "woodknives," were a sort of machete of peasant origin, but by the middle of the sixteenth century they had been adopted as practical tools of woodcraft by knights and nobles as part of their specialized hunting equipment. As the German name for these hunting swords – *Hirschfänger* – suggests, they were intended for the coup de grace of the downed stag, but at least in their sturdier examples they were also useful as all-purpose tools, such as for cutting a path through the underbrush, cutting wood and kindling for the campfire, as well as chopping the joints of a deer's carcass.

The design for such weapons was traditional and changed very little over the centuries. The asymmetrical pommel is found on late fifteenth-century German hunting swords (for example, cat. no. 44), as is the down-turned shell on the outside of the guard; the knuckle guard, also a common feature on hunting swords, is already found on the so-called "woodknife" of Henry VIII, datable to about 1544, at Windsor Castle.

These swords were usually accompanied by utensils (knife, fork, and bodkin) as a camping set, carried in the pocket of the scabbard. The knife and fork associated with this hanger are not the original set belonging to it.

Reference: Dean, *Swords*, 1929, no. 7, pl. XC.

Cat. no. 68

68

HUNTING HANGER
French (Paris), 1778
Steel, partly gilt, silver, porcelain
Length 28¼ in. (71.7 cm.)
Weight 13 oz. (0.37 kg.)
Ex collection: Jean Jacques Reubell, Paris
Gift of Jean Jacques Reubell, 1926, in memory of his mother, Julia C. Coster, and of his wife, Adeline E. Post, both of New York City (26.145.245)

The hilt has a slightly curved porcelain grip with gilt relief decoration, a silver guard with short counter-curved quillons and a shell in relief in its center, and a pommel cap of silver. The silver parts are stamped with the date-letter for 1778 of the Paris silversmiths' guild, and several illegible marks. The single-edged, slightly curved blade has a shallow groove on either side and is etched and formerly gilt in its upper third with rococo strapwork and a medallion enclosing a leaping stag. In the upper part of the groove is etched a sun in splendor surmounted by a royal crown. The relief decoration on the porcelain grip consists of motifs related to the hunt, such as a huntsman resting with his dog, Diana the Huntress, and Venus and Adonis, who fell asleep after a hunt.

As part of a gentleman's hunting attire, these swords tended to serve more of a symbolic – rather than functional – role and, like small-swords, became objects of luxury that were subject to every variety of decoration, however impractical.

Reference: Dean, Swords, 1929, no. 31, pl. XCVIII.

69

BILL
Italian, ca. 1480
Steel, wood
Length 97½ in. (247.7 cm.)
Weight 4 lb. 13 oz. (2.17 kg.)
Ex collection: Wiliam H. Riggs, Paris
Gift of William H. Riggs, 1913 (14.25.159)

The extraordinarily large head of the bill consists of a long, double-edged thrusting blade emerging from a body, which has on one side a cutting edge changing into a strongly curved hook, and on its back a sharp spike standing out at right angles. Two short spikes at the base of the blade serve as a guard. A simple ornament of dots and crescent lines is stamped along the back.

The bill is a weapon developed from an agricultural tool, the pruning hook, with which a farmer would lop off unwanted branches on his fruit trees. It was particularly popular in western European countries, where it was one of the equivalents of the halberd in central Europe. In England the call to arms was "Bills and Bows," for spearmen and archers. It seems to have been one of the few types of polearms that the Spanish conquistadores and the early English colonists used in the New World.

70

HALBERD
German, late 15th century
Steel, wood
Length 81³/8 in. (206.6 cm.)
Weight 4 lb. 12 oz. (2.13 kg.)
Ex collection: William H. Riggs, Paris
Gift of William H. Riggs, 1913 (14.25.51)

The head of this halberd incorporates three basic elements: an axe-like blade, an apical spike, and a beak. The axe blade, which gives the weapon its name (derived from the German *Halm*, long shaft, and *Barte*, axe) was used for hacking, the spike for thrusting, and the beak either for piercing a plate of armor (against which the cutting edge would have been useless), or for pulling a knight from his saddle.

The halberd was a foot-soldier's weapon particularly popular in Germany and Switzerland. It was the most versatile of shafted weapons a man on foot could use; though the pike was the main weapon for the massed squares of foot soldiers so important in fifteenth- and sixteenth-century battles, the halberd was preferred both by Swiss *Reisläufer* and German *Landsknecht* (mercenaries). It had the advantage that it could be used in a pinch by a single man, such as when ambushed on a foraging or plundering raid, while a twelve-foot-long pike was of use only by soldiers in massed formation, and for a single man was more of a hindrance.

In the formal development of the halberd, the offset socket pointing to the rear, as in this example, indicates a date before the middle of the sixteenth century.

71

POLEAXE
Western European, ca. 1500
Steel, wood
Length overall 817/8 in. (208 cm.)
Length of blade 87/8 in. (22.5 cm.)
Weight 5 lb. 7 oz. (2.46 kg.)
Ex collection: Ernest de Rozière, Paris;
William H. Riggs, Paris
Gift of William H. Riggs, 1913 (14.25.302)

The poleaxe was the western European equivalent of the halberd and was similarly designed for hacking and stabbing and for piercing armor plates. However, the heads of halberds were constructed in one integral piece, but the heads of poleaxes were composed from separate elements, held together by rivets. The basic element was the axe blade with a counter-balancing beak. The blade was overlaid by side straps, which in turn would have the apical spike attached. The long side straps reinforced the shaft against being chopped through in combat.

Though the poleaxe was one of the weapons used in the formal duels of foot combats, it was primarily a serious battle arm. In some cities the guards of the city gates were armed with poleaxes; in emergencies, when there was no time to raise the drawbridge, they could hack through the ropes that held up the portcullis, and the grill would drop to block the entrance.

Reference: Rozière sale, 1860, lot 219, ill.

72

BOAR SPEAR
German, second half of the 16th century
Steel, wood, staghorn, leather
Length overall 75½ in. (192 cm.)
Length of blade 14½ in. (36.9 cm.)
Weight 6 lb. (2.72 kg.)
Ex collection: Samuel J. Whawell, London;
William H. Riggs, Paris
Gift of William H. Riggs, 1913 (14.25.455)

The obtusely pointed oval head is reinforced by a heavy mid-ridge, and almost entirely covered with etched decoration of

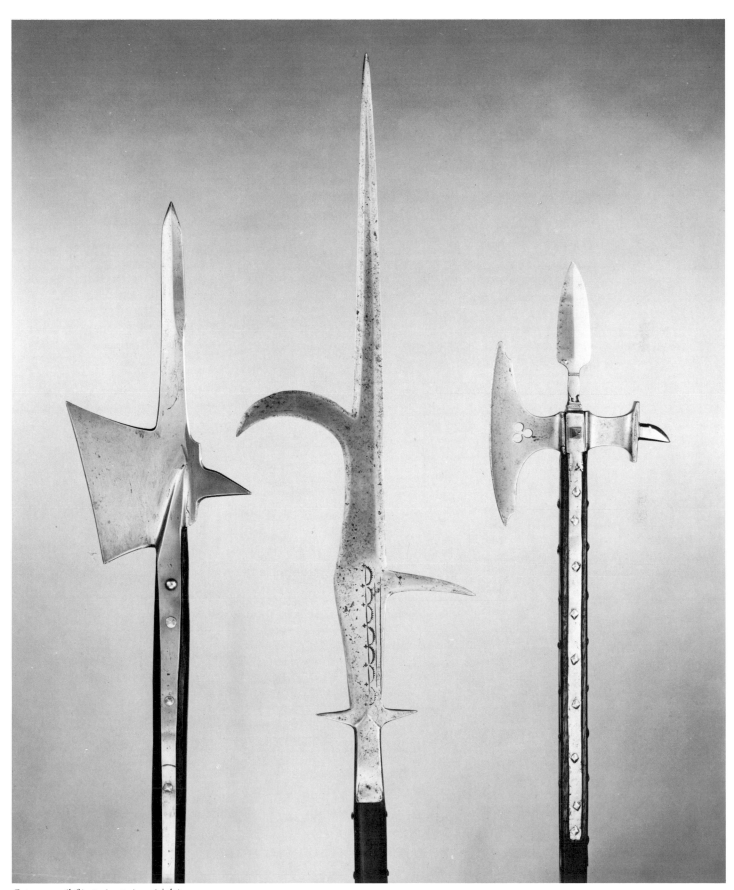

Cat. nos. 70 (left), 69 (center), 71 (right)

Cat. no. 72

foliate strapwork. A rivet at the bottom of the socket serves for attaching the toggle, carved from staghorn and tied on with leather straps. The strong wooden shaft is deeply grooved and crosscut, which creates a surface of short lobes for about two-thirds of its length.

These spears were specially designed for the hunt of boar and bear. The short but wide double-edged blade would inflict a heavily bleeding wound that would quickly disable the animal; the toggle would stop the on-rushing boar from impaling himself too deeply and would keep the huntsman at a reasonably safe distance from the slashing tusks. The heavily lobed surface of the shaft allowed the huntsman a firm grip, even if the wood were slippery with rain, dew, or blood. Sometimes ash saplings were selected, and while still alive their bark was nicked repeatedly in order to grow scar tissue to create the desired knobby surface (*gebickte Schäfte*).

References: Whawell sale, 1908, no. 299; Grancsay, 1953, no. 66.

73
GLAIVE OF THE BODYGUARD OF ARCHDUKE FERDINAND II OF AUSTRIA
South German, 1556 or after
Steel, wood
Length overall 99¹/₂ in. (252.1 cm.)
Length of blade 29¹/₄ in. (74.3 cm.)
Weight 6 lb. 4 oz. (2.834 kg.)
Ex collection: Maurice de Talleyrand-Périgord, Duc de Dino, Paris
Rogers Fund, 1904 (04.3.97)

The long, sharply pointed knife-like blade has a convex cutting edge and has a short back edge near the point. The rectangular socket was formerly mounted with two side straps (now cut off). Each side of the blade is etched with a shield bearing the arms of Archduke Ferdinand II of Austria (1529-1595), surrounded by a collar of the Order of the Golden Fleece and surmounted by an archducal bonnet, above which is the monogram F. The back and base of the blade are followed by an etched line, and at the base of the cutting edge is a tiny flower. The shaft is modern.

This weapon, called *Kuse* in German (derived from French *couteau*, knife), was a traditional arm carried by bodyguards at the imperial Hapsburg court. The present example bears the arms and monogram of Archduke Ferdinand II, who was governor of the Tyrol from 1564. The presence of the collar of the Order of the Golden Fleece indicates that this glaive may date from 1556, the year in which the archduke was received into the Order.

References: Cosson, 1901, no. H.26; Thomas, 1969, p. 62.

74
GLAIVE OF THE BODYGUARD OF EMPEROR RUDOLF II
Hans Stromaier (ca. 1524/25-1583), etcher
German (Augsburg), dated 1577
Steel, partly gilt, wood, velvet
Length overall 99¹/₄ in. (258.4 cm.)
Length of blade, with socket 29¹/₈ in. (74 cm.)
Weight 6 lb. 3 oz. (2.80 kg.)
Ex collection: Richard Zschille, Grossenhain, Saxony; Henry G. Keasbey, Eastbourne, England
Gift of George D. Pratt, 1925 (25.188.18)

The knife-like blade is similar to the preceding one. Two-thirds of each side are etched with a dense strapwork design on a dotted and blackened ground, with traces of gilding. The decoration includes the insignia of Emperor Rudolf II: on the left side, from top to bottom, the date 1577 and the emperor's motto AD SIT (literally "He [God] be with me," but also an acronym for the motto *Auxilium Domini Sit Iniquis Terror,* "The assistance of God is a terror to the evil ones"), a double-headed eagle surmounted by an imperial crown and holding an arrow in his right talon, the *Bindenschild* of Austria, and the number 24; on the right side the letter R surmounted by an imperial crown, and surrounded by a sword, scepter, orb, and cross above a shield bearing the arms of Hungary and Bohemia. Etched at the base of the left side of the blade, near the back, is the etcher's monogram H S (Hans Stromaier), and on the right side a tiny shield with a Greek cross with two pellets above, the etcher's coat of arms. The rectangular shaft of wood is original and retains traces of its brown velvet covering and iron nail heads; a tassel is fastened below the socket.

Cat. nos. 74 (left), 77 (center), 73 (right)

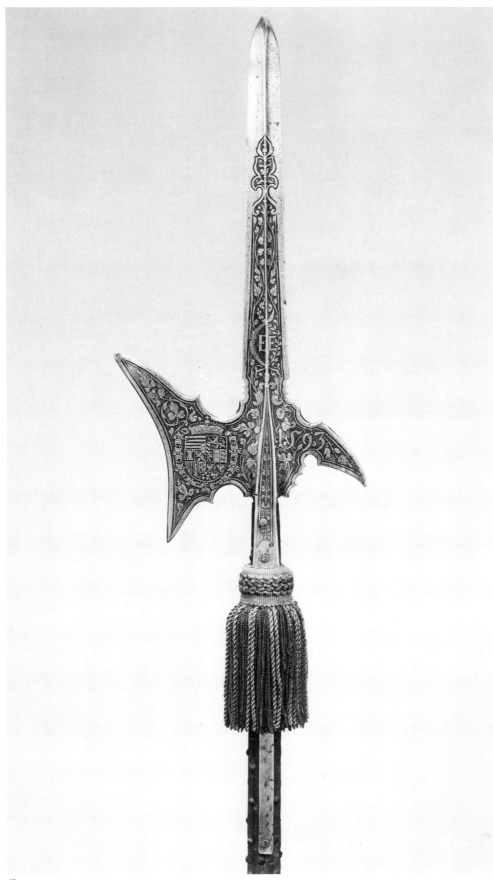

This glaive is one of a number of identical weapons carried by the bodyguard of *Hartschiere* of Emperor Rudolf II (reigned 1576-1612) and documented as having been made in Augsburg by the cutler Oswald Salzhuber and etched by Hans Stromaier. A full-scale color-washed pen and ink drawing of one of these glaives, presumably made by Stromaier himself, is preserved in the Vienna Archives, and probably served as a presentation design sent to the emperor in Prague for his approval. Six of these glaives are preserved in the Vienna Waffensammlung, each of them etched with a number, the highest being 74, which indicates that at least seventy-four similar arms were made. The Metropolitan Museum's glaive is the twenty-fourth of the series.

In the same year, 1577, Hans Stromaier is also known to have etched 110 halberds for the *Trabanten* bodyguards of the emperor. The Hapsburg court had two types of bodyguards: the *Hartschiere* (from French *archiers,* archers), who carried glaives, were noblemen; the *Trabanten,* who carried halberds, were commoners.

References: Forrer, p. 23, no. 702, pl. 180; Zschille sale, 1897, lot 452; Keasbey sale, 1925, lot 222; Thomas, 1969, pp. 61-73; Augsburg, 1980, II, pp. 89, and 520-521.

75
Parade halberd
German (Saxony), ca. 1586-91
Steel, partly gilt, wood
Length overall 105¹/4 in. (273.4 cm.)
Length of blade 26³/4 in. (68.1 cm.)
Weight 7 lb. 5 oz. (3.31 kg.)
Ex collection: Royal Saxon Armory, Dresden; Maurice de Talleyrand-Périgord, Duc de Dino, Paris
Rogers Fund, 1904 (04.3.80)

These halberds of characteristic shape, with elegantly S-shaped axe blade, long tapering spike with sharp mid-ridge, and fleur-de-lis shaped beak, were made for the *Trabantenleibgarde* (palace and body-guard) of the Prince Elector Christian I of Saxony (1586-91). An especially elaborate specimen – apparently an officer's weap-on – bears the name of the Elector Chris-tian and the date 1588 and is preserved in the Historische Museum Dresden, the former electoral arsenal. The entire surface

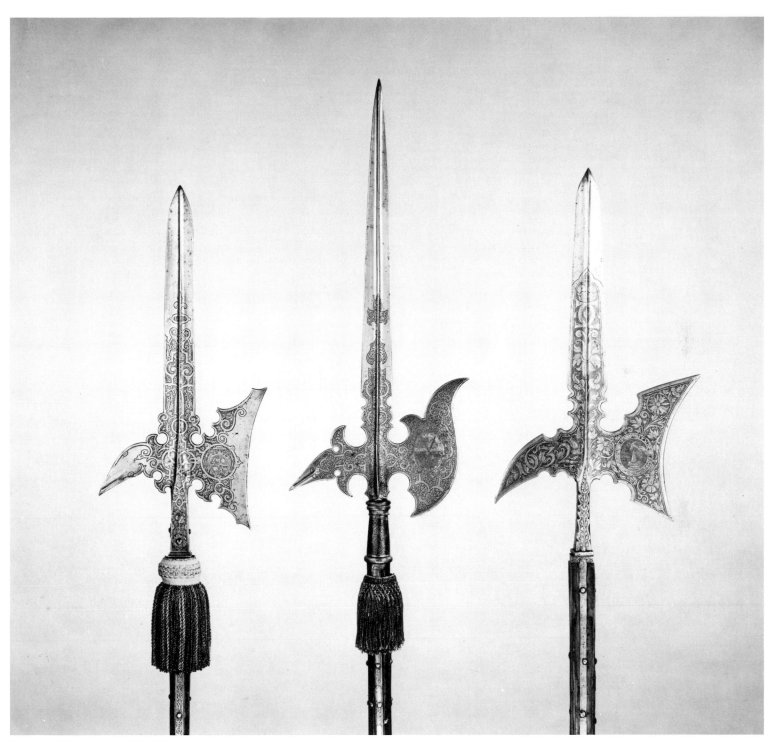

Cat. nos. 76 (left), 75 (center), 82 (right)

of these halberd heads, including their conical sockets and the long side straps, is covered with etched scrollwork. On one side of the axe blade is an oval cartouche with the arms of the archmarshalship of the Holy Roman Empire, *per fess, sable and argent, two swords gules in saltire overall*, and on the other side the arms of the duchy of Saxony, *barry of ten, or and sable, a crancelin vert in bend overall* (i.e., horizontally striped of gold and black, with a green coronet diagonally across). The *Trabantenleibgarde* consisted of more than one hundred men, and since there are enough of these halberds to make them highly desirable collector's items, no important collection seems to be without at least one.

References: Cosson, 1901, no. H. 51; Haenel, 1923, p. 140; Grancsay, 1933, no. 317.

76
PARADE HALBERD
German, 1589
Steel, brass, wood
Length overall 92 in. (233.7 cm.)
Length of blade 23¹/4 in. (59.1 cm.)
Weight 7 lb. 2 oz. (3.27 kg.)
Ex collection: William H. Riggs, Paris
Gift of William H. Riggs, 1913 (14.25.300)

This halberd, with its slightly concave axe blade, wide apical spike with sharp midridge, strongly curved beak, and fancifully scrolled general outline, is typical of the parade weapons used by palace guards of German princes during the second half of the sixteenth and throughout the seventeenth centuries. Its entire surface, including the square socket and the long steel straps (*Schaftfedern*) fastening the head to the shaft, is profusely etched with scrollwork and grotesques. On either side of the axe blade is an etched rondel containing the coat of arms of Wolfgang Dietrich von Raitenau, Prince Archbishop of Salzburg, *quarterly, 1 and 4 per pale, or, a lion sable, and gules, a fess argent (Salzburg); 2 and 3, argent, a ball sable (Raitenau)*, surmounted by a cardinal's hat. On a small cartouche approximately in the middle of the spike is etched the date 1589.

Reference: Potier, 1905, pp. 280-285, fig.3.

77
HALBERD OF THE BODYGUARD OF ARCHDUKE ERNST OF AUSTRIA
South German, dated 1593
Steel, brass, wood, silk
Length overall 94 in. (239 cm.)
Length of blade with socket 23¹/8 in. (58.7 cm.)
Weight 6 lb. 10 oz. (3.00 kg.)
Ex collection: Maurice de Talleyrand-Périgord, Duc de Dino, Paris
Rogers Fund, 1904 (04.3.67)

The head consists of a broad axe blade with concave cutting edge and decoratively cusped sides, a long spear blade with raised median rib, a down-turned hook with cusped edges, and a rectangular socket with two side straps. The etched decoration includes foliate scrolls on a blackened, dotted background, surrounding the emblems of Archduke Ernst of Austria (1553-1605): on each side of the spear blade is the monogram EE flanked by palm and laurel branches; on the left side of the axe blade are the archducal arms surrounded by the collar of the Order of the Golden Fleece and surmounted by an archducal bonnet; on the right side of the axe blade is the Burgundian Saint Andrew's cross and fire steels; and on either side of the hook is the date 1593. The original wooden shaft is octagonal in section, covered with red fabric and studded with brass nails; the tassel mounted at the top of the shaft is modern.

This halberd is one of a series made for the *Trabanten* (bodyguard) of Archduke Ernst of Austria and commemorates the year he assumed the title of regent of the Netherlands.

References: Cosson, 1901, no. H. 48, pl. 18; Laking, 1920-22, IV, fig. 1419 e; Thomas, 1969, p. 63.

78
GLAIVE OF THE BODYGUARD OF GIOVANNI BATTISTA BOURBON DEL MONTE
North Italian (Brescia), ca. 1590-1600
Steel, wood, gilt brass, fabric
Length overall 99³/8 in. (261 cm.)
Length of blade 30¹/2 in. (77.4 cm.)
Weight 6 lb. (2.72 kg.)
Ex collection: Bourbon del Monte family, Florence; Maurice de Talleyrand-Périgord, Duc de Dino, Paris
Rogers Fund, 1904 (04.3.89)

The long, knife-like blade has a convex cutting edge and flat back sharpened near the tip, with two molded spikes at the base. The back edge terminates in an ornamental scroll in the form of a dolphin, and a long, upward-curving parrying spike projects at an acute angle from the back. The lower half of the blade is etched on either side with a decorative cartouche enclosing the arms of Bourbon del Monte (*azure, three fleurs-de-lis or, with a bend gules overall*), surmounted by a seven-pointed crown, above a figure of a warrior in Roman armor. The octagonal socket and the side straps are etched with strapwork, rosettes, and tiny figures of warriors within oval medallions. The wooden shaft of flattened octagonal section is studded with gilt-brass nail heads beneath which are traces of the original fabric covering.

Italian staff weapons of this particular type, variously called *fauchards* in French, *falcioni* in Italian, are basically the same weapon as the German *Kuse* (cat. nos. 73, 74), but with the addition of a decorative spike on the back edge and two short spikes or lugs at the base of the blade. Like the *Kuse*, these glaives were carried by palace guards and, judging from the large number decorated with the arms of Venetian families, were particularly favored in Venice.

This example is one of eleven similar glaives from the Duc de Dino collection which bear the heraldic arms of the ancient Tuscan family Bourbon del Monte, marquises of Monte Santa Maria. However, the similarity of the del Monte arms with those of the cadet branch of the French Bourbon family lead Cosson in 1901 to identify these glaives as French and made for the bodyguard of Louis II de Bourbon, Duke of Montpensier (1513-1582). This error was perpetuated in arms and armor literature for seventy-five years, until corrected recently by L.G. Boccia. Giovanni Battista Bourbon del Monte (1541-1614) had a long military career in which he served in Africa, France, and Flanders, as well as in Italy. In 1587, Giovanni Battista entered Venetian service as captain-general of the infantry and inspector of fortresses on the mainland. These glaives, so common in Venice, were therefore probably carried by Giovanni Battista's Venetian bodyguard.

Cat. nos. 78 (left), 80 (center), 79 (right)

The Metropolitan Museum possesses a fragmentary armor of Giovanni Battista Bourbon del Monte (acc. no. 14.25.710) which also dates to about 1590, during the period of his Venetian service. The armor and the series of glaives bearing the del Monte arms were quite possibly made in Brescia, chief supplier of arms to the Venetian Republic.

References: Cosson, 1901, nos. H. 29-39; Boccia, Cantelli, Maraini, 1976, pp. 227-228 and 245.

79
GLAIVE OF THE PALACE GUARD OF THE TIEPOLO FAMILY
North Italian, ca. 1600
Steel, gold, wood, velvet
Length overall 106 in. (269 cm.)
Length of blade 30 1/2 in. (77.4 cm.)
Weight 6 lb. (2.72 kg.)
Ex collection: Tiepolo Palace, Venice; Prince Peter Soltykoff, Paris; William H. Riggs, Paris
Gift of William H. Riggs, 1913 (14.25.273)

Two rosettes pierce the long knife-like blade which has a spike set on a decoratively cut and pierced base at right angles to the back; between the blade and its socket are two trefoil-shaped lugs. The lower half of the blade, including the spike, is blued, chiseled, and damascened in gold; the decoration on each side includes flowers, grotesques, a sun, and a trophy composed of two cornucopias and a flaming torch. An oval medallion on the right side is painted with the arms of the counts of Tiepolo, and that on the left side contains the arms of the counts of Valmarana, both ancient Venetian families. Above the arms of Valmarana is a helmet crested with a palm tree and scroll inscribed MODVS. The octagonal wooden shaft is covered with red velvet (now rubbed) and is studded with gilt iron nails.

The palm tree was thought to grow stronger the more weight it bore, and so became an emblem for perserverance. Even more specific, in Italian symbolism, it seems to have been a gold palm on a blue background that stood for courage in the face of adverse fortune. The Latin motto *Modus*, "that way," emphasizes this virtue.

This is one of six identical glaives now in the Metropolitan Museum, of which four were purchased in 1860 by William Riggs from Prince Peter Soltykoff, who in turn had acquired them directly from the Tiepolo Palace in Venice. Not all of the heraldic arms on these glaives are the same. Three of them have medallions damascened in gold with the following arms: on the left side, *or, a fess sable;* on the right side, *sable, a lion rampant or.* These arms unfortunately have not yet been identified. The three other glaives, including this example, have these same gold-damascened arms painted over with the arms of Tiepolo and Valmarana. In light of the evidence we must conclude that these glaives were originally made for the palace guard of one family, and were subsequently acquired by the Tiepolo family, who added their own arms (and those of the Valmarana family, with whom the Tiepolo were probably intermarried) over those of the previous owners.

References: Grancsay, 1953, no. 73; Boccia and Coelho, 1975, p. 388, fig. 502.

80

GLAIVE OF THE PALACE GUARD OF CARDINAL SCIPIONE BORGHESE-CAFFARELLI

Italian, ca. 1600-10
Steel, copper, gold, silver, wood, velvet
Length overall 113³/₈ in. (296.5 cm.)
Length of blade 28¹/₂ in. (71.4 cm.)
Weight 5 lb. 13 oz. (2.64 kg.)
Ex collection: Villa Borghese, Rome; Rutherfurd Stuyvesant, Paris; Alan Rutherfurd Stuyvesant, Allamuchy, New Jersey
Bequest of Alan Rutherfurd Stuyvesant, 1954 (54.46.16)

The blade is very similar to the preceding one, but it is without the pierced rosettes. Except for the tip and the cutting edge, the blade is decorated similarly on both sides with a series of medallions and ornamental strapwork cartouches outlined in silver-encrusted dots and set against a blued background finely damascened with gold scrolls. The ornament within the medallions and cartouches is chiseled and gilt on a punched background and includes, from top to bottom, a grotesque, the papal tiara and crossed keys of Saint Peter, three palm branches projecting through a crown, a basilisk, the Borghese arms *(a dragon displayed, on a chief an eagle displayed)* surmounted by an archbishop's

hat with ten tassels, an eagle, and a grotesque. The side straps and their rivets are decorated with punched and gilt ornament to match the blade and its socket. A tassel of silver-colored thread is mounted at the base of the socket. The octagonal wooden shaft is covered with red velvet and studded with copper rivets, and terminates in a sharp iron point.

This glaive, one of two bearing the Borghese arms in the Metropolitan Museum, is surely one of the most elaborate and beautiful staff weapons ever produced, and combines all known techniques of metal decoration: bluing, gilding, engraving, and damascening, as well as encrustation with gold and silver. The owner of these glaives has traditionally been identified as Camillo Borghese (1552-1621), who became a cardinal in 1596 and who was elected to the papacy (as Paul V) in 1605. More recently, however, Boccia and Coelho have suggested that the owner may have been Cardinal Scipione Borghese-Caffarelli, a nephew of Paul V who was adopted into the Borghese family. Thirteen of these glaives remained in the Villa Borghese in Rome until 1892-93, when its contents were dispersed. A backplate for a child's armor decorated in the same technique and with the same motifs, which surely comes from the same workshop as these glaives, is in the Kienbusch Collection in the Philadelphia Museum of Art.

References: Borghese sales, 1892, no. 417, 1893, no. 433; Dean, 1914, no. 140, pl. XXXVIII; Laking, 1920-22, IV, p. 342; Kienbusch collection, 1963, no. 604, pl. CXXXI, and no. 138, pl. LXIII; Boccia and Coelho, 1975, p. 388, fig. 501.

81

LINSTOCK

North Italian, ca. 1575-1600
Steel, partly gilt, wood
Length overall 94⁷/₈ in. (240.9 cm.)
Length of blade 13¹/₄ in. (33.6 cm.)
Weight 3 lb. 13 oz. (1.728 kg.)
Ex collection: Kübach Collection, Innsbruck; William H. Riggs, Paris
Gift of William H. Riggs, 1913 (14.25.252)

The complex head of this weapon comprises the following elements (from top to bottom): a short triangular blade with convex sides, pierced along the center with two slits; a circular medallion,

chiseled in low relief at the center with a figure of a warrior in Roman armor, and framed by pierced foliate scrolls; two S-shaped arms terminating in stylized dragonheads whose curled tongues serve as match holders; and a circular socket with two straps, fit at the top with six semicircular prongs, each chiseled with a face in the center. The iron surfaces, except for the tip of the blade, are chiseled on a punched background and gilt; the ornament on the blade and socket includes stylized foliage and warriors within medallions.

Unlike the decorative halberds, glaives, and partisans with which palace bodyguards were armed, the linstock was strictly a military weapon. Its two arms, or prongs, held the smoldering matches used for igniting cannon, while the short blade also allowed it to be used as a weapon if necessary. Elaborate linstocks such as this one also served as a badge of rank for master gunners and artillery officers.

The punched and chiseled decoration of this piece recalls comparable decoration found on late sixteenth- and early seventeenth-century Italian armors. Two similar linstocks are in the Musée de l'Armée, Paris, and, like this example, have their match holders appropriately shaped as fire-breathing dragons.

Reference: Boccia and Coelho, 1975, pp. 379-380, figs. 452-453.

82

PARADE HALBERD

German (Liechtenstein), 1632
Steel, wood
Length 90⁵/₈ in. (230.1 cm.)
Length of blade 24¹/₄ in. (61.5 cm.)
Weight 7 lb. 7 oz. (3.36 kg.)
Ex collection: Princes Liechtenstein, Vaduz; Bashford Dean, New York
Gift of Mary Alice Dyckman Dean, 1949, in memory of Alexander McMillan Welch (49.120.13)

The halberd head—consisting of an axe blade with strongly concave cutting edge, a wide double-edged thrusting blade with strong mid-ridge, and a down-curved apical beak—is almost completely covered with etched decoration. On one side of the axe blade is etched the arms of the Princes Liechtenstein, and on the other an oval

Cat. nos. 81 (left), 83 (center), 84 (right)

medallion with the emblem of a hammer-wielding hand striking a pointed anvil, the personal device of Carl Eusebius (1611-1684), Prince of the Empire and Regent of the House of Liechtenstein, and the inscription VIRTUTE ELUDITUR ICTUS ("Through virtue he eludes the blow"). On the thrusting blade is the monogram of Prince Carl Eusebius, and on the beak is the date 1632. Both the armorial shield and the monograms are surmounted by the cap of state of a prince of the Empire. The angles between the three blades — axe, spike, and beak — are decoratively cusped; the socket is square in cross section and fastened to the four-sided shaft by four side straps.

The arms etched on one side of the axe blade show the family arms of Liechtenstein: *per fess, or and gules,* on the inescutcheon; the shield itself is quartered with an inserted point: in 1, *barry of or and sable, a crancelin vert in bend overall* (Dukedom of Saxony), in 2, *gules, a chevron sevenfold spiked or* (Czernahora von Boskowitz), in 3, *per pale, gules and argent* (Dukedom of Troppau), in 4, *or, an eagle sable, armed and beaked gules, with a crescent surmounted by a cross argent on its breast* (Dukedom of Silesia), and in the point, *azure, a huntinghorn or* (Dukedom Jägerndorf). These arms reflect the complicated family history and the complexity of territorial titles of the Princes of Liechtenstein (see *Siebmachers Grosses Wappenbuch; Die Fürsten des Heiligen Römischen Reiches, A-L,* vol. I, part III, section 3A, pp. 138-140, pls. 166-168). The Princes Liechtenstein are an ancient Austrian family; their ancestral castle (now ruined) is near Vienna. From the thirteenth through sixteenth centuries, they assembled vast holdings in Bohemia, Moravia, and Silesia (now Czechoslovakia and Poland). Prince Carl (died 1627), the father of Prince Carl Eusebius whose monogram is etched on this halberd, had added the Silesian Dukedom of Troppau in 1613, and that of Jägerndorf in 1623. Carl Eusebius's son, Johann Adam Andreas (1656-1712), acquired in 1708 the county of Vaduz, which in 1719 was elevated to the status of a principality by Emperor Charles IV, and which is now the Principality of Liechtenstein.

References: Grancsay, 1933, p. 183; Grancsay, Hagerstown-Newark, 1955, no. 55.

83
HALBERD
Northern European, ca. 1700-25
Steel, brass, wood
Length overall 82¾ in. (227 cm.)
Length of blade 13¼ in. (33.7 cm.)
Weight 3 lb. 11 oz. (1.67 kg.)
Ex collection: Samuel R. Meyrick, London; William H. Riggs, Paris
Gift of William H. Riggs, 1913 (14.25.377)

The elaborately pierced body of the halberd head consists of symmetrical floral scrolls, with a fleur-de-lis in its center; one side has a concave axe blade engraved with a crescent moon, and on the opposite side a sharply down-turned beak. A narrow spear blade is attached at the apex by ring moldings, the center ring inlaid with brass, and is also engraved with foliate scrolls. The tubular socket is attached to the blade by ring moldings, two near the upper end, one at the base, the larger two rings inlaid with brass. The shaft of wood is studded with nails and painted black overall, and it terminates in an iron cone.

The stout fighting halberd of the Swiss (see cat. no. 70) was transformed in the sixteenth century into the ceremonial weapon of palace guards throughout Europe, and by the seventeenth century had been adopted by the military as a symbolic weapon of rank for sergeants. This halberd may have been carried by a sergeant, but the quality of its delicately pierced and engraved designs suggest that it was a specially made piece rather than one of common military issue. Decoratively pierced and engraved halberds were also carried by noncommissioned officers in colonial America, the American-made halberds being copied after European examples of this type.

The heavy foliate scrolls that decorate this piece reflect the seventeenth-century baroque taste, and the foliated strapwork on the spear blade recalls the ornament of Jean Bérain the Elder (1637-1711). The general lightness and delicacy of the decoration, but without a hint of the rococo, suggest a slightly later dating, perhaps to the first quarter of the eighteenth century.

Reference: Skelton, 1830, II, pl. XC, fig. 7.

84
OFFICER'S SPONTOON
Central European (Austria or Hungary), ca. 1730
Steel, partly gilt, wood
Length overall 86½ in. (219.7 cm.)
Length of blade 12¾ in. (32.4 cm.)
Weight 2 lb. 14 oz. (1.303 kg.)
Ex collection: William H. Riggs, Paris
Gift of William H. Riggs, 1913 (14.25.405)

The wide, double-edged blade of flattened diamond section is flanked at its base by two cusped lugs with up-turned points. Turned moldings join the head to the socket, the latter with three ring moldings and side straps. The lower half of the blade and the socket are gilt, the blade etched with the following motifs: on one side is a double-headed eagle under an imperial crown, and on its breast an oval medallion bearing the monogram C VI (Carolus VI); on the other side are trophies of arms and two bound captives. The original shaft of wood is inlaid near the top with two brass letters on either side of the straps: Ö and Ẏ.

Throughout the eighteenth century, the spontoon was carried by military officers as a symbol of rank rather than as a weapon. Its form derives from the partisan, a weapon of similar shape but of larger proportions, that was commonly borne by household bodyguards (the "partisans") in the sixteenth and seventeenth centuries. This particular spontoon bears the monogram of Emperor Charles VI of Austria (reigned 1711-40), and similar examples, but with etching of much finer quality, are in the Vienna Waffensammlung and in the Historisches Museum der Stadt Wien. The somewhat crude and naive rendering of the decoration on this example suggests that it probably served a lower ranking officer and may have been made in a provincial center, copied after finer examples of Viennese make. The inlaid letters on the shaft may refer to the spontoon's owner, or to his regiment.

Reference: Thomas, 1969, p. 78, fig. 61.

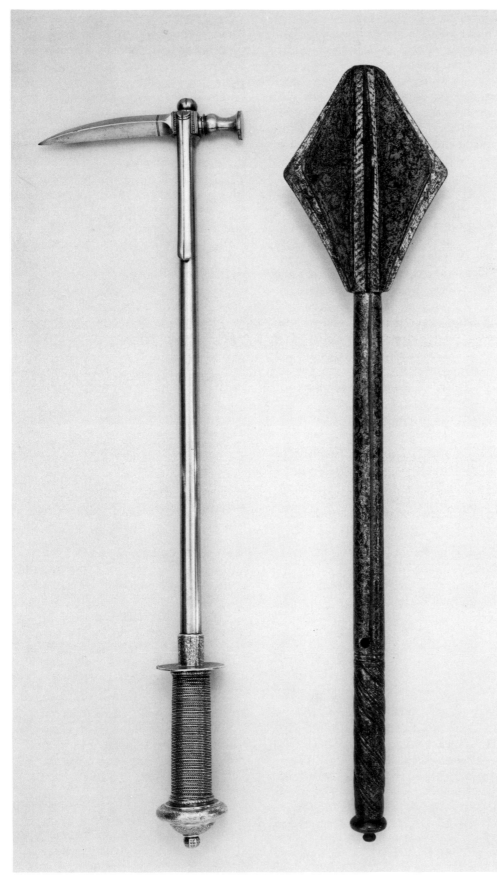

Cat. nos. 85, 86

WAR HAMMER
German (Saxony), second half of the
16th century
Steel, silver
Length 22¹/₂ in. (57.2 cm.)
Weight 2 lb. 8 oz. (1.23 kg.)
Ex collection: Royal Saxon Armory, Dresden;
Bashford Dean, New York
The Bashford Dean Memorial Collection,
1929 (29.158.674)

The slender steel shaft bears a baluster-
shaped hammerhead, and a sharp beak,
square in cross section; attached to one
side is a narrow belt hook. The cylindrical
grip is wrapped in silver wire, with a flat
disk as rondel guard and a bulbously
domed pommel of silver. The etched ornaments of floral arabesques are similar
in style to those found on Saxon silver
hilted cavalry swords *(Reitschwerter)* of
the period.

War hammers were used by knights as
auxiliary weapons during the fifteenth and
sixteenth centuries, after body armor of
plates had made attack by sword edge almost useless. The hammerhead was designed to deliver a stunning blow on a
steel helmet, but the sharp beak *(bec-de-
corbin)* would be able to penetrate the
chinks between plates and possibly even
pierce one of the lighter armor plates.

During the sixteenth century, war
hammers could be also borne as badges of
rank by leaders of mounted troops. The
precious material—solid silver grip—of
this war hammer indicates that it must
have been the weapon of an officer of the
mounted bodyguard of the Prince Electors of Saxony, the *Trabantenleibgarde zu
Ross*, in Dresden.

86
MACE
Italian, ca. 1570
Steel, gilt
Length 23¹/₁₆ in. (58.6 cm.)
Weight 3 lb. 14 oz. (1.75 kg.)
Ex collection: Giovanni P. Morosini,
New York
The collection of Giovanni P. Morosini,
presented by his daughter Giulia, 1932
(32.75.203)

The large steel head of this mace is composed of seven triangular flanges etched overall with trophies and scattered elements of armor on needle-dotted background; the spaces between the flanges are filled with twisted strapwork. The steel cylindrical shaft is hollow, its etched decoration en suite is arranged in four lengthwise bands, the spiral grip also etched en suite. The shaft is pierced just above the grip for a wrist strap. The decoration on this fully gilded mace is in the same style as on the armor shown in catalogue number 19a.

Maces became increasingly popular during the fifteenth and sixteenth centuries – a parallel to the use of the war hammer – due to the ineffectiveness of edged weapons against fully developed plate armor. Though the blow of a mace could not penetrate the armor plates, it might be enough to stun or disable an opponent. Maces were used by cavalrymen, and even became a badge of rank, as was certainly the case with this example.

Reference: Grancsay, 1953, no. III.

87

CROSSBOW

German, late 16th century
Steel, brass, wood, staghorn and bone,
hemp cord, wool
Length 24¹/2 in. (62.3 cm.)
Width 23⁵/8 in. (60 cm.)
Weight 8 lb. 4 oz. (3.73 kg.)
Ex collection: Prince Peter Soltykoff, Paris;
William H. Riggs, Paris
Gift of William H. Riggs, 1913 (14.25.1574a)

The straight walnut stock of this crossbow is inlaid with staghorn in an interlaced pattern of strapwork; upper and lower faces are veneered in staghorn engraved with masks and strapwork. Approximately in the middle of the stock is the nut – the pivoted bone cylinder with two cutouts, one for the string and one for the sear – and also a notch for butt of the bolt. Directly to the rear of the nut is the folding peep sight, adjustable vertically and horizontally. Farther back is a transverse peg, which serves as the rest for the winder. A hand's breadth from the butt end is an inserted brass thumb rest. The release mechanism is double, a long lever and a

hair trigger with three forward sears which can be set by inserting a peg through a set-hole in the stock. The folding hair trigger is under the lever.

Directly in front of the trigger is a safety swivel. The release nut is secured by eight strands of hemp thread bound around the stock. The steel bow is lashed to the forked forward end of the stock by heavy hemp cords, which also hold a suspension ring. Pompoms of green wool are attached to the bow as decoration (*Aufputz*).

Throughout the Middle Ages the crossbow was the most widely used missile weapon, though the English longbow has been much more popularized in modern romantic literature. Due to the extraordinary strength of its steel bow, the crossbow had superior penetration power and an accuracy barely surpassed by the modern rifle. It could have up to ten times the "pull" of a longbow, and therefore had to be spanned mechanically. As a consequence, its shooting speed was much slower than that of a longbow, but since both archers and crossbowmen carried only a limited supply of missiles – usually twenty-four arrows – into battle, shooting quickly might mean running out of ammunition too fast. Early crossbows had bows made of laminated horn or whalebone; steel bows were only introduced from the late fifteenth century onward, when technology was sufficiently advanced to produce good springy steel.

The crossbow was officially abolished as a military weapon in Germany in 1517 by order of Emperor Maximilian, though it was still used in other countries, as for instance Spain where Cortez and Pizarro armed their men with crossbows for the conquests of Mexico (1519-21) and Peru (1532-33). Though for military purposes firearms became more and more efficient, crossbows were prized as hunting weapons because of their silent release and the absence of a recoil. This explains the design of the straight crossbow stock, which was held lightly against the cheek and did not need to be braced against the shoulder.

References: Grancsay, Hagerstown-Newark, 1955, no. 85, ill.; Nickel, 1974, p. 228-229, ill.

Fig. 25.
"The Crossbowmaker." Woodcut by Jost Amman, from his
STÄNDEBUCH *(Frankfurt/Main, 1568).*

88

CROSSBOW WINDER (CRANEQUIN)

German, dated 1562
Steel, brass, hemp cord
Length 14¹/4 in. (36.2 cm.)
Weight 5 lb. 11 oz. (2.57 kg.)
Ex collection: Prince Peter Soltykoff, Paris;
William H. Riggs, Paris
Gift of William H. Riggs, 1913 (14.25.1574b)

The most practical spanner for heavy crossbows was the *cranequin*, consisting of a rack and reduction gear with handle. The gear box is usually almost circular, with a heavy loop of hemp rope attached to the underside. This loop would be slipped over the butt end of the crossbow stock and brought to rest against the transverse pegs to the rear of the release mechanism. The double claw of the rack, in extended position, would be slipped over the bow string, to be pulled back by turning the handle of the gears. The gear ratio of this winder is twelve to one.

Rack and gear housing are etched with floral scrolls and sea monsters; next to the claw is stamped the mark of the maker: a shield shape enclosing a purse sur-

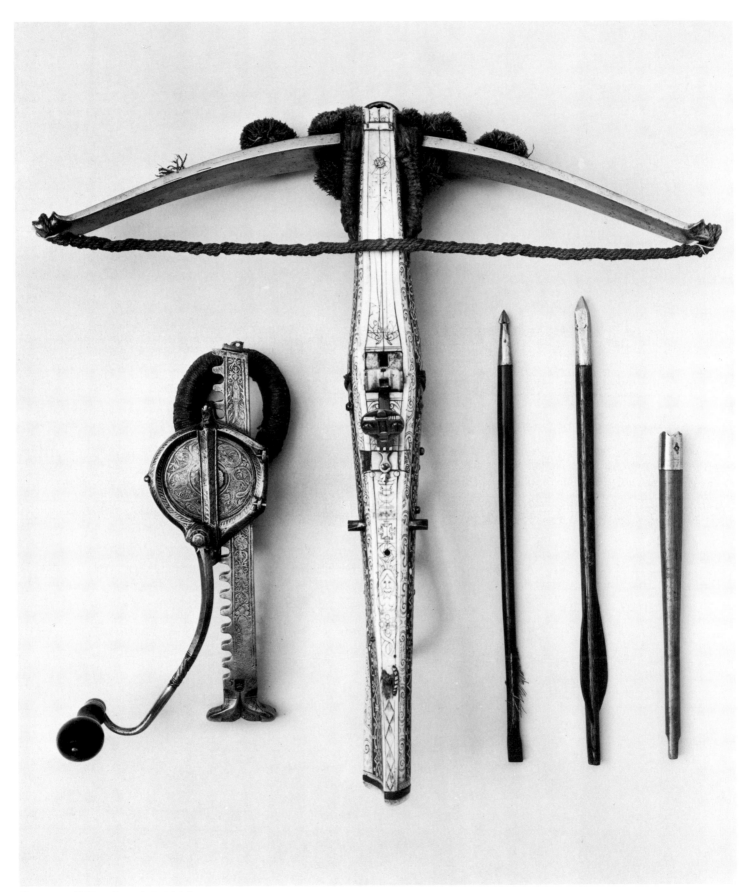

Cat. nos. 88 (left), 87 (center), 89 (right)

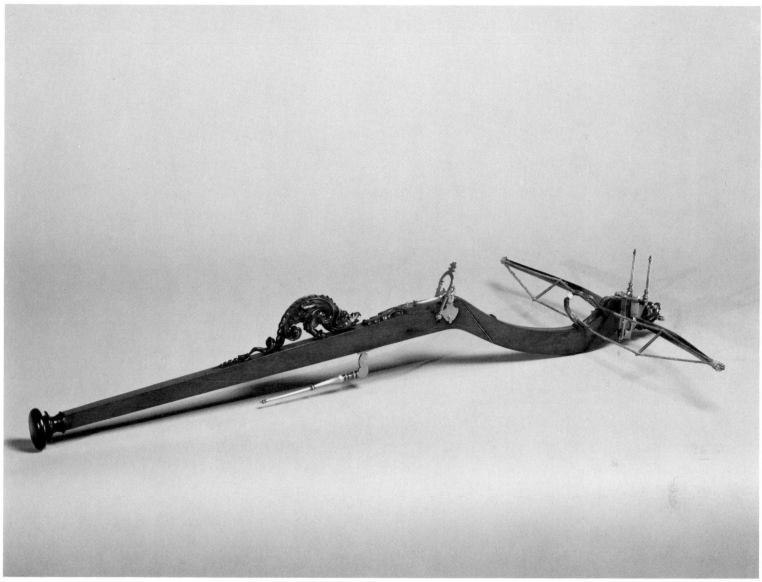

Cat. no. 90

mounted by the initials I and K, inlaid in brass, and flanked by the date 15-62.

Light crossbows with a "pull" of around 125 pounds could be spanned by setting them on the ground upside down. The crossbowman would squat down, pace a claw-like hook attached to his belt behind the string and stand up until the string would rest into the nut (the thigh muscles are the strongest muscles in the human body, the arms muscles would not be able to exert the necessary pressure). Another way of spanning light crossbows was with a "goat's-foot lever," which had a long arm with a short fork hinged to it.

The forward end of the arm was hooked into a ring at the fore-end of the stock, and the hinged fork set against the string. By pulling back the long arm the fork was made to move the string into the locking position. Oversize crossbows stationed on ramparts or castle walls were spanned with windlasses, using claws and pulleys. In the open field, however, this system was not practical, though it is still beloved by writers of historical novels who want to stress the differences between agile long-bowmen and cumbersome crossbowmen.

Reference: Grancsay, Hagerstown-Newark, 1955, no. 85, ill.

89
CROSSBOW BOLTS
German, 15th-17th century
Steel, wood, leather, feathers
Length 12 in. (30.5 cm.), 16 in. (40.6 cm.),
16^1/$_2$ in. (42 cm.)
Ex collection: William H. Riggs, Paris
Gift of William H. Riggs, 1913 (14.25.1591a,
1601b and c)

For reason of the greater power of the crossbow compared to the longbow, crossbows could not shoot slender arrows but had to use sturdy bolts. The bolt or quarrel (from French *carreau*, square) has a socketed head almost square in cross section and with an obtuse point that would not bend upon impact on plate armor; the rear end of the shaft was flattened in order to fit into the notch of the crossbow's nut. Two strips of stiff leather or thin wooden slats are set at an angle into grooves in the shaft, in order to give the bolt a flight-stabilizing spin. Later the idea of the spinning missile was adopted for rifle bullets.

Hunting bolts had lighter heads than quarrels for warfare; their fletchings are often made of three feathers, carefully set so that the bolt could lie flat on the crossbow's runner, with one feather sticking upward. Often these feathers were dyed bright colors or striking patterns to make identification of the hunting prey possible, and also to help in recovering stray bolts.

Crossbow bolts with cylindrical heads, filed with two crossing grooves at the fore-end in order to produce four blunt tips, were sporting bolts especially designed for shooting at man-size targets in the shape of heraldic eagles. These *Vogelschiessen* and *Schützenfeste* (marksmen's

festivals) are still held today in quaint little towns in Germany and Switzerland, but they were serious training in the days when the safety of a community depended on the military strength of its citizen's militia. Since the obvious way of defending a walled town was with as many crossbowmen as possible, every able-bodied man had to be trained in the use of this weapon, and failure to do so might result in facing an additional tax or even in losing one's voting rights. In shooting contests the target birds were made of wood, with all parts loosely doweled together, so that a lucky shot would knock off wing or tail feathers, head or leg. All parts were numbered for keeping score, and whoever either had the highest score or brought down the depleted torso with a final shot was the *Schützenkönig* ("King of the marksmen") for the year. In the good old days, that meant exemption from all city taxes for the period of his "reign"!

Reference: Grancsay, Hagerstown-Newark, 1955, nos. 86-88, ill.

90
PELLET CROSSBOW
Italian, ca. 1550-75
Steel, ebony, walnut
Length 39½ in. (100.3 cm.)
Width of bow 25¾ in. (65.2 cm.)
Weight 3 lb. 5 oz. (1.50 kg.)
Ex collection: William H. Riggs, Paris
Gift of William H. Riggs, 1913 (14.25.1581)

The slender stock of walnut is rectangular in section, straight at the butt, with a deep dip between the bow and release hook. The stock is carved on top with a crouching dragon-like creature and at the front end with a grotesque animal head. The butt tapers slightly and terminates in a turned ebony finial. The bow of polished steel is fitted with a bowstring made of two parallel cords, separated by wooden spacers, and fitted in the center with a basket into which the pellet or stone would fit. The spring-operated release lever is of polished steel and pivots within the stock; its front end is shaped as a hook to receive the basket of the bowstring. The arched rear sight of steel is decorated with moldings and is mounted on the stock behind the release hook; the front sight consists of two vertical steel columns between which a bead originally was suspended.

Pellet crossbows shot small stones or molded clay pellets rather than steel-tipped bolts (cat. no. 89) and were used solely for killing fowl and small animals such as squirrels, ermine, or marten. Though they lacked the power and range of conventional crossbows, pellet crossbows could be spanned by hand and their missiles stunned or killed the game without piercing the skin and ruining fur or feathers with bloodstains.

Pellet crossbows were used throughout Europe from the second half of the sixteenth century at least to the end of the seventeenth century. Bows of this particular type and design, with simple but beautifully carved sculptural ornament on the stock, recall the carving on similar examples from the Medici armory, now preserved in the Museo Nazionale del Bargello in Florence. These probably originated in the same workshop, perhaps in Florence itself.

Detail of cat. no. 90

Firearms

FIREARMS WERE INTRODUCED in Europe in the early fourteenth century, first as cannon and later also as hand-held guns, but some two hundred years had to pass before efficient hand firearms were developed for use in war and in hunting. This development was dependent on the invention and improvement of methods of ignition.

The earliest mechanisms, the matchlocks, had as their main component a match holder, which brought a slow-burning cord to the pan and ignited the priming powder. The resulting flash, in its turn, set off the charge in the barrel through a touchhole in the barrel wall. This principle of ignition through a touchhole remained unchanged up to the nineteenth century, regardless of the system of ignition, and was made obsolete only by introduction of the self-contained cartridge with built-in priming. Matchlocks were generally inexpensive and easy to repair; these were the reasons they remained in use for so long – until the second half of the seventeenth century – in infantry muskets and even in civilian guns and rifles designed for target shooting. The drawbacks inherent in such weapons included a complicated loading procedure, the danger of handling loose gunpowder in the immediate vicinity of a burning match, dependence on wind and weather which could blow out the match or dampen the powder, and the time required to provide the necessary fire with flint, steel, and tinder (unless the match was kept burning continuously).

So far the development of firearms was regarded with utter contempt and displeasure by the noble knights, whose steeds were spooked by the noisy guns, even if their own armor was only occasionally pierced by the foot soldiers' bullets. However, things were to change.

The first mechanism of automatic ignition was designed in the early 1500s. It probably derived from tinderboxes then in use, in which a small wheel of hardened steel, driven by a hand-pulled string, produced sparks by friction against a piece of pyrite. In the gun, the wheel was spun by a wound-up chain attached to a strong spring that had to be compressed with a special key, the spanner, after the weapon was loaded. Wheellock guns could be thus kept ready for instant firing, which required simply switching off the safety catch and pressing the trigger. Now the gun could be used easily even on horseback, and its shorter version, the pistol, was devised for use with one hand only. The wheellock was a fairly sophisticated and expensive mechanism, and therefore it became attractive to noblemen and knights, who had previously disdained the use of a firearm. By the mid-sixteenth century, south German and north Italian gunsmiths had acquired enough experience and had improved technology to such a degree that it became possible to equip entire cavalry formations with wheellock firearms, which in turn led to the development of entirely new military tactics. No less important was the use of the wheellock in hunting firearms, which were highly treasured possessions subject to lavish decoration.

Toward the middle of the sixteenth century, less complicated, and less expensive, mechanisms started a new line of development in firearms history. These devices were based on the old and homely strike-a-light, in which sparks are struck from a steel bar with a piece of flint. Flintlock mechanisms of various types – snaphaunce, miquelet, and of course the true "French" flintlock – performed on the same principle; they were in use in Europe and America up to the second quarter of the nineteenth century. Of all flintlock variations, the simplest and most reliable was the construction evolved in France by the 1620s and introduced in military and sporting firearms of most European countries by the end of the century. Interestingly, the development went from the complicated to the simple, as is almost universally the case with inventions. The French flintlock was pared down to the fewest moving parts, and remained in worldwide use and practically unchanged for more than two hundred years.

Cased set of flintlock pistols. French, ca. 1805 (cat. no. 115)

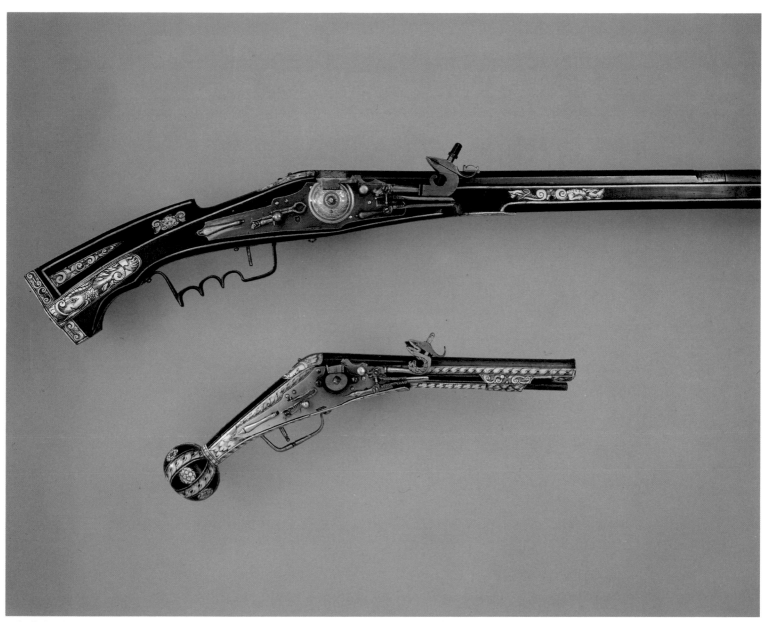

Wheellock gun. German, 1589 (cat. no. 96). Wheellock pistol. German, ca. 1570-80 (cat. no. 95)

Fig. 26.
"The Gunsmith's Shop." Woodcut by Jost Amman, from his STÄNDEBUCH
(Frankfurt/Main, 1568).

Fig. 27.
"The Gunstockmaker's Shop." Woodcut by Jost Amman, from his
STÄNDEBUCH *(Frankfurt/Main, 1568).*

The wheellock, attractive because of its smooth release, coexisted with the flintlock in central Europe up to the mid-1700s, while the matchlock had already been completely abandoned by the turn of the century everywhere in the Western world, though it lingered on in central and east Asia.

Other improvements of hand firearms were aimed at increasing accuracy, range, and speed of reloading and firing. From the mid-1500s, rifled barrels were coming into wider use, particularly in hunting guns. In rifles, the bullet tightly fit the bore of the barrel and was given a rotation by the twist of grooves, assuring a more stable trajectory, a longer range, and greater accuracy. This was based on experience gained from spinning crossbow bolts. During the same century, various breech-loading systems were devised. These eased the loading procedure, which was particularly time-consuming in muzzle-loading a rifle, that is, forcing a tight-fitting bullet through the entire length of the barrel.

To provide a shooter with more than one ready charge, multi-shot guns and pistols were constructed. The simplest way to resolve this problem was to make a firearm with two or more barrels, but these tended to be heavy and sometimes very cumbersome. A more convenient method was a rotating cylinder containing several charges which were fired successively through a single barrel. This system appeared in revolvers toward the 1600s and remains in use today.

Hand firearms as military weapons played an important role in the evolution of the art of warfare and thus had great influence on political and social development. As efficient means of self-defense and attack, as well as hunting weapons, they were highly valued possessions. These deadly objects were naturally given a great deal of attention not only by designers and gunmakers, but also by decorators, who embellished firearms for wealthy owners. Many artists in large and small arms-producing centers of Europe applied their skills to decorating firearms according to contemporary artistic trends as well as local traditions and tastes. All techniques used in the applied and decorative arts were successfully practiced in ornamenting firearms and other weapons, and armor, and many a great artist of the Renaissance contributed to making weapons works of art either by decorating them directly (Benvenuto Cellini took great pride in his hunting gun, which he had made himself) or by designing ornamental patterns which were then adapted by armorers and arms decorators.

Fig. 28.
Musketeer. Engraving by Jacob de Gheyn, one of a series illustrating the military manual WAFFENHANDLUNG VON DEN RÖREN, MUSQUETTEN, UNDT SPIESSEN *(Amsterdam, 1608). The matchlock musket was too heavy (about 12-15 pounds) to be fired freehand; it had to be supported by a forked musket rest. The premeasured charges (powder and ball) were carried in containers hung from a bandoleer. The match had to be kept burning during action.*

Cat. no. 91

91
SHIELD WITH BREECHLOADING HAND GUN

English, second quarter of the 16th century
Steel, wood, leather, canvas, wool
Diameter 18³/4 in. (47.6 cm.)
Caliber .55 (44 mm.)
Weight 10 lb. 4 oz. (4.653 kg.)
Ex collection: Prince Peter Soltykoff, Paris;
William H. Riggs, Paris
Gift of William H. Riggs, 1913 (14.25.746)

The base of the shield is formed by two layers of wood covered by embossed steel plates. Eight reinforcing bosses were lined with washers of red wool, now completely worn, which served as decoration. In the center is a heavy umbo with an aperture for the round barrel and, above it, an aiming slot and a grilled observation window. Inside, the shield is lined with a canvas pad under the enarmes (grips). A metal rim was formerly attached around the outer edge.

The hand gun of simple, massive construction is one of breechloading type, which opened for the insertion of reloadable steel cartridges; it is provided with a touchhole on the top. The cartridge was locked into the chamber by a hinged iron loop with a retaining spring catch; the loop is additionally secured to the breech by a pin passing through two lugs fitting the slots in the breech extension. Shield was held on the left arm, the gun operated by the right hand; once the breech had been loaded and locked closed, the charge could be ignited by hand with a match held ready in a special bracket (now lost) attached to the right of the breech.

This shield is one of a large group thought to have been made for the bodyguard of King Henry VIII of England, of which thirty-five are recorded in the inventory of the Tower Armoury drawn up in 1547 following the king's death. They are usually associated with a document of 1544, in which a Maestro Giovanni Battista, painter of Ravenna, offered his company's service to the English king, listing among the inventions he could supply, "several round shields and arm pieces with guns inside them that fire upon the enemy and pierce any armor." However, except for several shields finely decorated with etching in the Italian style, there is little evidence to connect these shields with the otherwise unknown Maestro Giovanni Battista. The majority of the shields are rather crude in workmanship, including this example, which suggests that they may have been made locally, perhaps in the Tower itself after Italian models.

This shield, together with another in the Metropolitan Museum (acc. no. 14.25.745), was purchased by Prince Peter Soltykoff from the London dealer Samuel Pratt, who in turn is said to have acquired them directly from the Tower of London. At least two other shields from this group

Cat. no. 91. Back of shield, chamber closed

Cat. no. 91. Back of shield, chamber open and cartridge partially withdrawn

are also preserved in American museums, one in the Walters Art Gallery, Baltimore, and another in the George F. Harding Museum, Chicago.

References: Viollet-le-Duc, 1858-75, VI, pp. 250-252; Ffoulkes, 1916, I, p. 195; Wilson, 1960, pp. 8-10; Hayward, 1965, no. 10.

92

MACE WITH WHEELLOCK PISTOL
German, mid-16th century
Steel, partly gilt
Length 23¼ in. (59 cm.)
Caliber .45 (11 mm.)
Weight 4 lb. 10 oz. (2.09 kg.)
Ex collection: Prince Peter Soltykoff, Paris;
William H. Riggs, Paris
Gift of William H. Riggs, 1913 (14.25.1324)

This combination weapon is made entirely of steel, though there must once have been a cover of leather or fabric on the grip. The shaft is hollow to serve as the pistol's barrel; the head consists of six sharply pointed flanges attached to the fore-end of the shaft. The hollow grip is set between two roundels; the pommel roundel has a hinged lid for access to the cavity of the grip, which was presumably used for the storage of wads, pyrites, and other accessories. The handguard roundel has a semicircular cutout to facilitate reaching the trigger button of the wheellock, which is attached along the shaft. The lock has a sickle-shaped mainspring curving around the wheel, with an extension spur for the cock (this was a feature in use during the period of about 1545-60); it also has a pivoted lever safety catch. Just behind the breech there is a transverse hole in the shaft for a wrist strap. All parts are etched with dense foliate scrollwork, and traces of gilding are extant.

On the breech is stamped a shield-shaped maker's mark: a fleur-de-lis surmounted by the letters S and H (Støckel 4474), possibly a member of the Herold family, gunsmiths in Dresden.

Combination weapons such as this pistol-mace were attempts to overcome the inherent weaknesses of early firearms, their cumbersome method of loading and the resulting slow rate of fire. Once the one pistol shot was fired at the enemy at close range, it was hoped that the weapon would still be useful as a mace in hand-to-hand combat. Unfortunately, most of these hybrid arms were too clumsy – particularly because of the additional weight of gun barrel and lock – to be of much use.

Reference: Grancsay, Hagerstown-Newark, 1955, no. 103.

93

BOAR SPEAR WITH TWO WHEELLOCK PISTOLS
German, second half of 16th century
Steel, wood
Length overall 89¾ in. (228 cm.)
Length of barrels 12 in. (30.5 cm.)
Caliber .41 (11 mm.)
Weight 9 lb. 4 oz. (4.19 kg.)
Ex collection: Maurice de Talleyrand-Périgord, Duc de Dino, Paris
Rogers Fund, 1904 (04.3.77)

The blade is lanceolate in its forward part, entirely covered with etched decoration of interlaced strapwork, and with two curved parrying hooks shaped as dolphins in its rearward section. The blade is placed between two pistol barrels, its median ridge is eliminated and changed into a shallow channel on either side aligned with the bore of the barrels. Between the blade and the heavy cylindrical socket are attached the two wheellocks with covered wheels. The folding triggers are halfway down the shaft, inserted into long steel straps covering the pulls of the mechanisms. The shaft is plain and smooth, with a large conical steel mount on its butt end.

It has generally been speculated that the combination of boar spear and pistol was designed to be used to break the onrush of the charging boar or the rampant bear, and the double pistols could be fired before the animal was received on the blade. However, the blade is unusually thin, and as an accommodation to the bullets fired at the raging animal, its stiffening midridge was supplanted by grooves which thinned the material even more. Additionally, the rather small caliber of the pistol barrels makes it doubtful that a boar or bear would have been much impressed. On the contrary, such a relatively light wound might have inflamed its rage.

During the second half of the seventeenth century, before the invention of the bayonet, musketeers were often equipped with boar spears *(Schweinsfedern)* in addition to their firearm. These *Schweinsfedern* served a dual purpose: they could be used as musket support instead of the older musket fork, and they could be used in square formation to repel cavalry charges when there was no time to reload the musket.

Since the shaft of this combination weapon is quite smooth and not made slip proof by knobs or nails, it is another reason to suspect that this was not a hunting weapon, but was designed for antipersonnel use. This *Schweinsfeder* with pistols might have been the weapon of a noncommissioned officer, perhaps a sergeant, who would not carry a musket but who did not want to be left in an emergency without a firearm.

References: Cosson, 1901, no. H. 54; Grancsay, 1953, no. 67; Nickel, 1974, ill. p. 194.

94
MATCHLOCK PETRONEL
French, ca. 1570-80
Steel, wood, bone
Length overall 45¹/4 in. (114.9 cm.)
Length of barrel 37¹¹/16 in. (95.8 cm.)
Caliber .51 (13 mm.)
Weight 7 lb. 11 oz. (3.49 kg.)
Ex collection: Giovanni P. Morosini, New York
The collection of Giovanni P. Morosini, presented by his daughter Giulia, 1932 (32.75.111)

The octagonal barrel is mounted with a front sight and tubular rear sight; it bears the barrelsmith's mark at the breech: a five-pointed star in a shield. The sear matchlock has a long hand lever acting on the sear inside the lock plate; when the lever is pressed, the sear activates the match holder, which brings the match to the pan. On the pan cover is chiseled a warrior bust. The stock is provided with a strongly curved massive butt which was pressed against the breast when the gun was fired (hence the name of this type of gun, from French *poitrinal* deriving itself from *poitrine,* breast) and is decorated with inlaid pieces of bone engraved with floral motifs partly tinted green. This kind of decoration was widely used by German, French, Dutch, and English gunmakers in the second half of the sixteenth century and in the early seventeenth century. Although not very sophisticated in artistic design or difficult in technical execution, this decoration nevertheless produced a pleasing aesthetic effect by contrasting materials and color.

Although at this time much more advanced ignition systems were already used in Europe, like the wheellock and snaphaunce, simple and inexpensive matchlocks were employed for another hundred years on hunting and target guns as well as on infantry muskets. A very similar petronel, made in the same workshop, is in the Kienbusch Collection, Philadelphia Museum of Art. The same barrelsmith's mark is stamped on a later sixteenth century French wheellock pistol in the Hermitage Museum (inv. no. 3.0.N.6660).

References: Hayward, 1962-63, I, p. 278, pl. 1b; Kienbusch collection, 1963, no. 635, pl. CXLVI; Lindsay, 1967, p. 40; Tarassuk, 1971, no. 62; Kennard, 1972, p. 5.

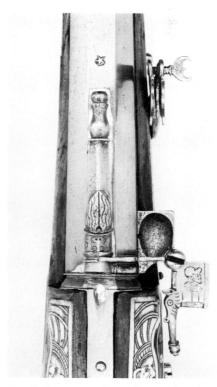

Detail of cat. no. 94. Gunmakers' marks on barrel (star) and pan cover (helmeted head)

Cat. no. 93

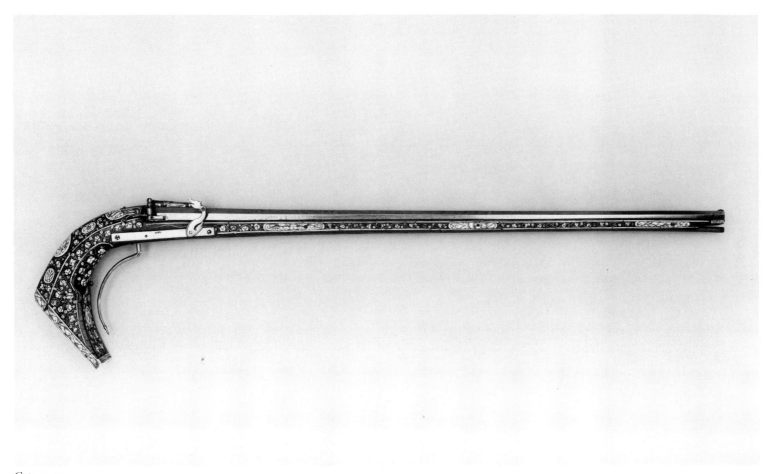

Cat. no. 94

95
WHEELLOCK PISTOL

German (Augsburg), ca. 1570-80
Steel, wood, staghorn
Length overall 19 in (48.3 cm.)
Length of barrel 11 7/16 in. (29.1 cm.)
Caliber .52 (13 mm.)
Weight 3 lb. 6 oz. (1.536 kg.)
Ex collection: William H. Riggs, Paris
Gift of William H. Riggs, 1913 (14.25.1402a)

The blued barrel is in two stages, round at
the front with a flaring muzzle, octagonal
at the breech, and it is ornamented with
chiseled roping, stamped crescents, and
circles. It bears two marks: a hunting horn
in a shield, the gunmaker's mark (similar
Støckel 5223), and a pine cone, the control
mark of the city of Augsburg. The wheellock has a spring-closed pan cover with
release button, and safety catch; the cock
is chiseled with a stylized dragon.

The ebonized stock is inlaid with staghorn engraved with stylized foliage and
geometric patterns, and with a lion's
mask on the forestock, two crowned
female heads on the grip, and two grotesque dragons with devil's faces on the
left side. The incisions were blackened to
make the designs stand out.

After the automatic-ignition mechanism – the wheellock – was devised
around 1500, it was first applied to firearms used on horseback. In fact, the appearance of pistols – weapons handled
with one hand – was due to the invention
of the wheellock, and by the middle of the
sixteenth century they became part of the
equipment of middle and light cavalry, not
just weapons available exclusively to men
of high rank as had initially been the case.
Since an ordinary pistol could deliver only
one shot and had to be reloaded to fire the
next round, pistols were commonly made
in pairs and carried in leather holsters, one
on each side of the saddle. A large ball-
shaped pommel on the pistol grip made it

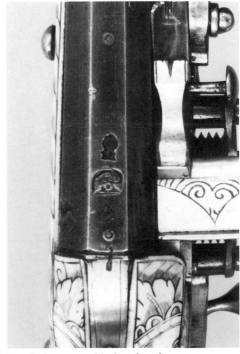

Detail of cat. no. 95. Marks on barrel

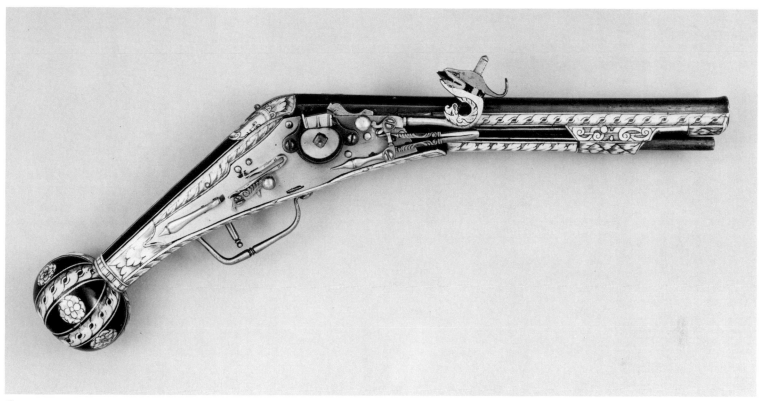

Cat. no. 95

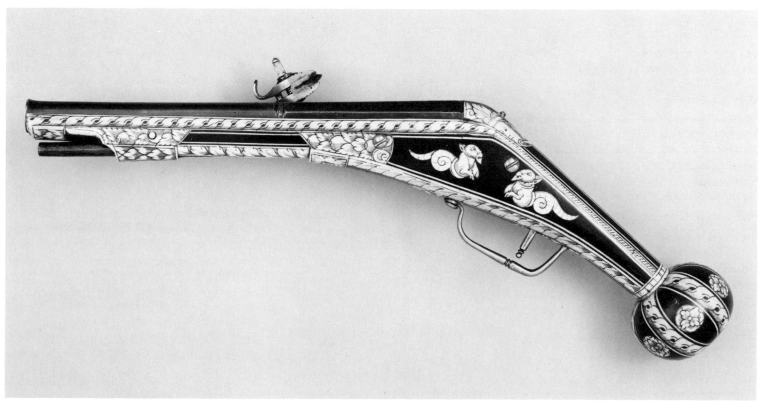

Cat. no. 95

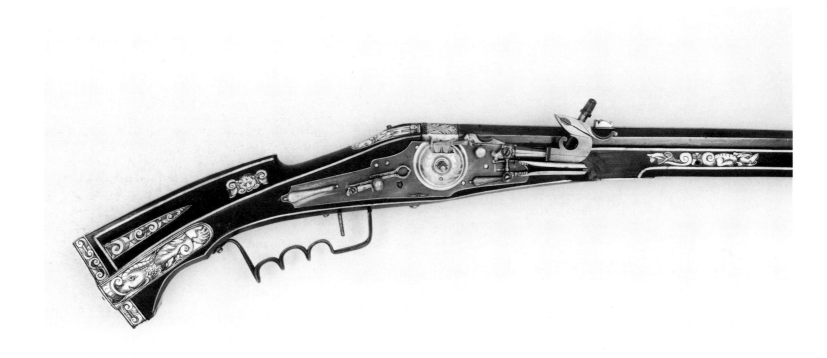

Cat. no. 96

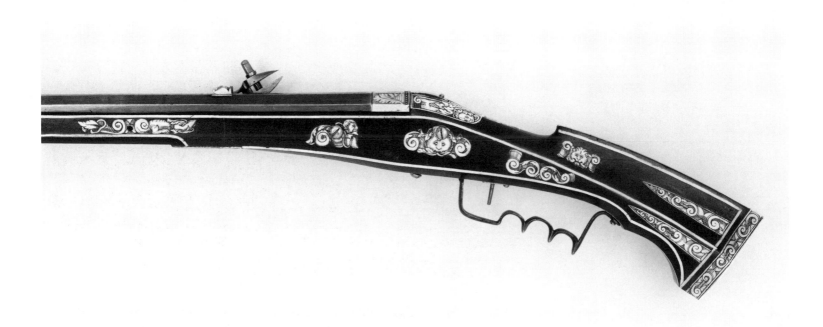

Cat. no. 96

easier to retrieve from the holster and also helped to counterbalance a heavy barrel.

The city of Augsburg was one of the foremost arms-producing centers in Europe, and its armorers were among the first to produce wheellock pistols and carbines. Since wheellock firearms were fairly expensive, even pistols of military type, as represented by this example, rarely left the gunmaker's shop undecorated. The preferred decorative technique of German stockmakers from the sixteenth century on was the inlay of engraved staghorn plaques into the wood. Apart from the simple decorative effects of contrasting materials, use of staghorn inlays also reinforced the wooden stock, which was particularly vulnerable to the rough use of military firearms.

Reference: Grancsay, 1967, no. 72

96
WHEELLOCK GUN
Zacharias Herold, recorded 1586-1618
German (Dresden), dated 1589
Steel, brass, gold, walnut, staghorn
Length overall 54 in. (137.1 cm.)
Length of barrel 40 1/2 in. (102.8 cm.)
Caliber .64 (16.25 mm.)
Weight 11 lb. 11 oz. (5.31 kg.)
Ex collection: Royal Saxon Armory, Dresden
Gift of Prince Albrecht Radziwill, 1928
(28.100.7)

The barrel is in two stages, the rear half faceted, the front half round, and is blued, with a band of engraved and gilt floral patterns at both ends and in the center. The front and rear sights are also gilt. On the barrel are stamped the initials Z H of Zacharias Herold (Støckel 513), the date 1589, and the initials M B of an unidentified barrelsmith (Støckel 3879). On the breech plug is the number 8.

The lock is fitted with a safety catch and a spring-closed pan cover with button release. The wheel is housed under a domed cover of gilt brass engraved with Saxon coat of arms. On the lock plate is the fleur-de-lis mark of Zacharias Herold (Støckel 512). The trigger is provided with a screw regulating the pull (which is generally very sensitive in wheellocks).

The walnut stock is inlaid with staghorn carved and engraved with fantastic animals, human and animal mask, an eagle, a bust of a warrior, scrolls, and floral motifs. The patch-box cover is marked inside with the monogram M A, probably that of the stockmaker. The numbers 31 and 32 are incised on the butt and are probably inventory markings. The stock of this gun probably belonged to another arquebus from the same series and was at some time assembled with this barrel and lock (possibly because the original stock was in bad condition).

Since the wheellock was quite expensive to produce and repair, its use was limited to cavalrymen's pistols and light guns, and better-quality hunting firearms affordable to the wealthy. Infantry used much simpler matchlock guns but some élite guard units were issued wheellock arquebuses like this gun, one of a series of a hundred made by Dresden gunmakers for the bodyguard on foot (*Trabantenleibgarde*) of the Prince Elector Christian I of Saxony (reigned 1586-91).

References: Grancsay, 1953, no. 117; Grancsay, 1967, no. 73; Schaal, 1975, pp. 32-33, nos. 71-74, pp. 38-39, nos. 107-108.

97
DOUBLE-BARRELED WHEELLOCK PISTOL
German (Augsburg), ca. 1570-80
Steel, gilt copper, leather
Length overall 25 3/8 in. (64.5 cm.)
Length of barrels (upper) 17 1/8 in. (43.5 cm.),
(lower) 15 1/4 in. (38.7 cm.)
Caliber .358 (9 mm.)
Weight 4 lb. 4 oz. (1.80 kg.)
Ex collection: William H. Riggs, Paris
Gift of William H. Riggs, 1913 (14.25.1420)

The two round barrels are mounted one over the other, the upper one faceted at the breech end and furnished with front and rear sights; the barrels are etched overall with scrolls and arabesques. On the breech is the control mark (the pine cone) of the city of Augsburg.

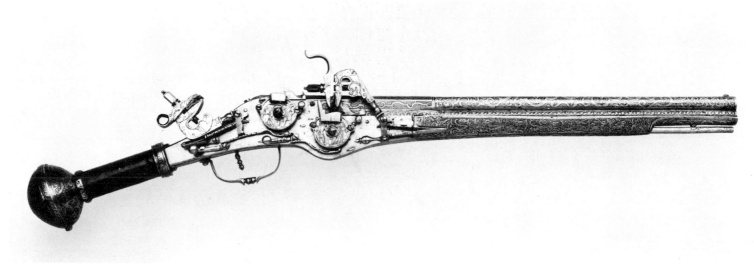

Cat. no. 97

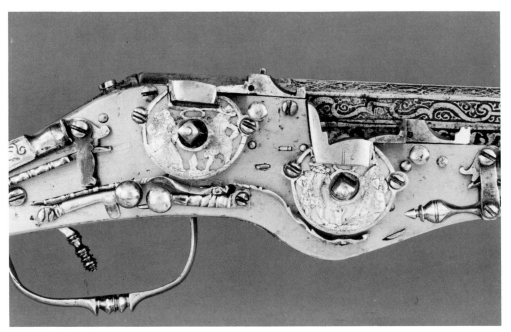

Detail of cat. no. 97. Lock

The lock plate serves to mount a double lock – two mechanisms to set off charges in the two barrels. The lock is fitted with spring-closed pan covers, their release buttons, two independent safety catches, and a single trigger acting on both sears. The cocks are engraved with monsters. Each wheel cover is of gilt copper, chiseled and engraved with a dancing couple. The stock of steel is etched on the sides with a hunting scene in a forest, the rest of the surface with strapwork and arabesques. The grip is bound with dark leather. The spherical pommel is hollow, its lower half hinged as a lid to serve as a box for spare pyrites.

Since ordinary firearms of the early period could deliver only one shot and reloading was an awkward task on horseback, gunmakers devised various multi-shot systems to provide the soldier and hunter with several ready shots. One was a firearm with two or more barrels. Such weapons required, in turn, a special ignition mechanism, like the double lock fitted to this pistol. The presence of two safety catches and a single trigger permitted the firing of both loads simultaneously or either one of them in turn. With two such pistols at his saddle, the owner thus had

four shots ready at his disposal. Due to the weight of the barrels and the large lock, the stock for such pistols was often made of steel instead of wood for greater strength of the whole construction. German gunmakers used all-metal stocks also for single-barreled pistols, decorating them either with chased designs or, more often, with etched ornament, usually copied from some published graphic source.

Reference: Grancsay, Hagerstown-Newark, 1955, no. 105.

98

WHEELLOCK RIFLE

Peter Danner, recorded 1583-1602
German (Nürnberg), dated 1594
Steel, wood, ivory, mother-of-pearl
Length overall 45³/₄ in. (116.2 cm.)
Length of barrel 34¹¹/₁₆ in. (88.1 cm.)
Caliber .53 (13.46 mm.)
Weight 8 lb. 11 oz. (3.94 kg.)
Ex collection: Maurice de Talleyrand-Périgord, Duc de Dino, Paris
Rogers Fund, 1904 (04.3.165)

The octagonal barrel is rifled with eight grooves and is decorated on the breech

with incised arabesques. The barrel is provided with a frontsight and three-leaf rear sight. It bears these marks: P D, both letters surmounted by a serpent (similar Støckel 4251), the initials of Peter Danner; the control mark of the city of Nürnberg (similar Støckel 1582), struck twice, surmounted by a cartouche with the letter N and figure 94 for the year 1594; the incised monogram V E (VF or VI ?), probably that of the owner; and a trumpet in a shield (similar Støckel 5966), the mark of a late seventeenth-century gunmaker who carried out a repair.

The lock has a spring-closed pan cover with button release. The plate, the domed wheel cover, the cock, and the pan cover are finely engraved, mostly with floral motifs, and partly gilt. On the lock plate are a lockmaker's mark, C S over scissors (Støckel 2303), and the Nürnberg control mark (similar Støckel 1592-1595).

The massive straight butt of typical German form, with a sloping plane on the left side, was pressed against the cheek when aiming and firing. The butt plate is reinforced with a brass knob to protect it when the gun was put on the ground. The steel trigger guard is chiseled, blued, and gilt. This is a type of good-quality gun widely used in central Europe for hunting and target shooting, with a rear sight for three different distances and a set trigger for a very light pull.

The stock is decorated with carved and engraved inlays of ivory and mother-of-pearl displaying figures of animals, fantastic and grotesque figures, Venus with a dove, scrolls, putti, and soldiers. Arms decorators often relied on contemporary prints or albums of designs compiled by professional ornamentalists for inspiration, and in this instance the stock decorator chose, among other sources, a popular series of engravings issued in 1587 by Jacob de Gheyn (after drawings by Hendrick Goltzius) showing various types of infantry soldiers in costumes with deeply pointed peascod breasts that were popular in the last third of the sixteenth century.

Reference: Cosson, 1901, no. J.3.

Detail of cat. no. 98. Marks on barrel

Detail of cat. no. 98. Underside of stock

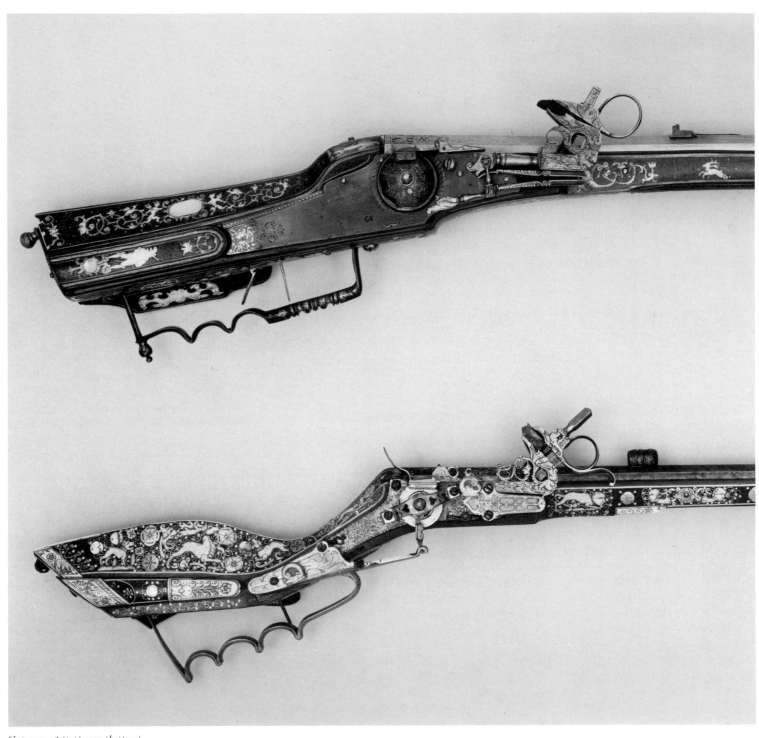

Cat. nos. 98 (top), 100 (bottom)

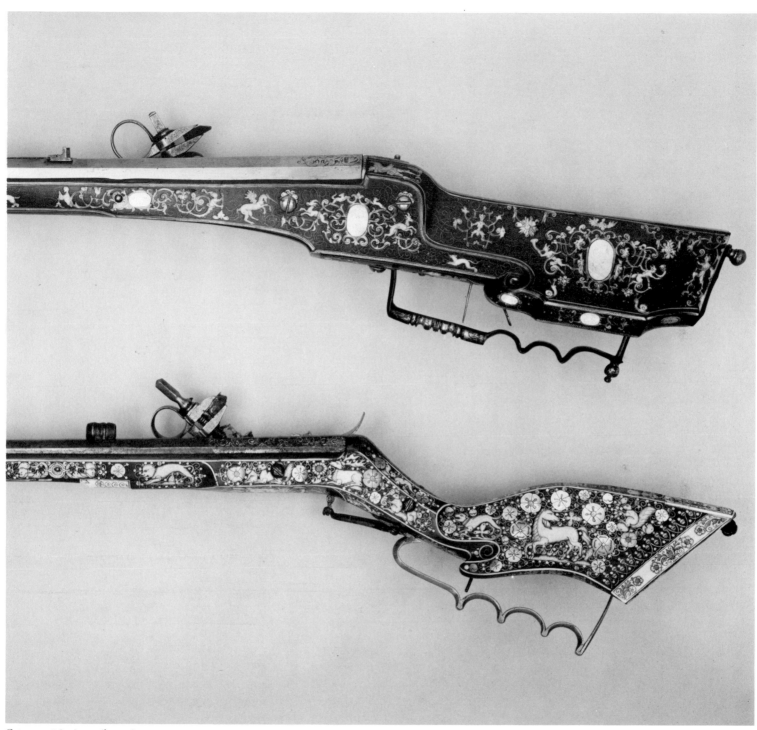

Cat. nos. 98 (top), 100 (bottom)

Detail of cat. no. 99. Reverse, signature on barrel

99

WHEELLOCK PISTOL *(one of a pair)*
François Du Clos, active in the first half
of the 17th century
French (Paris), ca. 1640
Steel, gilt, cherry wood, silver, mother-of-pearl
Length overall 23¹/₈ in. (58.7 cm.)
Length of barrel 15¹/₂ in. (39.4 cm.)
Caliber .52 (13.2 mm.)
Weight 2 lb. 3 oz. (.993 kg.)
Ex collection: Maurice de Talleyrand-
Périgord, Duc de Dino, Paris
Rogers Fund, 1904 (04.3.192)

The barrel is in two stages, round at the muzzle end and octagonal at the breech, the juncture encircled by a multi-faceted molding and a narrow chiseled band. The breech and tang are decorated with fine symmetrical foliate designs in gold on a blued background. Amid the ornament is the gunmaker's signature: F DU CLOS.

The wheellock is of French construction, with hand-closed pan cover; the cock, its spring, and wheel bridle are decorated with foliate scrolls chiseled, engraved, and gilt.

The stock of cherry wood is inlaid around the lock emplacement with silver wire; the S-shaped side plate of gilt brass is delicately chiseled and is surrounded by foliage of inlaid silver wire and mother-of-pearl. The mounts, including pommel, grip strap, and trigger guard, are of blued steel decorated with gold foliate ornament to match the barrel.

By the middle of the sixteenth century, French gunmakers devised their own distinctive form of wheellock construction. Its main features included a long, elastic main spring shaped to the curvature of the grip (or small of the butt in long guns) and placed into a recess cut inside the grip—not mounted on the lock plate as it was in wheellocks of other types. The spindle of the wheel was supported by a bearing (side) plate on the left side of the stock instead of being mounted with a heavy bridle inside the lock plate. To reinforce the stock where the wood was weakened by a hollowed-out recess for the mainspring, the grip was provided with a steel strap under the trigger guard. As a result of these innovations, the French wheellock was distinguished by its small size, light weight, and gracefulness of outline which greatly contributed to the general elegance of its appearance.

At the time this pistol was produced, French gunmakers and decorators ranked among the very best in Europe, and French firearms exerted great influence on stylistic and mechanical development of guns and pistols in other countries. Fine decoration in gold as seen on the barrel and furniture of this pistol was apparently executed in the technique of *Goldschmelz* (smelted gold in German). In this process the design was first traced and etched on the steel parts, then the recessed areas filled with an amalgam of powdered gold and mercury; the latter was evaporated by

heating, leaving the gold adhering to the base and producing a striking contrast against the blued steel.

That François Du Clos was an artisan of high repute is confirmed by the fact that in 1636 he was granted a patent of *logement* (literally "lodging") for his workshop in the galleries of the royal palace of the Louvre, a special honor given to select artists and craftsmen in royal employment. Du Clos's patron at this time was Louis XIII (reigned 1610-43), a great admirer and collector of firearms (and more popularly remembered as the king in Alexandre Dumas's *Three Musketeers*). The gold foliate decoration on the barrel and mounts of this pistol appear to derive from Thomas Picquot's *Livre de diverses Ordonnances de Feuillages, Moresques...*, a patternbook of engraved ornament for gunmakers, dedicated to Louis XIII and published in Paris in 1638. The association of Du Clos and Picquot (who described himself on the patternbook frontispiece as a painter) is not accidental as both received their patent of *logement* in 1636 and shared the same atelier. It is even possible that Picquot himself decorated the steel parts of this pistol.

References: Cosson, 1901, no. K.8; Lenk, 1943, p. 18, fig. 9; Hayward, 1962-63, I, pp. 132, 289, pls. 37a, 37b; Lenk, 1965, pp. 42, 130, pls. 19:2, 134:17; Hoff, 1969, II, p. 179; Grancsay, 1970, pp. 9 and 154; Gusler and Lavin, 1977, p. 18.

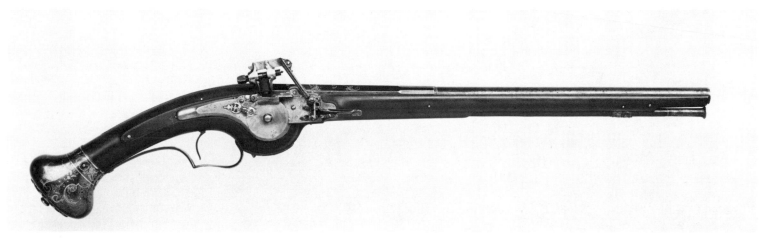

Cat. no. 99

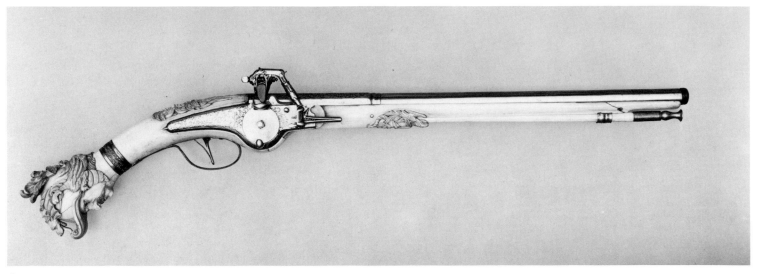

Cat. no. 101

100

WHEELLOCK RIFLE (TESCHINKE)

*Polish (Teschen, now Cieszyn in Poland),
middle of the 17th century
Steel, partly gilt, gilt brass, walnut, bone,
mother-of-pearl
Length overall 48¹/₂ in. (123.1 cm.)
Length of barrel 37¹/₄ in. (94.6 cm.)
Caliber .344 (8.73 mm.)
Weight 6 lb. 13 oz. (3.09 kg.)
Ex collection: Count Saint Maur, Toulouse,
France; William H. Riggs, Paris
Gift of William H. Riggs, 1913 (14.25.1389)*

The octagonal barrel is rifled with eight
grooves, blued, and decorated at both
ends and the center with arabesques engraved, dotted and gilt; it is mounted with
a copper front sight and tubular rear sight.
On the breech are the stamped initials
T R, possibly those of Thomas Ritter, a
gunmaker recorded in Teschen during
1639-67.

The lock is typical for *Teschinke* rifles. Its
main spring is mounted on the outside,
which made it possible to reduce the size
of the lock plate and, consequently, of the
butt. Instead of a conventional sear with a
strong spring, this sear is provided with an
arming button, which had to be pressed
with the left thumb when the lock was
spanned. The cock is chiseled and engraved with grotesque figures and scrolls.

The lock plate is engraved with arabesques, and gilt. The bridles for cock
spring, wheel, and main spring, as well as
pan cover and release buttons are covered
with brass mounts pierced and gilt.

The full stock is provided with a light,
strongly curved butt, which was pressed
against the cheek. The recoil was partly
absorbed by the gun due to its heavy barrel, and partly contained by the shooter's
hands and arms (for a stronger grip, the
trigger guard is shaped to accommodate
the fingers). The stock is profusely inlaid
with staghorn and mother-of-pearl carved
and engraved with animals, grotesque
masks, scrolls, and floral motifs in eastern
European folk-art style. On the top of the
butt, behind the barrel, is engraved a
monogram H K, possibly the initials of
Hans Kaluza, a Teschen stockmaker and
decorator recorded during 1628-70.

The gunmakers of Teschen specialized
in producing light rifles of small caliber
intended for hunting small game and
birds; their characteristic form and decoration are well represented by this specimen. The small-caliber rifles produced in
Teschen were very popular in central
Europe in the seventeenth century, being
widely known as *Teschinke,* and even today
in Germany BB guns are called *Tesching.*

Reference: Karger, 1964, pp. 36-38.

101

WHEELLOCK PISTOL *(one of a pair)*

*Dutch (Maestricht), ca. 1655-65
Steel, gilt brass, ivory
Length overall 22¹/₂ in. (57.1 cm.)
Length of barrel 14⁷/₈ in. (37.8 cm.)
Caliber .51 (13 mm.)
Weight 2 lb. (.972 kg.)
Ex collection: Prince Peter Soltykoff, Paris;
William H. Riggs, Paris
Gift of William H. Riggs, 1913 (14.25.1432a)*

The barrel is in two stages, the front end
round with a molding before the breech,
the rear part octagonal, chiseled with dogs
chasing animals amid foliation. On the
underside is the barrelsmith's mark, I R
divided by a six-point star (similar Støckel
3220).

The small lock has a spring-closed pan
cover with button release. The lock plate is
chiseled with flowers and foliate scrolls.
The upper jaw of the cock is carved with a
lion's mask, the stem of the cock, with
acanthus leaves. In front of the wheel is
engraved *Maest [richt]* surrounded by
scrolls.

The stock is carved of one piece of ivory,
with exception of the separately sculpted
pommel in shape of a helmeted head. On
the grip behind the barrel tang is a grotesque mask in relief; on the forestock, at
the base of the ramrod channel, is a dra-

gon's head. The ramrod is also of ivory, with a gilt brass tip. The mounts are of gilt brass; the ring enclosing the pommel joint is stamped with symmetric foliate pattern.

In the sixteenth and seventeenth centuries, the Netherlands had an advanced arms industry employing many outstanding craftsmen and artists. During the Thirty Years' War (1618-48), Dutch armorers provided weapons for all belligerent armies and exported firearms even to Muscovy. Dutch gunmakers developed a type of wheellock for cavalry pistols and carbines, which technically was based on German construction but was made as light, compact, and graceful as French wheellocks. Holster pistols and carbines with such locks became standard cavalry weapons, and even after a better ignition mechanism, the flintlock of French design, was introduced, Dutch wheellocks continued in use by some armies up to the early eighteenth century.

Pistols with ivory stocks produced during a few decades starting about 1650 in the city of Maestricht. Ivory was available

Detail of cat. no. 101. Pommel

to craftsmen and artists through merchant importers from the colonies, this exotic material being highly valued for its beauty and for the possibilities it offered to sculptors and decorators. Although in general ivory-stocked pistols look like normal cavalry weapons of the period, they were too expensive and rare to be used in ordinary ways. Such pistols were ordered by wealthy and noble customers more for display and presentation purposes, which explains the fact that a sizable number of these firearms has been preserved in hereditary princely armories.

References: Soltykoff sale, 1854, no. 266; Ilgner, 1931, p. 212, fig. 13; Scofield, 1941, p. 10, fig. 10; Peterson, 1962, p. 67, fig. 5; Thomas, Gamber, Schedelmann, 1964, no. 82; Lindsay, 1967, p. 212; Hoff, 1978, p. 211, fig. 8.

102
SNAPHAUNCE REVOLVING GUN

Dutch, ca. 1660-70
Steel, brass, wood, paint
Length overall 52¼ in. (132.9 cm.)
Length of barrel 34⁷/₁₆ in. (87.5 cm.)
Caliber .51 (13 mm.)
Weight 9 lb. 4 oz. (4.20 kg.)
Ex collection: Princes Liechtenstein, Vaduz;
William G. Renwick, Scottsdale, Arizona
Bequest of William G. Renwick, 1972
(1972.44)

The barrel is octagonal, engraved with foliation on the breech, and is mounted with a blade front sight of brass and a rear sight of steel, attached with a long tang chiseled with floral scrolls. The cylinder is of brass with eight chambers, each provided with a pan and manually operated sliding pan cover retained in position by a spring. The cylinder was also turned by hand, and was locked in firing position by a spring catch released by a lever in front of the trigger guard. The chambers were loaded in turn from the front where the stock has a special recess. The chambers and pan covers are numbered 1 to 8.

The combined frizzen-pan cover and its spring are mounted in front of the cylinder, separate from the rest of the lock mechanism. All parts of the lock and the side plate are chiseled and engraved with floral motifs, including tulips.

The ebonized wooden stock is painted on the butt and the cheekpiece with birds

amid foliation, in gold, red, and green, now badly rubbed, and the butt-plate tang is an engraved number 171, probably an inventory number. Decoration imitating Chinese and Japanese lacquerwork was popular on Dutch furniture, inspired by objects brought back from the Orient by the ships of the Dutch East India Company. The design of the engraved and chiseled floral decoration shown here was widely applied in the seventeenth century to Dutch firearms, as well as to Russian guns and pistols made under the strong influence of Dutch gunmakers and decorators.

In early firearms the slow rate of fire was one of the serious problems, and various multi-shot firearms were devised so that several shots could be fired in quick succession. From the late sixteenth century, revolving firearms came into use. They had a cylinder containing a number of chambers for loads that could be fired as quickly as the lock could be cocked and the cylinder rotated in position. This system was fairly widely employed in civilian firearms but was too expensive for ordinary military use. The revolving system was greatly improved in the 1830s by the American inventor Samuel Colt, who devised a mechanism to turn and lock the cylinder by cocking the hammer.

Reference: Liechtenstein sale, 1926, no. 210.

103
SNAPHAUNCE CARBINE

Barrel: Giovanni Lazarino Cominazzo,
active ca. 1635-64
Lock: Carlo Botarelli, recorded ca. 1660-90
Italian (Brescia), ca. 1660-70
Steel, walnut
Length overall 37⁹/₁₆ in. (95.4 cm.)
Length of barrel 25⁵/₈ in. (65.1 cm.)
Caliber .59 (15 mm.)
Weight 4 lb. 2 oz. (1.85 kg.)
Ex collection: Rutherfurd Stuyvesant, Paris;
Alan Rutherfurd Stuyvesant, Allamuchy,
New Jersey
Gift of Alan Rutherfurd Stuyvesant, 1949
(49.163.5)

The barrel is in two stages, twelve-sided at the fore-end and octagonal at the breech, and is decorated with ridges and grooves.

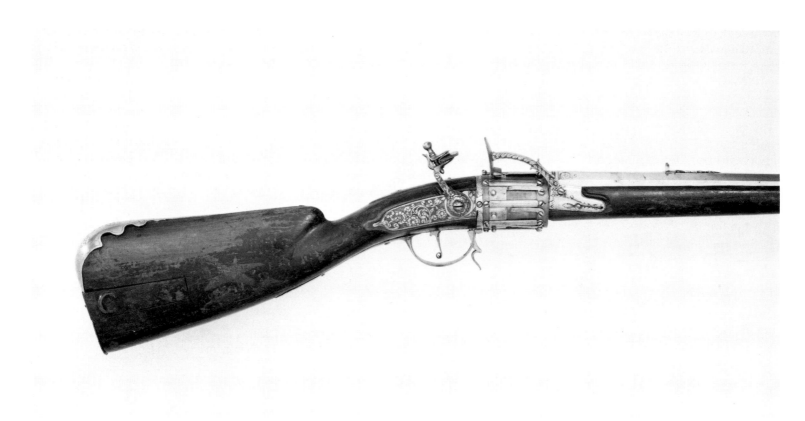

Cat. no. 102

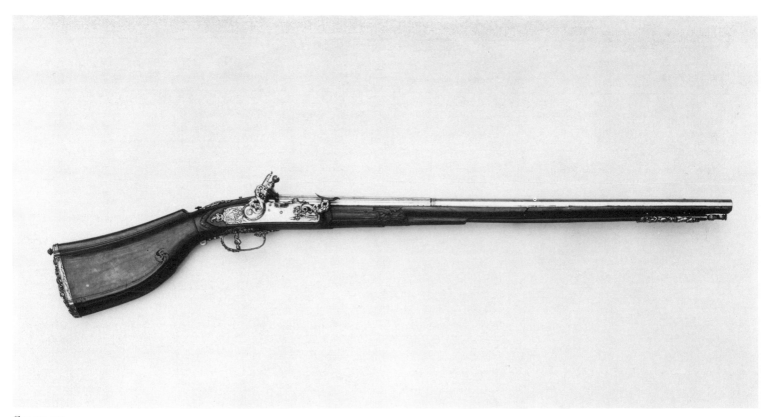

Cat. no. 103

On the underside of the breech is the stamped initial L; on the upper facet of the breech is the signature of the gunmaker, GIO LAZARINO COMINAZZO (Neuer Støckel, p. 235), a member of the famous gunmaking clan of Brescia.

The snaphaunce lock, of the type conventionally called *alla fiorentina*, represents a developed form of ignition mechanism in which a piece of flint held by the cock strikes against the frizzen to produce sparks, which set off the priming powder in the pan; the latter has a sliding cover that opened automatically when the cock moved forward. This type of lock was widely used in the central and northern parts of Italy. On the lower edge of the lock plate is the engraved signature in script *Carlo Botarelli*, a steel chiseler-decorator recorded in Brescia about 1660-90 (Neuer Støckel, p. 129). All parts of the lock are chiseled with floral motifs and figures of dragons; in center of the lock plate is an engraved bird on a branch.

The stock has a folding butt hinged to the trigger guard and locked with a spring catch behind the barrel tang, which allowed it to be carried in the confined space of a coach. A long hook and a loop on the left side served, respectively, to attach the carbine to the saddle, or to suspend it from the shoulder belt if carried on horseback. Trigger guard, butt plate, and other mounts are profusely chiseled in high relief with foliation, grotesque masks (trigger guard), eagle (tang mount), dragons (ramrod pipe and ramrod tip) and a child riding on a dragon (butt plate). The quality of the design and chiseling of the steel parts ranks this gun among the finest ever produced in Brescia, a city famed for her ironwork.

References: Dean, 1911, p. 79, no. 199; Dean, pp. 125-126, no. 170, pl. XLII, fig. 170 a-h.

Detail of cat. no. 103. Lock

Detail of cat. no. 103. Butt plate

Detail of cat. no. 103. Signature on barrel

Detail of cat. no. 103. Signature of Carlo Botarelli on lock plate

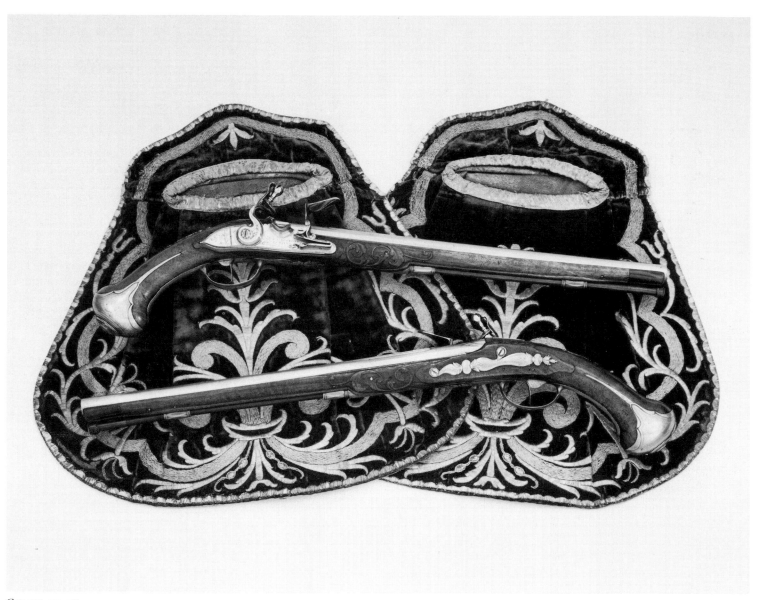

Cat. nos. 105, 106

104

FLINTLOCK PISTOL (one of a pair)
Girolamo Francino, active ca. 1650-60
Italian (Gardone, Val Trompia and Brescia),
mid-17th century
Steel, walnut
Length overall 22¹/₂ in. (57.1 cm.)
Length of barrel 15¹³/₁₆ in. (40.2 cm.)
Caliber .52 (13.2 mm.)
Weight 1 lb. 15 oz. (.869 kg.)
Ex collection: Theodore Offerman, New York
Rogers Fund, 1928 (28.196.18)

The faceted barrel is in two stages, the muzzle end polygonal, the breech end octagonal, chiseled with fine ridges. On the top of the barrel is the stamped signature GIROLAMO FRANCINO. On the underside is a barrelsmith's mark: in a hexagon, the initials G M, with a six-pointed star above, and three dots below (Neuer Støckel, p. 853, no. 7969). The flintlock is chiseled and engraved with foliate motifs. Pan, pan cover, and touchhole are lined with gold to preserve them from corrosion. The walnut stock is carved under the barrel with grooves and ridges, and is inlaid with lace-like mounts of steel, chiseled and pierced with fine arabesques and enhanced with engraving. On the side plate are traces of two apertures, originally for the attachment of a belt hook.

Girolamo Francino belonged to an illustrious family of gunmakers recorded working in Gardone, Val Trompia and Brescia from the sixteenth to the eighteenth centuries. This pistol is made and decorated in the style typical of Brescian craftsmen, reputed for the quality of their firearms, especially for their unusually light and thin-walled barrels, as well as for their embellishment with fine steel chiseling. The stockmaker's skills had to match those of the chiseler since the sophisticated, delicate scrolls of the pierced mounts were to be set into corresponding recesses cut into the wood.

References: Grancsay, 1953, no. 131; Nickel, 1974, p. 258.

105

PAIR OF FLINTLOCK
HOLSTER PISTOLS
Georg Keiser (1647-ca. 1740)
Austrian (Vienna), ca. 1710-20
Steel, brass, rosewood, horn
Length overall 22³/₄ in. (57.8 cm.)
Length of barrel 15¹⁵/₁₆ in. (40.5 cm.)
Caliber .65 (16.5 mm.)
Weight (28.100.12) 2 lb. 4 oz. (1.16 kg.),
(28.100.13) 2 lb. 9 oz. (1.32 kg.)
Ex collection: Royal Saxon Armory, Dresden
Gift of Prince Albrecht Radziwill, 1928
(28.100.12, 13)

The barrels are round, with a flat longitudinal sighting facet and a large facet on each side of the breech. The rear sight on the barrel tang is of chiseled steel, the front sight is of brass. The breech is decorated with chiseled moldings and is lightly engraved with floral motifs. On the sighting facet, the maker's signature is inscribed: GEORG KEISER IN WIENN.

The locks are chiseled and engraved with foliate and linear motifs; on the lock plates, a girl picks flowers and winds a wreath, and Cupid waters a garden and holds a bouquet. The same signature that is on the barrels is found under the pan.

The stocks are of rosewood, with carved foliation in the center and around the barrel tang; the forestock tip is of black horn. The mounts are of cast brass, chiseled and engraved with stylized foliate designs. Impressed into each grip is the number 1689, presumably a nineteenth-century Dresden inventory number.

Georg Keiser became a master-gunmaker in 1674 (Støckel, p. 615). He was the outstanding master of the Vienna school, working for the imperial court for more than half a century. This pair of pistols, of robust construction and simple finish and decoration, is typical of the kind commonly carried in saddle holsters by officers and gentlemen on horseback throughout most of the eighteenth century.

Reference: Schedelmann, 1972, p. 190.

106

PAIR OF PISTOL HOLSTERS
Spanish, 18th century
Leather, velvet, gold thread, silver galloon,
canvas
Length 18 in. (45.5 cm.)
Width 18 in. (45.5 cm.)
Rogers Fund, 1942 (42.59.2,3)

Each holster is of soft brown leather shaped to pistol form and covered with canvas-lined red velvet; the seams are trimmed with silver galloon. The velvet is embroidered with gold thread in symmetrical foliate designs. Holsters were attached to either side of the saddlebow; they preferably matched the decoration of the saddlecloth and other pieces of the horse trappings. This particular form was in use from the mid-seventeenth to the early nineteenth century.

107

SNAPHAUNCE PISTOL (one of a pair)
Italian (Pistoia), ca. 1750-75
Steel, wood
Length overall 18³/₈ in. (46.7 cm.)
Length of barrel 13³/₈ in. (34 cm.)
Caliber .46 (11.7 mm.)
Weight 1 lb. 8 oz. (.681 kg.)
Ex collection: Theodore Offerman, New York
Rogers Fund, 1928 (28.196.16)

The barrel is in two stages, round at the muzzle and octagonal at the breech, and is engraved with foliate ornament. On the breech are two rectangular marks, deeply stamped and gold-plated: the first is inscribed PIS/TO/IA under a crown; the second shows a lion (Neuer Støckel, nos. 7774, 7775), possibly the mark of the gunmaker Christiano Leoni of Pistoia.

The lock is of the type conventionally called a snaphaunce *alla fiorentina* since it was widespread in central Italy, even after this construction and style had been abandoned elsewhere in favor of French-type flintlocks. As in all snaphaunces, the frizzen and the pan cover are separate; the latter opens automatically when the cock falls forward thus exposing the priming powder to a shower of sparks. The lock is chiseled with foliation, dogs' heads, and grotesque busts.

The stock of rosewood is decorated with carved foliate scrolls and leaves which incorporate two grotesque heads in the center of the forestock. The steel mounts are chiseled and engraved with floral scrolls, acanthus leaves, and busts *all' antica*. On the side plate, a long belt hook is attached, enabling the user to carry the pistol not only in a saddle holster but alternatively tucked onto his waist belt.

The style and motifs of the decoration follow patterns first set by French oramentalists and fashionable in western Europe in the late seventeenth and early eighteenth centuries. These patterns were still used for a few decades outside the main arms-producing centers by conservative artisans strongly adhering to established traditions and local artistic tastes often influenced by folk art. These trends are sometimes expressed in decoration by rather humorous interpretations of copied motifs and subjects – particularly the classical profile busts – that were essentially quite alien to the mentality of native craftsmen. These provincial features can be seen on many pieces produced by armorers in small workshops of central Italy and are well illustrated by this pistol.

The mark on the barrel indicates that this pistol, or at least the barrel, originated at Pistoia, a Tuscan city north of Florence, and a noted center of firearms production since the sixteenth century. The term "pistol" has even been thought to derive from Pistoia, though the exact origins of the word are obscure.

References: Carpegna, 1962, pp. 120-128; Carpegna, 1974, p. 7.

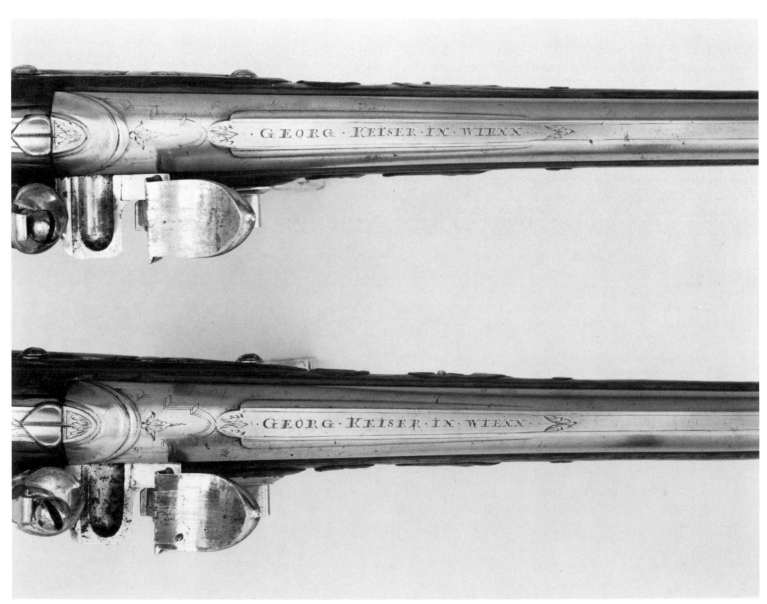

Cat. no. 105. Signature on barrels

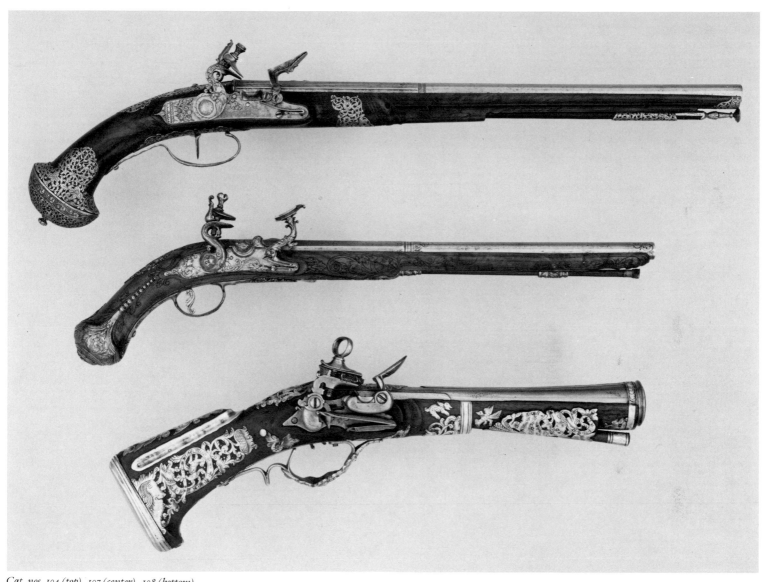

Cat. nos. *104 (top)*, *107 (center)*, *108 (bottom)*

Detail of cat. no. *107. Marks on barrel*

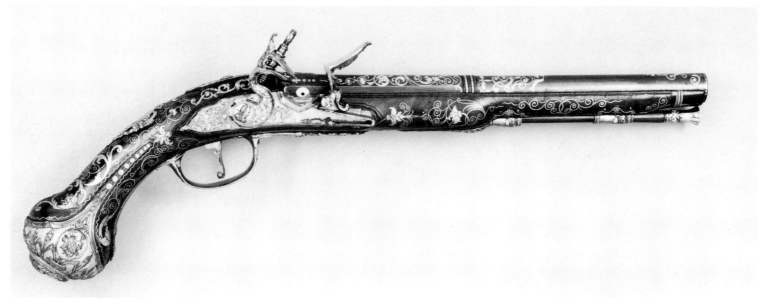

Cat. no. 109

108

MIQUELET BLUNDERBUSS PISTOL
(*one of a pair*)
Spanish (Ripoll), ca. 1750-75
Steel, silver, walnut
Length overall 16⁷/8 in. (42.9 cm.)
Length of barrel 9³/16 in. (23.3 cm.)
Caliber (at muzzle) 1.15 (29.2 mm.)
Weight 2 lb. 13 oz. (1.27 kg.)
Ex collection: Charles M. Schott, Jr., New York
Gift of Charles M. Schott, Jr., 1917 (19.53.51)

The barrel is round, flaring toward the muzzle; the breech has a flat facet on each side, and the muzzle is encircled by a ring molding. The barrel is inlaid with heavy silver decoration at the breech, on a lengthwise strip, and at the muzzle; this decoration is engraved with scrolls, shells (rocailles), and flowers typical of the rococo style.

The lock is of the type conventionally called "miquelet," in which all parts except for the sear are mounted on the outside of the lock plate. Introduced into the Iberian Peninsula by the end of the sixteenth century, this mechanism was subsequently adopted by many countries around the Mediterranean, in the Middle East, and in the Caucasus. In Spain it was preferred over the French-type flintlock and continued in use up to the middle of the nineteenth century.

The stock is decorated with large silver plaques pierced and engraved with floral motifs, a bird, a rabbit, and on the underside of the forestock, a double-headed crowned eagle. The decoration on the grip includes dragons, lions, and foliate scrolls. The comb and the heel of the butt are reinforced with solid silver mounts. The trigger guard is of heavy cast silver chiseled with rococo shells and scrolls. The side plate is mounted with a long belt hook of steel. The ramrod is provided with a retaining spring catch and a worm to extract unfired wads and bullets.

Short guns and pistols of large caliber, with barrels flaring at the muzzle (blunderbusses), had developed in Europe by the mid-seventeenth century. They were designed for shooting at close range, and were loaded with buckshot or even several pistol bullets. As such, they were popular as traveling and boarding weapons, the flaring muzzle making it easier to reload while in a swaying stagecoach, onboard a ship, or on horseback. It is a peculiarity of the blunderbuss, whether full-size or pistol, that it often retains the butt shape of a carbine.

In the seventeenth and eighteenth centuries, the town of Ripoll, not far from Barcelona, was an important center of arms production, a considerable part of which was exported to the Mediterranean

and, particularly, to Spanish America. In spite of these worldwide trade connections, the often exuberant decoration of Catalan firearms has a distinct folk-art flavor.

References: Grancsay, Hagerstown-Newark, 1955, no. 116; Lavin, 1965, p. 270, fig. 119.

109

FLINTLOCK PISTOL (*one of a pair*)
Michele Battista, active ca. 1760-ca. 1778
Barrel: Emanuel Esteva, recorded in 1773
Italian (Naples), ca. 1768
Steel, gilt, silver, horn
Length overall 17¹/4 in. (43.8 cm.)
Length of barrel 11¹/16 in. (28.1 cm.)
Caliber .63 (16 mm.)
Weight 2 lb. (1.95 kg.)
Ex collection: Princes Liechtenstein, Vaduz
Gift of Henry Walters, 1926 (26.259.6)

The barrel is in two stages, round at the muzzle, octagonal at the breech, the two sections divided by transverse ring moldings. The blued surface of the barrel is engraved and gilt with symmetrical floral ornament and birds. On the breech are two deeply stamped and gold-plated marks: the monogram CR beneath a crown, for Carolus Rex (King Charles); FAB:R:/DI/NAP, for Fabbrica Reale di Napoli (Royal Factory of Naples). In front and to the side of these marks are three gold-inlaid fleurs-de-lis (for the reigning Bourbon family), the upper group surmounted by a gold-inlaid Calvary Cross. On the underside of the breech is the barrelsmith's mark, the stamped letters EM · ES ·, probably for Emanuel Esteva. The breech is also stamped with a crowned monogram CL, the ownership mark of the Liechtenstein Collection. The breech tang of polished steel is chiseled in relief and engraved with a grotesque mask and foliation against a gilt background.

The flintlock is of conventional French type, and is decorated with foliage, a shell, a mask, and a medallion with a profile head crowned with a laurel wreath, all ornamental elements of bright steel chiseled in relief against a gilt background. The pan is lined with gold, as is the touchhole. The trigger guard is decorated with gold-inlaid floral scrolls and an undulating border. On the lock plate, among engraved military trophies, is a stamped and gold-plated mark: a monogram F R beneath a crown, for Ferdinandus Rex (King Ferdinand); and on the inside of the lock plate is the engraved signature in script *Michele Battista*.

The stock of dark root walnut is profusely inlaid with silver wire and engraved silver sheet displaying foliate scrolls, strapwork, and sea monsters. The tip of the forestock is of black horn bound with a strap of silver-gilt. On the grip, near the pommel, is incised the number 286 (probably an inventory number from the Liechtenstein armory). The stock mounts are of highly polished steel, chiseled with baroque ornament in relief against a matt gold background. On the rear branch of the trigger guard is the gunmaker's signature MICHAEL · BAPTISTA · F · (the last letter standing for the Latin *fecit,* made). On the grip is a crowned escutcheon with a monogram of unusual ribbon-like form, possibly a stylized rendering of the letters F R (Ferdinandus Rex). The decoration of the pommel cap includes, at the sides, oval medallions with profile heads of classical warriors, swags of drapery held in the maws of lions' masks, and bowls of fruit; inset at the base of the pommel is an oval portrait medallion of a young man, presumably King Ferdinand IV of Naples

and Sicily, wearing the insignia of the Order of the Golden Fleece.

The Royal Arms Factory at Torre Annunziata, just outside Naples, was founded in 1757 by order of Charles III, King of Naples and Sicily (1735-59) and King of Spain (1759-88). A number of gunmakers from Spain, highly reputed for the quality of its firearms, were invited to Italy to give a start to the new plant. This accounts for the pronounced Spanish character evident in many of the firearms produced there, and in the Spanish-type barrel marks, surmounted by a Calvary Cross, found on this pistol. One of these Spanish craftsmen, Emanuel Esteva, is recorded in a document dated 1773 as one of the factory's chief masters. It is on this basis that the mark EM · ES · on the underside of the barrel is attributed to Esteva. The same document of 1773 also mentions Michele Battista, who signed the locks and trigger guards of the pistol, as another chief master.

It is presumably the young King Ferdinand IV who is represented on the portrait medallion on the pommel cap. On the second pistol of the pair (not exhibited) the medallion encloses the portrait of a young woman, almost certainly

Ferdinand's wife, Queen Karoline. These matching portraits suggest that this pair of pistols was made to commemorate the marriage of Ferdinand to Princess Karoline, daughter of the Holy Roman Emperor Franz I Stefan, in 1768, when the couple were aged respectively 17 and 16.

The profuse and very beautiful decoration of this pistol is French-inspired and derives from the pages of engraved ornament for gunsmiths issued by De Lacollombe in Paris in 1730. The heads of classical warriors, chiseled in steel on the lock, side plate, and sides of the pommel cap, and the silver wire scrolls and dragons' heads of engraved silver sheet that are inlayed into the stock, appear to have been copied directly from De Lacollombe's patternbook. Very similar decorative motifs derived from De Lacollombe are also found on a miquelet fowling piece by Michele Battista in the Clay P. Bedford collection, Scottsdale, Arizona, which is dated 1770, and on another pair of pistols by Battista in Cracow.

References: Liechtenstein sale, 1926, no. 241; Grancsay, Hagerstown-Newark, 1955, no. 115; Hayward, 1962-63, II, p. 250; Gusler and Lavin, 1977, pp. 188-189, no. 75; Terenzi, 1978, pp. 14, 23.

Detail of cat. no. 109 and matching pistol (not exhibited). Pommel caps

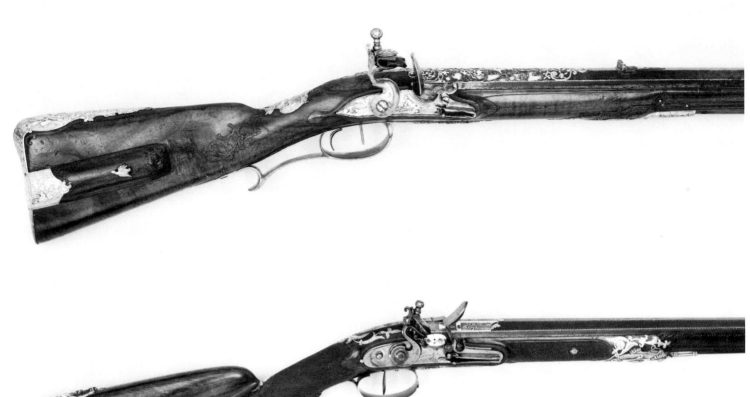

Cat. nos. 110 (top), 114 (bottom)

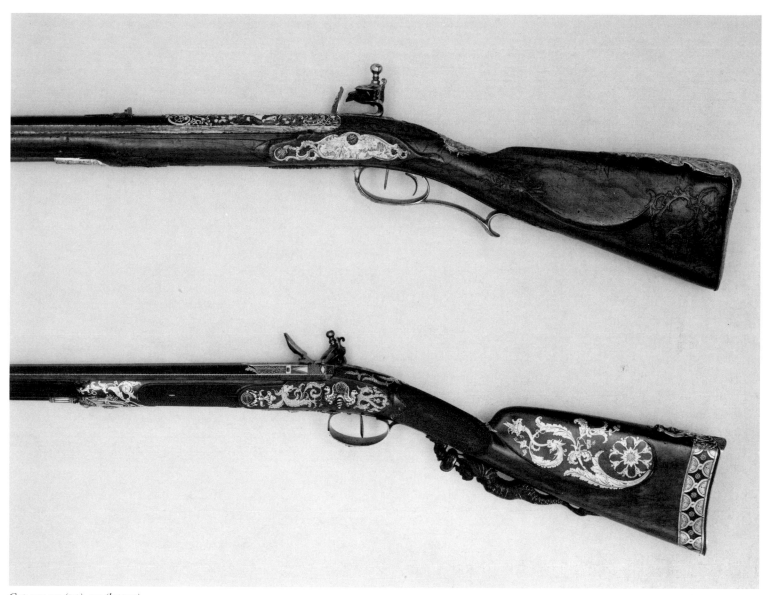

Cat. nos. 110 (top), 114 (bottom)

Details of cat. nos. 110 (left), 114 (right). Butts

Detail of cat. no. 110. Top of barrel

Detail of cat. no. 114. Trigger guard

110

FLINTLOCK RIFLE
Bohemian (Carlsbad, now Kárlovy Vary,
Czechoslovakia), ca. 1750-60
Steel, gold, silver-gilt, brass, wood
Length overall 44 in. (111.4 cm.)
Length of barrel 29³/8 in. (74.6 cm.)
Caliber .60 (15.24 mm.)
Weight 8 lb. 9¹/2 oz. (3.9 kg.)
Rogers Fund, 1910 (10.99)

The heavy, octagonal barrel is blued and
mounted with front and rear sights; its
bore is rifled with seven grooves. At the
breech, tang, and sights, the barrel is
chiseled with rocailles against gilt background and is inlaid with gold and silver;
amidst the decoration on the breech is a
hunter with his dog, inlaid in silver-gilt.
On the underside of the barrel is a barrelsmith's mark, HIW, and below, the
letter Z, possibly for Zella, an arms-
producing center in Thüringen, Germany,
which exported barrels and gun parts all
over Europe.

Cat. no. 111

The flintlock of conventional French type is provided with a hair trigger for precision shooting. The lock plate is decorated with the scene of a boar hunt, inlaid in silver and multi-colored gold.

The walnut stock has a patch box and is embellished with carved rocailles and floral motifs at the tang, rear ramrod pipe, and butt. Heavy mounts of gilt-brass are profusely chiseled with rococo patterns and hunting scenes amid landscapes. The figure of a flying bird on the sliding patch-box cover serves as a button to unlock the box.

Heavy rifles of this type were widely used in central Europe in deer hunting, as well as for chasing other big game such as bear and wild boar. Though unsigned, this gun may have been made in Carlsbad, whose arms were especially popular because of their quality and their attractive, colorful decoration using blued steel or dark wood in contrast with bright gilt mounts ornamented with hunting motifs.

Detail of cat. no. 111. Butt

III
FLINTLOCK PISTOL
Bohemian (Carlsbad, now Kárlovy Vary, Czechoslovakia), ca. 1760-70
Steel, silver-gilt, wood, horn
Length overall 15⅞ in. (40.3 cm.)
Length of barrel 9¾ in. (24.8 cm.)
Caliber .51 (12.95 cm.)
Weight 1 lb. 11 oz. (.752 kg.)
Rogers Fund, 1916 (16.85)

The barrel is round, with a narrow sighting facet along the top and a silver fore sight at the muzzle; on each side of the breech is a flat facet. The breech is decorated with the figure of a standing Roman warrior amid trophies, shells, and scrolls, all chiseled in relief against a matted gold background.

The flintlock of conventional French type is chiseled with trophies, scrolls, and foliation against a partly gilt background. The walnut stock is profusely decorated with carved foliation and rococo scrolls;

the tips of the forestock and of the ramrod are of bone.

The trigger guard and mounts are of cast silver, chiseled with classical figured motifs in rococo frames against a gilt background. On the rear branch of the trigger guard are scratched four letters: VKBI (probably an owner's initials). This pistol exhibits many of the same qualities as the flintlock gun shown in catalogue number 110, and, though unmarked, is also tentatively attributed to a Carlsbad workshop.

Detail of cat. no. 111. Top of barrel

112

FLINTLOCK TURN-OFF PISTOL
(*one of a pair*)
Daniel Moore, recorded 1758-ca. 1800
Silver: John King, recorded from 1775
English (London), 1775-80
Steel, silver, wood
Length overall 11 3/4 in. (28.5 cm.)
Length of barrel 6 13/16 in. (17.3 cm.)
Caliber .59 (15 mm.)
Weight 1 lb. 3 oz. (.539 kg.)
Ex collection: Giovanni P. Morosini, New York
The collection of Giovanni Morosini, presented by his daughter Giulia, 1932 (32.75.137)

The round barrel has chiseled molding at the muzzle and two chiseled moldings on the otherwise smooth polished surface. At the rear is a lug for the wrench to unscrew the barrel from the breech which is made in one piece with the lock plate and the grip strap. The breech is engraved on the top with trophies and a shield bearing the inscription LONDON. On the underside is the gunmaker's signature, D: MOORE, his mark (Støckel 798), and two proofmarks of the British Board of Ordnance used for private proofing (Støckel 1316); it is also marked number 1 (to distinguish this weapon from its companion piece). The tang is engraved with foliation. The flintlock with rounded surfaces is of conventional French construction except for the frizzen spring, which is mounted around the pan, making the lock more compact.

The grip is carved with a shell behind the breech tang which is engraved with foliation. The mounts on the grip are of silver, cast and chiseled: the side plate depicts military trophies, the butt cap is shaped as a monster face framed in rococo ornaments, and the escutcheon is engraved with the (unidentified) owner's monogram P W, the shield supported by a trophy and surmounted by a crested helmet. On the butt cap are the hallmark of London (leopard) and the initials I K under a crown, the mark of John King, a London silversmith recorded from 1775.

Turn-off pistols were loaded directly into the breech after the barrel was unscrewed (turned off) with a special wrench that engaged a lug on the barrel. This method made it possible to use bullets tightly fitting the caliber and thus to increase the accuracy and range of the shot, though of course to the detriment of the rate of fire. Such pistols were first introduced by the middle of the seventeenth century and remained in use for some two hundred years. Turn-off pistols were particularly popular in England, mostly as a light civilian weapon carried at the waist belt or in the pocket.

Reference: Grimwade, 1976, nos. 1445-1446.

113

FLINTLOCK PISTOL (*one of a pair*)
John Campbell, active in the second half of the 18th century (d. 1807)
Scottish (Doune), late 18th century
Steel, silver
Length overall 13 3/4 in. (34.9 cm.)
Length of barrel 8 11/16 in. (22.1 cm.)
Caliber .58 (14.7 mm.)
Weight 1 lb. 15 oz. (.880 kg.)
Ex collection: Rutherfurd Stuyvesant, Paris; Alan Rutherfurd Stuyvesant, Allamuchy, New Jersey
Bequest of Alan Rutherfurd Stuyvesant, 1954 (54.46.6)

The blued barrel is in three stages, octagonal at the slightly flared muzzle, round in the center, and grooved and ridged at the breech; the surface is chiseled with floral scrolls and arabesques against a hatched background. The touchhole is lined with gold.

The lock is of the type used exclusively in Scotland and conventionally classified as "Scottish snaphaunce": its mechanism incorporates a long sear lever, with a hooked half-cock sear protruding through the lock plate to engage the front of the cock at the safety position. This reliable safety device was particularly important since the Scottish pistols were carried at the belt and had no trigger guards. The trigger takes the form of a silver button engraved with a four-petaled flower. The flash screen has a slot to let out moisture from the frizzen. On the lock plate is the engraved signature *John Campbell* (in script), a member of a family of gunmakers active during the eighteenth and nineteenth centuries in Doune, Glasgow,

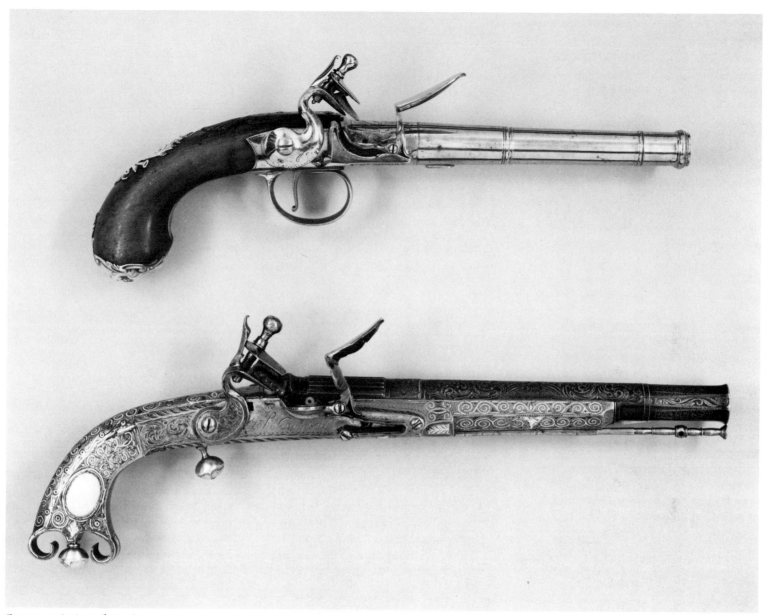

Cat. nos. 112 (top), 113 (bottom)

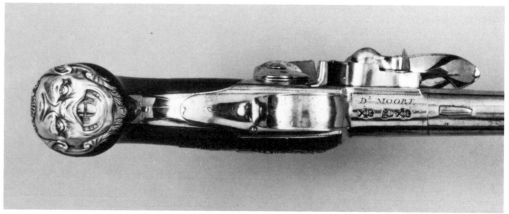

Detail of cat. no. 112. Underside

and other Scottish towns (Neuer Støckel, p. 185).

The stock is entirely of steel, engraved and silver-inlaid with Celtic ornaments, and on the left side is a long belt hook of steel chiseled and pierced with scrolls, foliation, and roping. The ramrod is also of steel, with chiseled moldings at the fore-end.

This pistol represents well the most typical form of all-steel pistols worn in Scotland both with military uniforms and as an accessory of Scottish national dress from the mid-seventeenth to the mid-nineteenth centuries.

References: Dean, 1914, pp. 146-147, no. 196, figs. 196a-e, pl. XLVII; Whitelaw, 1977, p. 43.

114

FLINTLOCK RIFLE
Nicolas Noël Boutet, active ca. 1780-1833
French (Versailles), ca. 1800
Steel, gold, silver, walnut, ebony
Length overall 40 1/2 in. (102.8 cm.)
Length of barrel 25 13/16 in. (65.5 cm.)
Caliber .60 (15.24 mm.)
Weight 5 lb. 15 oz. (2.69 kg.)
Ex collection: Giovanni P. Morosini, New York
The collection of Giovanni P. Morosini, presented by his daughter Giulia, 1932 (32.75.107)

The blued barrel is octagonal, with a front sight and four-leaf rear sight; its bore is rifled with thirty-two fine grooves. The three upper facets of the barrel are decorated along the ridges with a stamped and punched foliate pattern; both ends are engraved with garlands and geometric patterns on a gold background. In an octagonal frame of gold dots on the upper facet is the engraved signature in script, *Boutet Directeur Artiste/Manufacture à Versailles.* The barrel bears numerous markings: Boutet's monogram within an octagon (Støckel 97); another mark of Boutet in a rectangle (Støckel 96); the letters J B (as a monogram) and C in an octagon (Neuer Støckel, p. 224; possibly a mark of the barrelsmith Jean Baptiste Le Clerc, active about 1775-1820); L C in an octagon (Neuer Støckel, p. 224, no. 3741; attributed to Jean Nicolas Le Clerc, also a barrelsmith); D B in a wreath (Neuer

Støckel, p. 150; probably a mark of Denis Brouilly, active 1793-1801 at the Versailles factory where he became a controller before he moved to Rouen in 1801); B incised on the breech (probably the controller's initial); B L Y NO 1 laid in octagon (possibly the controller's quality stamp); *Pour Brouilly* scratched in script (an indication that the piece was intended personally "for Brouilly"); and the engraved serial number, NO 35. The barrel tang is finely engraved with a cornucopia, garlands, and a figure of a drummer "sansculotte" (revolutionary soldier).

The lock is fitted with a frizzen-spring roller for smoother operation, and an additional safety — an externally operated bolt for half-cock position. Both the pan and the touchhole are lined with gold to reduce corrosion. On the lock plate is the engraved signature in script, *Boutet/Directeur Artiste.* The lock has a set trigger with adjustable pull. The pan and the trigger guard are an incised with the letter B (probably for Brouilly).

The dark walnut stock is checkered in front of the lock and on the small of the butt; the forestock is bordered with carved geometric patterns. The wood is inlaid with silver chiseled and engraved with floral motifs to match the mounts. On the underside of the stock behind the trigger guard is finely carved in ebony a dragon supporting a flaming urn.

The heavy silver mounts are cast and chiseled with neoclassical motifs on a matted background. The rear ramrod-pipe mount displays a Medusa head on a shield framed by a helmet, banners, weapons, and oak branches. On the trigger guard is a winged head of Mercury, a globe within laurel branches, and artists' tools — emblems of world peace, commerce, and the arts; the frontal extension is chiseled with a winged bull supporting a cornucopia. The tang of the butt plate is modeled as a naked female figure in Egyptian headdress supporting a flaming urn. The mounts bear the French hallmarks for 1798-1809, a silversmith's mark (in a lozenge, I · M under a five-point star, with six dots forming a triangle under the initials), and the letter B (probably for Brouilly); on the butt plate, *Brouilly* incised in script. On the inside of the rear side plate is the name *Leon Fletcher,* finely

scratched in script, perhaps the name of an owner or a craftsman who at one time carried out a repair.

The fact that all parts are marked with the name or the initial of Brouilly and, in one instance, there is a direct indication to his ownership ("for Brouilly") suggest that the carbine was made for the factory's controller, perhaps to his personal order or as a farewell gift before he left Versailles for his new assignment in Rouen in 1801. This dating seems to be supported by two decorative motifs: a figure of a uniformed sansculotte, typical for the earlier period of the French Revolution, and a female figure in Egyptian headdress, which may reflect a vogue following Napoleon's Egyptian campaign of 1798-99.

Nicolas Noël Boutet (1761-1833) was the leading figure among French gunmakers from the last years of the Ancien Régime to the end of the First Empire. Appointed a gunmaker to the king in 1788, he was appointed *Directeur-Artiste* of the Manufacture d'armes de Versailles in 1793 by the newly-installed revolutionary regime. The high artistic qualities of the firearms made by Boutet were fully appreciated by the First Consul (and after 1804, Emperor) Napoleon Bonaparte, who granted the artist an eighteen-year concession (1800-18) to direct the factory as an arms plant and school for armorers and decorators. Apart from standard weapons for the armed forces, the Versailles factory produced deluxe weapons for Napoleon and his court, as well as presentation weapons awarded to soldiers, officers, and foreign dignitaries.

References: Grancsay, Hagerstown-Newark, 1955, no. 101; Pyhrr, 1973, pp. 270-271, fig. 10.

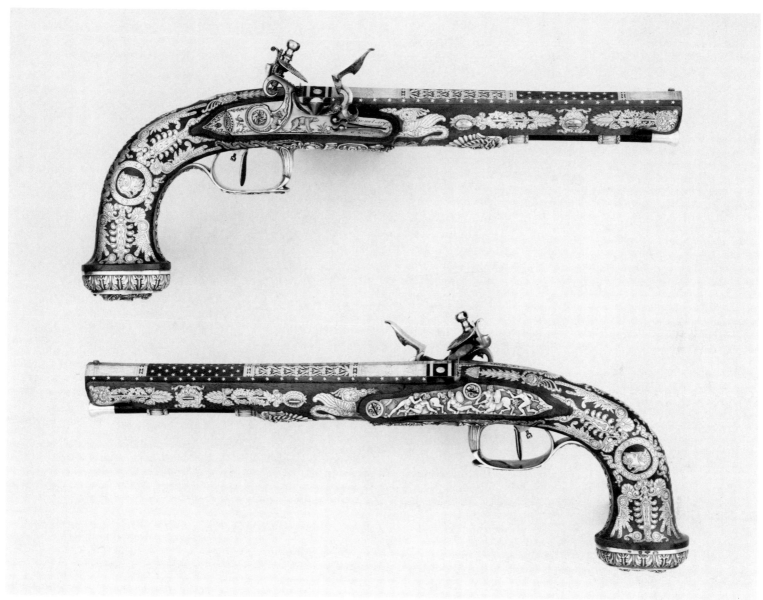

Cat. no. 115

115

CASED SET OF FLINTLOCK PISTOLS
F. Pirmet, recorded 1779–1818
French (Paris), ca. 1805
Steel, gold, silver, wood, tortoise shell, velvet
Both pistols have identical measurements
Length overall 15¹/₁₆ in. (38.2 cm.)
Length of barrel 9³/₈ in. (23.8 cm.)
Caliber .48 (12 mm.)
Weight 4 lb. 14 oz. (2.21 kg.)
Size of the case 12¹/₂ x 18¹/₈ in. (31.7 x 46 cm.)
Ex collection: Frederick S. Rook, New York;
Theodore Offerman, New York
Rogers Fund, 1928 (28.196.1-2)

Identical in design and decoration, the pistols have octagonal barrels slightly flared at the muzzle, and with fine poly-groove rifling. Each breech plug, of the design patented by H. Nock in 1781, is provided with a screwed-in ignition chamber – a cylinder connected with the touchhole and the breech; loose powder in the cylinder procured faster ignition which was vitally important in dueling. Each touchhole is lined with gold. The front blade sight is of silver, the rear sight of gold. The five upper facets of the barrel are decorated in four stages: at the muzzle

and at the breech are wide gold bands engraved with diamond patterns and winged thunderbolts; of the remaining two sections, the one nearest the breech is encrusted in gold with lace-like neoclassical foliage, and the one nearest the muzzle is dotted with tiny golden stars on a matt gray background. On the breech are three gold-plated oval marks with a fleur-de-lis (Støckel 5454).

The flintlock is provided with a flash screen, a roller bearing on the steel spring, a sliding bolt as an additional safety for the half-cock position, a main-spring link, and

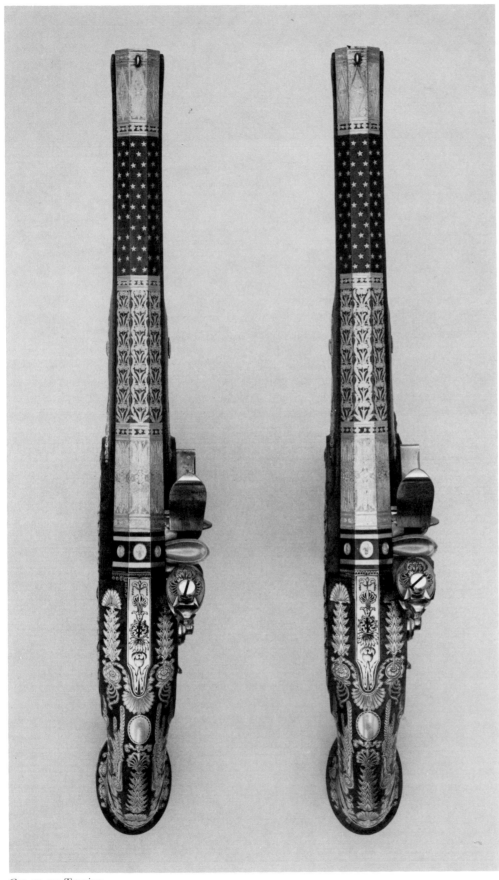

Cat. no. 115. Top view

a detent—a tiny pawl in the tumbler to prevent the sear engaging the half-cock notch when the weapon is fired. The pan is lined with gold to prevent corrosion. The lock parts are decorated with fine engraving displaying foliate motifs, a dragon (on the cock), a swan (on the frizzen), a bear (on one pistol's lock plate), and a wolf (on the other lock plate, this being the only essential difference in the decoration of the two pistols). The set trigger is provided with a pull-adjusting screw. At the forward end of the lock plate, above and below the frizzen spring, is engraved in script the signature *Pirmet arq*[*uebusier*] / *à Paris* ("Pirmet Gunmaker/in Paris").

The stock carved of walnut is profusely inlaid with openwork silver plaques engraved with foliage, two confronted dragons (in front of the lock), and a classical Corinthian-type helmet within a wreath (one on each side of the grip). The trigger guard, butt cap, and other mounts are of cast and chiseled silver: the finial of the rear ramrod pipe takes the shape of a winged Gorgon's head, the mount in front of the trigger guard displays a trophy composed of Roman armor and weapons, the trigger guard bears a winged female demi-figure with a star on her forehead and a palm branch in either hand. The side plate depicts in relief a battle of the Lapiths against the Centaurs. The pommel cap is surrounded by acanthus leaves enclosing an oval medallion with the head of Heracles wearing his lion's skin.

The trigger guard and the pommel bear hallmarks established for use in 1798-1809: cock and numeral 1 in vertical octagon, old man's head and number 88 (for Département de Seine-Inférieur), lictor's fasces. The fourth mark is a lozenge with the initials N B separated by a pistol—a mark of the gunmaker Nicolas Noël Boutet (1761-1833). All steel and silver parts, even the screws, are further marked with the letter P, an asterisk, and a number of dots (1 to 4) as assembly marks.

The case of mahogany is mounted with ebony and silver, lined with green velvet, and contains fitted compartments for the two pistols and a number of loading and cleaning accessories, including a mallet of mahogany, a small hammer of steel with mahogany handle, a bullet mold with a plug wrench of steel engraved with floral patterns and birds, an oil can of chiseled steel, a loading rod with silver powder measure, a ramrod with silver tip, a powder flask of tortoiseshell mounted in silver, a triple screwdriver with mahogany handle, a scouring stick of steel, and a detachable worm to extract unfired bullets.

In the 1770s, the flintlock firearms entered the final phase in their development and reached an epitome both in construction and decoration. To a great extent, this was due to the spreading vogue for dueling with pistols, which resulted in a number of technical improvements brought about mainly by British and French gunmakers. High-quality hunting guns and dueling pistols required special care for good performance, and to this effect they were kept in cases provided with tools necessary for maintenance and loading. In France during the Consulate and the Empire, Napoleon, as the head of state and commander-in-chief, used similar cased sets of elaborately decorated arms as presentation gifts for heads of state and diplomats, and as rewards to soldiers of outstanding bravery and service.

The maker of these pistols, Pirmet, was one of the leading gunmakers of Napoleonic France, though he, like most other French gunmakers of this period, was overshadowed by Nicolas Noël Boutet, *Directeur-Artiste* of the government arms manufactory at Versailles. Pirmet was apparently well established in Paris and had a shop on the prestigious rue de la Loi, on which were also found the shops of the other great Parisian gunsmiths Boutet and Le Page; he also held the title "gunmaker to the King of Westphalia" (that is, to Napoleon's brother Jérôme) and so enjoyed official recognition and patronage. It is surprising, then, that little else is known about Pirmet. Even his first name does not seem to have been recorded, though what is probably his personal silver mark, found on a double-barreled fowling piece in the Metropolitan Museum, incorporates the letter F P separated by a gun. This mark is analogous in form to the mark frequently encountered on Boutet firearms, described above. Pirmet's first name thus presumably begins with F. It is very curious to observe that these beautiful pistols, signed prominently on

Cat. no. 115. Underside

the locks with Pirmet's name, and with each mount stamped with his initial P, nevertheless has silver mounts stamped with Boutet's personal mark. These mounts – the pommel cap, trigger guard, and side plate – are of a design frequently found on Boutet firearms, and so were clearly made to his order. Exactly why Pirmet should have utilized Boutet's silver mounts remains a subject for further speculation.

References: Dean, 1911, no. 207, pl. XLIII; Rook sale, no. 554; Howard, 1979, pp. 195-197.

116
POWDER FLASK
Italian, second half of the 16th century
Leather, steel
Height 7 1/2 in. (19 cm.)
Width 6 in. (15.2 cm.)
Weight 13 oz. (.360 kg.)
Ex collection: Charles M. Schott, Jr., New York
Gift of Charles M. Schott, Jr., 1916 (19.53.89)

The body of this flask is made of *cuir bouilli* (molded and hardened leather). Its lower half is semispherical with roped ribs; in the deep grooves between them are arabesques painted in gold and silver. The narrow upper part is embossed with an oval heraldic shield, surmounted by a crown and surrounded by the collar of the Order of the Golden Fleece; the remaining space is filled with sphinx-like chimeras and is framed by a rectangular wreath. The flat back of the body is pierced with holes for attaching a belt hook (now missing).

Grooved steel mounts reinforce the body. The columnar nozzle also served as a powder measure and is fitted with a spring-operated cutoff screen. To measure the powder charge, the open end of the nozzle was covered with a finger, the flask turned upside down, and the screen opened for a moment. The nozzle thus filled with powder. When the screen closed again, the flask could be reversed and the measured powder charge poured down the barrel.

The heraldic shield shows faint traces of a coat of arms. Though these arms are now unidentifiable, the owner, as a Knight of the Order of the Golden Fleece, must have been of exalted position.

117
PRIMING FLASK
German (Saxony), late 16th century
Gilt brass, wood, velvet
Height 5 3/4 in. (14.6 cm.)
Weight 13 oz. (.357 kg.)
Ex collection: Royal Saxon Armory, Dresden; Giovanni P. Morosini, New York
The collection of Giovanni P. Morosini, presented by his daughter Giulia, 1932 (32.75.181)

The body of truncated triangular shape with concave sides is made of wood covered with black velvet and encased in heavy mounts of cast brass, chiseled and gilt overall. The front and back are cast from the same mold and differ only in minor engraved details, both depicting the classical legend of Marcus Curtius leaping into the abyss. The scene is framed by a baroque ornament composed of floral motifs, masks, a swag, and architectural elements. The cover has grooved borders and a slender nozzle (the stopper is missing). On the cover are engraved the initials B C, probably those of the owner. On each side a pair of lion's masks hold rings for the suspension cord.

This priming flask belongs to a set of firearms equipment, including bandoliers and powder flasks together with a hundred wheellock arquebuses made by Dresden masters for the bodyguard on foot of the Prince Elector Christian I (reigned 1586-91). Both the priming flasks and the much larger powder flasks are of the same form, with gilt-brass mounts and furniture, including lion's masks with suspension rings. Similar masks decorate the bandoliers and the morions of the guard (cat. no. 23). The guns of this group are also mounted with gilt-brass furniture (cat. no. 96).

On the powder flasks the coat of arms of Saxony is the central decorative motif whereas on the priming flasks the decoration refers to the legend of Marcus Curtius as a patriotic example. According to the legend, a flaming abyss opened in the Roman Forum in the fourth century B.C., and the augurs forecast that only the sacrifice of the most treasured possession of the Roman people would close the chasm. The young Marcus Curtius proclaimed that civic courage was the worthiest possession of a Roman citizen, and in full armor and on horseback he leaped into the abyss – which immediately closed.

References: Blair, 1974, pp. 365-366, no. 150; Schaal, 1975, pp. 37-39, nos. 104-105, 107-108.

118
CARTRIDGE BOX
German (Saxony), late 16th century
Silver, wood, velvet
Height 4 1/2 in. (11.5 cm.)
Weight 10 oz. (.309 kg.)
Cartridge caliber .60 (15.2 mm.)
Ex collection: Royal Saxon Armory, Dresden; Bashford Dean, New York
The Bashford Dean Memorial Collection, 1929 (29.158.700)

The body of this box is of wood, hollowed out to fit four cylindrical cartridges, and was once covered with black velvet, now completely worn. The mounts are of silver engraved with arabesques, geometric patterns, a pheasant on the front strap, a standing horse on the bottom, and a fox

Detail of cat. no. 118. Lid

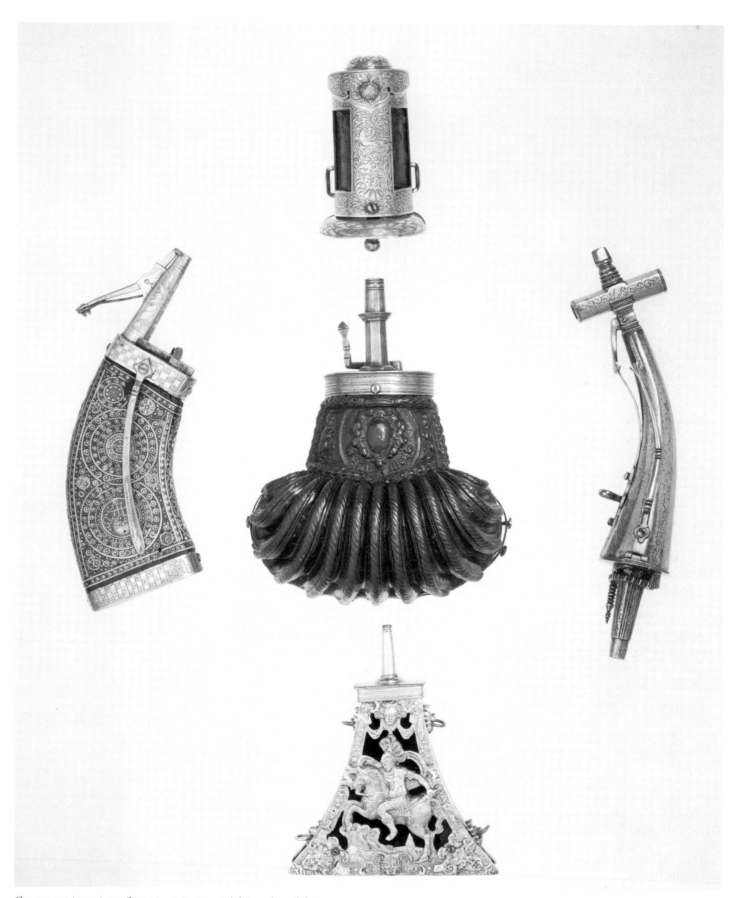

Cat. nos. 116 (center), 117 (bottom), 118 (top), 119 (right), and 120 (left)

on the back. On the cover is the coat of arms (a storming ladder) and the initials H G W of Hans Georg Wehse, the court marshal *(Hofmarschall)* of Saxony. The hinged cover is locked by a spring-catch released by a knob on the underside. Three brackets held the carrying straps. The silversmith's mark, B P within a heart-shaped shield, is stamped inside the box between the four openings for the cartridges. The back and the bottom are further marked with the Roman numeral I.

In the sixteenth century, paper cartridges were introduced for faster reloading of firearms. Each cartridge contained a premeasured powder charge and a bullet; after one end of the paper wrapping was torn open, the powder and bullet were poured down the barrel, followed by the paper which served as a wad.

Hans Georg Wehse was the commander of the *Trabantenleibgarde,* the bodyguard of the Prince Electors of Saxony at Dresden, during the reigns of Christian I (1586-91), and Christian II (1601-11), as well as during the interim regency of Frederick Wilhelm (1591-1601). Wehse is recorded as having supplied equipment for the *Trabantenleibgarde* at his own expense. This cartridge box, serial number I, with his personal arms, was probably his own as commander of the guard.

Reference: Grancsay, 1933, p. 240, no. 195, pl. LXII.

Detail of cat. no. 118. Bottom

119
COMBINATION WHEELLOCK SPANNER, PRIMING FLASK, AND SCREWDRIVER
Western European, late 16th-early 17th century
Steel
Length 9³/₄ in. (24.7 cm.)
Weight 11 oz. (.298 kg.)
Ex collection: Giovanni P. Morosini, New York
The collection of Giovanni P. Morosini, presented by his daughter Giulia, 1932 (32.75.184)

The faceted horn-shaped body is engraved with abstract wavy patterns. For filling the flask, the lid hinged at the wide end can be opened; it is fitted with a nozzle, chiseled and engraved, and a spring-activated semicircular release lever. The opposite end of the flask is provided with a screwdriver and a spring-held pivoted spanner. One end of the spanner is fitted to the wheel spindle, while the other, smaller, end was used to tighten the jaws of the cock holding a piece of pyrite.

On the body are a long narrow belt hook and a loop for a cord because these flasks were hung around the neck to speed up reloading.

Reference: Grancsay, 1953, no. 143.

120
POWDER FLASK
Eastern European, 17th century
Horn, staghorn, gilt brass
Length 8¹⁵/₁₆ in. (22.7 cm.)
Weight 12 oz. (.328 kg.)
Rogers Fund, 1957 (57.47)

The body of flattened cow horn is decorated overall with a series of large and small concentric circles inlaid with wood and staghorn (some tinted green), and studded with crosslets, stars, and dots of brass. In the centers of the largest circle on the front and back is an orb and cross. Gilt-brass mounts at each end are engraved with foliate scrolls and geometric patterns. The nozzle, which also served as a powder measure, has a spring-operated cap and a cutoff screen. A screw attaches a long belt hook to the left side of the cover.

REFERENCES CITED

Anonymous sale, 1980
Anonymous collection, sale catalogue. Galerie Ineichen, Zurich, November 4, 1980.

Augsburg, 1980
Welt im Umbruch: Augsburg zwischen Renaissance und Barock (exhibition catalogue). Armor catalogued by B. Thomas. 2 vols. Augsburg, 1980.

Austin sale, 1917
Samuel H. Austin collection, sale catalogue. American Art Galleries, New York, April 24-28, 1917.

Beardmore, 1844
Beardmore, John. *A Catalogue with Illustrations of the Collection of Ancient Arms and Armour at Uplands, near Fareham, Hampshire.* London, 1844.

Belous, 1969
Belous, Russell E., ed. *A Distinguished Collection of Arms and Armor on Permanent Display at the Los Angeles County Museum of Natural History.* Los Angeles, 1969.

Biorci, 1839
Biorci, D. *L'Armeria del Signore C. Ambrogio Uboldo, Nobile de Villareggio.* Milan, 1839.

Blackmore, 1972
Blackmore, Howard. *Hunting Weapons.* New York, 1972.

Blair, 1962
Blair, Claude. *European and American Arms c. 1100-1850.* London, 1962.

Blair, 1968
Blair, Claude. *Pistols of the World.* London, 1968.

Blair, 1970
Blair, Claude. "A Royal Swordsmith and Damascener: Diego de Çaias." *Metropolitan Museum Journal,* III (1970), pp. 149-198.

Blair, 1974
Blair, Claude. *The James A. de Rothschild Collection at Waddesdon Manor. Arms, Armour and Base-Metalwork.* Fribourg, 1974.

Boccia, Cantelli, Maraini, 1976
Boccia, L. G.; Cantelli, G.; and Maraini, F. *Il Museo Stibbert a Firenze; Volume Quarto: i Depositi e l'Archivio.* 2 vols. Milan, 1976.

Boccia and Coelho, 1967
Boccia, L. G., and Coelho, E. T. *L'Arte dell'Armatura in Italia.* Milan, 1967.

Boccia and Coelho, 1975
Boccia, Lionello G., and Coelho, Eduardo T. *Armi Bianche Italiane.* Milan, 1975.

Bohlmann, 1914
Bohlmann, Robert. "Die Braunschweigischen Waffen auf Schloss Blankenburg am Harz." *Zeitschrift für historische Waffenkunde,* VI (1912-14), pp. 335-358.

Bohlmann, 1935
Bohlmann, Robert. "Zeughaus und Harnischkammer der Herzöge von Braunschweig in Wolfenbüttel und seit 1730 in Braunschweig." *Zeitschrift für historische Waffenkunde,* XIV [n.s. 5] (1935-36), pp. 40-41.

Borghese sales, 1892-93
Prince Borghese collection, sale catalogues. Giacomini et Capobianchi, Rome, March 28-April 9, 1892; Capobianchi, Rome, March 13-24, 1893.

Bosson, 1964
Bosson, Clément. "Les Dagues Suisses." *Genava,* n.s. 12 (1964), pp. 167-168.

Brunswick, 1953
Exhibition of Arms, Armour and Militaria lent by H. R. H. the Duke of Brunswick and Lüneburg at the Armouries of the Tower of London. Catalogue by James G. Mann. 2nd ed. London, 1953.

Carpegna, 1962
di Carpegna, Nolfo. "Armi da Fuoco dell' Italia Centrale." *Waffen- und Kostümkunde,* IV (1962), pp. 120-128.

Carpegna, 1974
di Carpegna, Nolfo. "Notes on Central Italian Firearms of the Eighteenth Century, Part II." *Journal of the Arms and Armour Society,* VIII (1974), pp. 1-84.

Carrington-Peirce, 1937
Carrington-Peirce, P. *A Handbook of Court and Hunting Swords, 1660-1820.* London, 1937.

Cosson sale, 1893
Baron [C. A.] de Cosson collection, sale catalogue. Christie, Manson and Woods, London, May 2-3, 1893.

Cosson, 1901
Baron [C. A.] de Cosson. *Le Cabinet d'Armes de Maurice de Talleyrand-Périgord, Duc de Dino.* Paris, 1901.

Dean, 1905
Dean, Bashford. *Catalogue of European Arms and Armor.* The Metropolitan Museum of Art Handbook no. 15. New York, 1905.

Dean, 1911
Dean, Bashford. *Catalogue of a Loan Exhibition of Arms and Armor.* The Metropolitan Museum of Art, New York, 1911.

Dean, 1914
Dean, Bashford. *The Collection of Arms and Armor of Rutherfurd Stuyvesant, 1843-1909.* n.p., 1914.

Dean, 1915
Dean, Bashford. *Handbook of Arms and Armor, European and Oriental, Including the William H. Riggs Collection.* The Metropolitan Museum of Art, New York, 1915.

Dean, 1922
Dean, Bashford. "Two Horse Panoplies in the Armor Gallery." *The Metropolitan Museum of Art Bulletin,* XVII (1922), pp. 190-193.

Dean, 1925
Dean, Bashford. "Gift of Two Embossed Sixteenth-Century Round Shields." *The Metropolitan Museum of Art Bulletin,* XX (1925), pp. 290-292.

Dean, 1928
Dean, Bashford. "Recent Accessions in the Armor Department." *The Metropolitan Museum of Art Bulletin,* XXIII (1928), pp. 16-24.

Dean, *Daggers,* 1929
Dean, Bashford. *Catalogue of European Daggers.* The Metropolitan Museum of Art, New York, 1929.

Dean, *Swords,* 1929
Dean, Bashford. *Catalogue of European Court Swords and Hunting Swords.* The Metropolitan Museum of Art, New York, 1929.

Demmin
Demmin, August. *Zweiter Ergänzungs-band für die vier Auflagen der Kriegswaffen in ihren geschichtlichen Entwickelungen; eine Encyclopädie der Waffenkunde.* Wiesbaden, n.d.

Erizo sale, 1929
Count Erizo collection, sale catalogue. American Art Association Inc., New York, January 18-19, 1929.

ffoulkes, 1916
ffoulkes, Charles J. *Inventory and Survey of the Armouries of the Tower of London.* 2 vols. London, 1916.

Florence, 1980
Firenze e la Toscana dei Medici nell' Europa del Cinquecento. Palazzo Vecchio: committenza e collezionismo medicei (exhibition catalogue). Armor catalogued by L. G. Boccia. Florence, 1980.

Forrer
Forrer, R. *Die Waffensammlung des Herrn Stadtrath Rich. Zschille in Grossenhain (Sachsen).* Berlin, n.d.

Gall, 1965
Gall, Gunter. *Leder im Europäischen Kunsthandwerk.* Brunswick, 1965.

Grancsay, "Swords," 1929
Grancsay, Stephen V. "Swords from the Dresden Armory." *The Metropolitan Museum of Art Bulletin,* XXIV (1929), pp. 56-58.

Grancsay, "Helmet," 1929
Grancsay, Stephen V. "An Embossed Parade Helmet." *The Metropolitan Museum of Art Bulletin,* XXIV (1929), pp. 209-210.

Grancsay, 1930
Grancsay, Stephen V. "The Bashford Dean Memorial Collection." *The Metropolitan Museum of Art Bulletin,* XXV (1930), pp. 86-94.

Grancsay, 1931
Grancsay, Stephen V. *Loan Exhibition of European Arms and Armor.* The Metropolitan Museum of Art, New York, 1931.

Grancsay, 1933
Grancsay, Stephen V. *Loan Exhibition of European Arms and Armor.* Brooklyn Museum, New York, 1933.

Grancsay, 1937
Grancsay, Stephen V. "A Hapsburg Locking Gauntlet." *The Metropolitan Museum of Art Bulletin,* XXXII (1937), pp. 188-191.

Grancsay, 1939
Grancsay, Stephen V. "The Bequest of Giulia P. Morosini: Arms and Armor." *The Metropolitan Museum of Art Bulletin,* XXXIV (1939), pp. 15-19.

Grancsay, 1953
Grancsay, Stephen V. *Loan Exhibition of Medieval and Renaissance Arms and Armor from The Metropolitan Museum of Art.* Los Angeles County Museum, Los Angeles; California Palace of the Legion of Honor, San Francisco; Department of Fine Arts, Carnegie Institute, Pittsburgh, 1953-54.

Grancsay, Louisville, 1955
Grancsay, Stephen V. *A Loan Exhibition of Equestrian Equipment from The Metropolitan Museum of Art.* The J. B. Speed Art Museum, Louisville, 1955.

Grancsay, Hagerstown-Newark, 1955
Grancsay, Stephen V. *A Loan Exhibition of Medieval and Renaissance Arms and Armor from The Metropolitan Museum of Art.* Washington County Museum of Fine Arts, Hagerstown, Md.; Newark Museum Association, Newark, N.J., 1955.

Grancsay, "Helmet," 1955
Grancsay, Stephen V. "A Helmet Made for Philip II of Spain." *The Metropolitan Museum of Art Bulletin,* n.s. XIII (1955), pp. 3-7.

Grancsay, 1956
Grancsay, Stephen V. "New Galleries of European Arms and Armor." *The Metropolitan Museum of Art Bulletin,* n.s. XIV (1956), pp. 205-236.

Grancsay, 1963
Grancsay, Stephen V. "Sculpture in Steel: A Milanese Renaissance Barbute." *The Metropolitan Museum of Art Bulletin,* n.s. XXI (1963), pp. 182-191.

Grancsay, "Lucio Piccinino," 1964
Grancsay, Stephen V. "Lucio Piccinino, Master Armorer of the Renaissance." *The Metropolitan Museum of Art Bulletin,* n.s. XXII (1964), pp. 257-271.

Grancsay, Allentown, 1964
Grancsay, Stephen V. *Arms and Armor: A Loan Exhibition from the Collection of Stephen V. Grancsay, with Important Contributions by The Metropolitan Museum of Art, New York, and the John Woodman Higgins Armory, Worcester, Massachusetts.* Allentown Art Museum, Allentown, Pa., 1964.

Grancsay, 1967
Grancsay, Stephen V. *The Art of the Armorer* (exhibition catalogue). Flint Institute of Arts, Flint, Mich., 1967.

Grancsay, 1970
Grancsay, Stephen V. *Master French Gunsmiths' Designs of the XVII-XIX Centuries.* New York, 1970.

Grancsay, 1977
Grancsay, Stephen V. "Renaissance Arms and Armor." *The Triumph of Humanism: Visual Survey of the Decorative Arts of the Renaissance* (exhibition catalogue). San Francisco, 1977, pp. 43-51.

Grancsay and Kienbusch, 1933
Grancsay, Stephen V., and von Kienbusch, C. O. *The Bashford Dean Collection of Arms and Armor in the Metropolitan Museum of Art.* Portland, Me., 1933.

Grimwade, 1976
Grimwade, A. G. *London Goldsmiths, 1697-1837: Their Marks and Lives.* London, 1976.

Gusler and Lavin, 1977
Gusler, Wallace B., and Lavin, James D. *Decorated Firearms, 1540-1870, from the Collection of Clay P. Bedford.* Williamsburg, Va., 1977.

Haenel, 1923
Haenel, Erich. *Kostbare Waffen aus der Dresdner Rüstkammer.* Leipzig, 1923.

Hayward, 1948-49
Hayward, J. F. "The Origin of Small-Sword Ornament." *Apollo,* XLVIII (1948), pp. 33-35, 86-88, 103-104, 107-108; XLIX (1949), pp. 76-78, 80.

Hayward, 1962-63
Hayward, J. F. *The Art of the Gunmaker.* 2 vols. London, 1962-63.

Hayward, 1965
Hayward, J. F. *European Armour.* 2nd ed. Victoria and Albert Museum, London, 1965.

Hodnett, 1971
Hodnett, Edward. *Marcus Gheeraerts the Elder of Bruges, London and Antwerp.* Utrecht, 1971.

Hoff, 1969
Hoff, Arne. *Feuerwaffen.* 2 vols. Brunswick, 1969.

Hoff, 1978
Hoff, Arne. *Dutch Firearms.* London, 1978.

Howard, 1979
Howard, Gordon T. "Pirmet à Paris." *The Journal of the Arms and Armour Society,* IX (1979), pp. 195-197.

Ilgner, 1931
Ilgner, E. "Maastrichter Elfenbeinpistolen." *Zeitschrift für historische Waffenkunde,* XII [n.s. III] (1931), pp. 210-214.

Indianapolis, 1970
Catalogue of the Inaugural Exhibition of the Indianapolis Museum of Art: Treasures from the Metropolitan. Indianapolis, 1970.

Innsbruck, 1954
Die Innsbrucker Plattnerkunst (exhibition catalogue). Text by B. Thomas and O. Gamber. Innsbruck, 1954.

Karger, 1964
Karger, V. "Neue Teschner Beiträge zur Herkunftsfrage der Teschinken." *Waffen- und Kostümkunde,* 1964, pp. 29-42.

Kaunitz sale, 1935
R. von Kaunitz collection, sale catalogue. Galerie Fischer, Lucerne, September 3, 1935.

Keasbey sale, 1924
Henry G. Keasbey collection, sale catalogue. American Art Galleries, New York, December 5-6, 1924.

Keasbey sale, 1925
Henry G. Keasbey collection, sale catalogue. American Art Galleries, New York, November 27-28, 1925.

Kennard, 1972
Kennard, A. N. *French Pistols and Sporting Guns.* London, 1972.

Kienbusch collection, 1963
The Kretzschmar von Kienbusch Collection of Armor and Arms. Princeton, 1963.

Kolasinski sale, 1917
Adalbert von Kolasinski collection, sale catalogue. Lepke, Berlin, March 27-31, 1917.

Laking sale, 1920
Sir Guy F. Laking collection, sale catalogue. Christie, Manson and Woods, London, April 19-22, 1920.

Laking, 1920-22
Laking, Sir Guy F. *A Record of European Armour and Arms Through Seven Centuries.* 5 vols. London, 1920-22.

Lavin, 1965
Lavin, James D. *A History of Spanish Firearms.* New York, 1965.

Lenk, 1943
Lenk, Torsten. "De franska hjullåsvapen." *Vaabenhistoriske Aarbøger,* IV (1943), pp. 5-24.

Lenk, 1965
Lenk, Torsten. *The Flintlock: Its Origin and Development.* J. F. Hayward, ed.; G. A. Urquhart, trans. (original ed., 1939). London, 1965.

Liechtenstein sale, 1926
[Prince Liechtenstein collection], sale catalogue. American Art Association Inc., New York, November 19-20, 1926.

Lindsay, 1967
Lindsay, Merrill K. *One Hundred Great Guns.* New York, 1967.

Macomber sale, 1936
Frank G. Macomber collection, sale catalogue. American Art Galleries, New York, December 10-12, 1936.

Mann, 1929
Mann, James G. "Notes on the Armour of the Maximilian Period and the Italian Wars." *Archaeologia,* LXXIX (1929), pp. 217-244.

Mann, 1961
Mann, James G. "The Master of the Snails and Dragonflies." *Waffen- und Kostümkunde,* III (1961), pp. 14-26.

Moscardo, 1672
Moscardo, Lodovico. *Parte Seconda delle Note Overo Memorie del Museo del Conte Lodovico Moscardo, Nobile Veronese.* Verona, 1672.

Müller, 1904
Müller, Bernhard. "Die Rüstung Philipps des Grossmütigen." *Philipp der Grossmütige, Beiträge zur Geschichte seines Lebens und seiner Zeit.* Marburg, 1904.

Müller-Hickler, 1923
Müller-Hickler, Hans. *Führer durch die Kunst- und historischen Sammlungen: Waffensaal.* Hessisches Landesmuseum, Darmstadt, 1923.

Neuer Støckel
Heer, Eugène, ed. *Der Neue Støckel. Internationales Lexikon der Büchsenmacher, Feuerwaffenfabrikanten und Armbrustmacher von 1400-1900.* 3 vols. Schwäbisch Hall, 1978-80.

Nickel, 1969
Nickel, Helmut. "English Armour in the Metropolitan Museum of Art." *Connoisseur,* CLXXII (1969), pp. 196-203.

Nickel, 1974
Nickel, Helmut. *Ullstein Waffenbuch.* Berlin, 1974.

Norman and Barne, 1980
Norman, A. V. B., and Barne, Catherine. *The Rapier and Small-Sword, 1460-1820.* London, 1980.

O'Dell-Franke, 1977
O'Dell-Franke, Ilse. *Kupferstiche und Radierungen aus der Werkstatt des Virgil Solis.* Wiesbaden, 1977.

Offerman sale, 1937
Theodore Offerman collection, sale catalogue. American Art Association, New York, November 11-13, 1937.

Peterson, 1962
Peterson, Harold L. *The Treasury of the Gun.* New York, 1962.

Potier, 1905
Baron Potier, O. "Die Paradewaffen der erzbishöflichen Trabanten am Hofe von Salzburg." *Zeitschrift für historische Waffenkunde,* III (1905), pp. 280-285.

Pyhrr, 1973
Pyhrr, Stuart W. "Hidden Marks on Boutet Firearms." *Arms and Armor Annual,* I (1973), pp. 266-274.

Reid, 1965
Reid, William, "Biscotto me fecit." *Armi Antiche,* 1965, pp. 3-27.

Reitzenstein, 1962
von Reitzenstein, Alexander. "Hohenaschauer Waffen." *Waffen- und Kostümkunde,* 1962, pp. 34-50.

Richards sale, 1890
Raoul Richards collection, sale catalogue. Giacomini et Capobianchi, Rome, March 3-29, 1890.

Robert-Dumesnil, 1865
Robert-Dumesnil, A. P. E. *Le peintre graveur français.* 10 vols. Paris, 1865.

Rook sale
Frederick S. Rook collection, sale catalogue. Silo's Fifth Avenue Art Galleries, New York, [ca. 1920].

Rozière sale, 1860
Ernest de Rozière collection, sale catalogue. Hôtel Drouot, Paris, March 17-18, 1860.

Schaal, 1975
Schaal, D. *Katalog Dresdener Büchsenmacher 16.-18. Jh.* Dresden, 1975.

Schallaburg, 1977
Das Wiener Bürgerliche Zeughaus: Rüstungen und Waffen aus 5 Jahrhunderten. Austellung im Schloss Schallaburg bei Melk (exhibition catalogue). Vienna, 1977.

Schedelmann, 1972
Schedelmann, Hans. *Die grossen Büchsenmacher: Leben, Werke, Marken vom 15. bis 19. Jahrhundert.* Brunswick, 1972.

Schele, 1965
Schele, Sune. *Cornelis Bos. A Study of the Origins of the Netherland Grotesque.* Stockholm, 1965.

Schneider, 1977
Schneider, Hugo. *Der Schweizerdolch.* Zurich, 1977.

Schöbel, 1975
Schöbel, Johannes. *Fine Arms and Armor: Treasures from the Dresden Collection.* New York, 1975.

Scofield, 1941
Scofield, J. K. "Old Firearms in America." *Connoisseur,* CVIII (1941), pp. 8-12.

Shrewsbury sale, 1857
Bertram Arthur Talbot, 17th Earl of Shrewsbury collection, sale catalogue. Christie and Manson, London, July 6 and 29, 1857.

Skelton, 1830
Skelton, Joseph. *Engraved Illustrations of Antient Arms and Armour from the Collection at Goodrich Court, Herefordshire, from the Drawings and with the Descriptions of Dr. Meyrick.* 2 vols. London, 1830.

Soltykoff sale, 1854
Prince Peter Soltykoff collection, sale catalogue. Hôtel Drouot, Paris, April 18-22, 1854.

Souchal, 1973
Souchal, Geneviève. "Un grand peintre français de la fin du XVᵉ siècle, le maître de la 'Chasse à la Licorne.'" *Revue de l'Art,* no. 22 (1973), pp. 22-49.

Spitzer collection, 1892
La Collection Spitzer. 6 vols. Paris, 1892.

Spitzer sale, 1895
Frédéric Spitzer collection, sale catalogue. Galerie Georges Petit, Paris, June 10-14, 1895.

Støckel
Støckel, Johan F. *Haandskydevaabens Bedømmelse.* 2 vols. Copenhagen, 1938-43.

Stöcklein, 1908
Stöcklein, Hans. "Eine bisher unbekannte Augsburger Ätzerfamilie." *Zeitschrift für historische Waffenkunde,* IV (1908), pp. 382-387.

Stöcklein, 1918-20
Stöcklein, Hans. "Münchner Klingenschmiede." *Zeitschrift für historische Waffenkunde,* VIII (1918-20), pp. 198-205.

Stöcklein, 1928
Stöcklein, Hans. "Neuerwerbungen des Metropolitan Museums." *Pantheon,* 1928, pp. 269, 274.

Stone, 1934
Stone, George C. *A Glossary of the Construction, Decoration and Use of Arms and Armor in All Countries and at All Times.* Portland, Me., 1934.

Tarassuk, 1971
Tarassuk, L. *Antique European and American Firearms at The Hermitage Museum.* Leningrad, 1971.

Terenzi, 1978
Terenzi, Marcello. *Michele Battista e il suo tempo.* Rome, 1978.

Thomas, 1969
Thomas, Bruno. "Zwei Vorzeichnungen zu Kaiserlichen Gardestangenwaffen von Hans Stromaier 1577 und Johann Bernhard Fischer von Erlach 1705." *Jahrbuch der Kunsthistorischen Sammlungen in Wien,* LXV (1969), pp. 61-78.

Thomas, 1974
Thomas, Bruno. "Die Innsbrucker Plattnerkunst – Ein Nachtrag." *Jahrbuch der Kunsthistorischen Sammlungen in Wien,* LXX (1974), pp. 179-220.

Thomas, Gamber, Schedelmann, 1964
Thomas, B.; Gamber, O.; and Schedelmann, H. *Arms and Armour of the Western World.* New York and Toronto, 1964.

Trapp and Mann, 1929
Trapp, O., and Mann, J. G. *The Armoury at the Castle of Churburg.* London, 1929.

Tulsa, 1979
Gloria dell' Arte: A Renaissance Perspective (exhibition catalogue). Philbrook Art Center, Tulsa, Okla., 1979.

Uboldo, 1841
Descrizione degli Scudi Posseduti da Ambrogio Uboldo. Milan, 1841.

Uboldo sale, 1869
Ambrogio Uboldo collection, sale catalogue. Hôtel Drouot, Paris, May 21, 1869.

Valencia de Don Juan, 1898
Conde Valencia de Don Juan. *Catálogo historico-descriptivo de la Real Armeria de Madrid.* Madrid, 1898.

Viollet-le-Duc, 1858-75
Viollet-le-Duc, E. *Dictionnaire raisonné du mobilier français de l'époque carlovingienne à la renaissance.* 6 vols. Paris, 1858-75.

Weyersberg, 1926
Weyersberg, Albert. *Solinger Schwertschmiede des 16. und 17. Jahrhunderts und ihre Erzeugnisse.* Solingen, 1926.

Weyersberg, 1932-34
Weyersberg, Albert. "Klingen mit der In-
schrift MEVES PERNS." *Zeitschrift für historische Waffenkunde*, XIII [n.s. IV]
(1932-34), pp. 137-138.

Whawell sale, 1908
[Samuel J. Whawell collection], sale cata-
logue. Galerie Helbing, Munich,
November 10, 1908

Whawell sale, 1927
Samuel J. Whawell collection, sale catalogue. Sotheby and Co., London, May
3-6, 1927.

Whitelaw, 1977
Whitelaw, Charles E. *Scottish Arms Makers*.
Sarah Barter, ed. London, 1977.

Williams sale, 1921
Morgan S. Williams collection, sale cata-
logue. Christie, Manson and Woods,
London, April 26-28, 1921.

Wilson, 1960
Wilson, R. L. "Gonne-Shields." *Muzzle
Blasts*, XXII (1960), pp. 8-10.

Zschille and Forrer, 1891-99
Zschille, Richard, and Forrer, Robert.
Der Sporn in seiner Formen-Entwicklung.
2 vols. Berlin, 1891-99.

Zschille and Forrer, 1896
Zschille, Richard, and Forrer, Robert. *Die
Steigbügel in ihrer Formen-Entwicklung*.
Berlin, 1896.

Zschille sale, 1897
Richard Zschille collection, sale cata-
logue. Christie, Manson and Woods,
London, January 25-February 1, 1897.